ALSO BY COURTNEY ANGELA BRKIC

Stillness: And Other Stories

THE STONE FIELDS

THE
STONE FIELDS

*An Epitaph for
the Living*

Courtney Angela Brkic

FARRAR, STRAUS AND GIROUX

NEW YORK

Farrar, Straus and Giroux
19 Union Square West, New York 10003

Library of Congress Cataloging-in-Publication Data
Brkic, Courtney Angela, 1972–
    The stone fields : an epitaph for the living / Courtney
Angela Brkic.— 1st ed.
        p.   cm.
Includes bibliographical references and index.
    ISBN 0-374-20774-7 (hard : alk. paper)
    1. Yugoslav War, 1991–1995—Atrocities—Bosnia and
Hercegovina.   2. Yugoslav War, 1991–1995—Personal
narratives, Bosnian.   3. Brkic, Courtney Angela, 1972–   I. Title.

DR1313.7.A85B75 2004
949.703—dc22

                                                    2003024285

EAN: 978-0-374-20774-8

Designed by Cassandra J. Pappas

www.fsgbooks.com

1   3   5   7   9   10   8   6   4   2

For my father,
last survivor of those days

I have learned how faces fall to bone . . .

—Anna Akhmatova, from "Requiem"

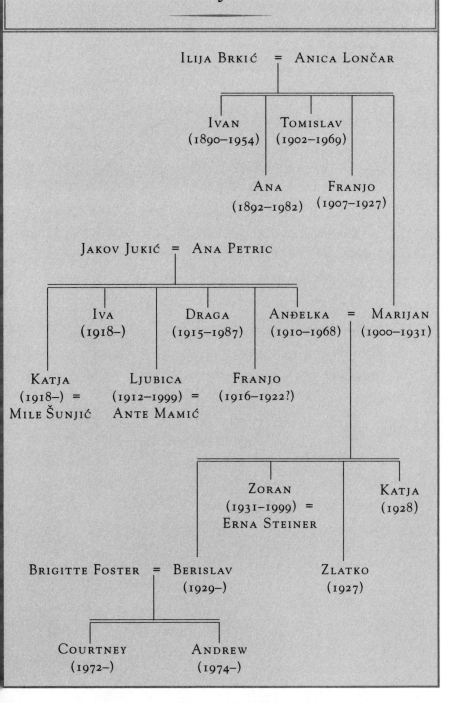

Family Tree

ILIJA BRKIĆ = ANICA LONČAR

IVAN
(1890–1954)

TOMISLAV
(1902–1969)

ANA
(1892–1982)

FRANJO
(1907–1927)

JAKOV JUKIĆ = ANA PETRIC

IVA
(1918–)

DRAGA
(1915–1987)

ANĐELKA = MARIJAN
(1910–1968)   (1900–1931)

KATJA
(1918–) =
MILE ŠUNJIĆ

LJUBICA
(1912–1999) =
ANTE MAMIĆ

FRANJO
(1916–1922?)

ZORAN
(1931–1999) =
ERNA STEINER

KATJA
(1928)

BRIGITTE FOSTER = BERISLAV
(1929–)

ZLATKO
(1927)

COURTNEY
(1972–)

ANDREW
(1974–)

CROATIA AND
BOSNIA-HERZEGOVINA

AUSTRIA

SLOVENIA

HUNGARY

Drava River

Danube River

Zagreb

CROATIA

Rijeka

Vukovar

Sava River

BOSNIA-
HERZEGOVINA

Tuzla

Srebrenica

Sarajevo

YUGOSLAVIA

Posušje

Mostar

ITALY

Dubrovnik

ALBANIA

Adriatic Sea

0 Miles   50   100
0 Kilometers   100

© 2004 Jeffrey L. Ward

Pronunciation Key

C, c = *ts* as in "*ts*ar"

Ć, ć = *ch* as in "*ch*eck"

Č, č = *ch* as in "*ch*ore"

Đ, đ = *j* as in "*g*entleman"

J, j = *y* as in "*y*ellow"

Š, š = *sh* as in "*sh*ore"

Ž, ž = *zh* as in "gara*g*e"

THE STONE FIELDS

Prologue

I placed a hand on his forehead, careful not to wake him, and let my fingers rest on the vein that pulsed in evening's thin light. Beneath the warm skin were the plates of his cranium, the sutures where entire continents met in his childhood and fused over the ocean of his mind. The gentle, breakable bones of his face were like china, or the hollow bones of birds. They were as fragile as calcified breath.

The flow of his blood was like water singing through rock, and in my concentration, I was only vaguely aware of figures standing on all sides of the bed. Lifting my head, I found myself looking through their bodies as through the fluid of memory; I turned them into glass and buried my face in him once again. Whether this angered or saddened them, I could not tell.

Wind from the open window made the curtains dance and crept over my naked legs.

Stjepan's vertebrae reminded me of dinosaur exhibits at a

museum. There was something salamander-like about them. They started out small and graceful, and metamorphosed into the sturdiness of the lumbar region, where they were the trunk of a stout oak.

"Ribs are the tines of a cage," I recited under my breath, "and the sternum the thing that joins them. The sternum is variable: it can bow inward or out." It can have holes down its middle, tiny pinpricks, or be as smooth as the inside of a solid piece of bark. I brushed my eyelids against him, wondering what shape his had taken.

I examined his hand, which rested on my hip. Undone, it is a jigsaw puzzle, and reassembling it takes concentration and patience. I had been told that you get better with time. The skin on Stjepan's hip was taut and smooth. Although the pelvis is called the "innominate" because there is no other shape in nature that it resembles, the construction had seemed elephantine to me. Here you can discern a man from a woman definitively.

He stirred in his sleep. Soon—sooner than I would have liked—he would return to the base, and I would go back to my Zagreb apartment. I moved my right leg, which had become entangled in his. They had been like that in the ground, all arms and legs, and I shivered. I had not wanted to let that picture intrude while he held me, but it was inevitable, as was every memory of bones.

Stjepan sighed and stretched toward me in his sleep, burrowing his face into my neck. I continued to avoid the faces around the bed, realizing that his ghosts were vying with mine for position.

Months had passed since my return from Bosnia, but at

times they dwindled down to moments, and now I looked at Stjepan, wondering if his ghosts looked the same to him. They started to bend their heads over us, as if attempting resuscitation, and I closed my eyes. I found that I could not bring myself to look at them from one day to the next.

A sudden change in breathing told me that he had awakened, and a moment later he wrapped legs and arms around me in a bear hug. He opened his eyes and looked at me solemnly, his breath making a few strands of my hair shiver as the curtains had done. My heart beat faster, and I smiled.

I wondered whether I would recognize him by his bones.

TUZLA

1996

Wind carries the sudden smell of burning
  From the charred ruin of my village;
The smell from which all memory rises:
  All weddings, harvests, dances, and celebrations,
All funerals, lamentations, and dirges;
All which life sowed and death took away.

—*Ivan Goran Kovačić*, The Pit, *Stanza* X

I N 1995 I had brought my field boots with me from America to Croatia. They were thick leather, reached mid-calf, and had steel plates over the toes so that I would not accidentally remove part of my foot with a sharpened shovel. Red Virginia dirt was still wedged in the tread when I reached Zagreb, two months after the war ended.

The boots were comfortable in winter and unbearable in summer, but during my months of work as a field archaeologist in America I wore them constantly, plagued by memories of the snake that passed over my foot in the woods outside Baltimore in a burst of clay-colored red, as if the ground itself had grown a living and mobile appendage. A colleague behind me had yelled while I stood dumbstruck, watching the rustling of the high grass into which the snake disappeared. Later I wondered whether I had imagined its length or the dark hourglass markings of its back. Copperhead venom is unpleasant, I have since been told, causing fever, night sweats, and hallucinations, but rarely death.

The boots were also put to good use in Croatia, though for less openly pernicious reasons. I had worn them to tramp through the yards of several refugee camps, mud rising to my ankles. The camps were scattered throughout the country, and housed displaced persons from occupied areas of Croatia, as well as refugees from neighboring Bosnia-Herzegovina. Invariably, the camps seemed to occupy haphazard spaces: former army barracks or unused buildings in factory complexes.

Regardless of how many socks I wore, my feet often cramped from the cold that followed me indoors. I never mentioned my discomfort to anyone, my sense that cold stuck like shadow to the edges of refugee rooms, but more than one elderly woman sensed it in their young interrogator. They made gifts of thick woolen socks that they had knitted themselves after the dishes were washed and the grandchildren asleep, while the late news hummed from the radio. I imagined these women, intent on the length that grew from their knitting needles as they listened with half an ear to news of the war's end. In most cases, the fact that it had ended meant nothing, and they knew that they would not be returning home.

I had been conducting research on women in the war-affected population: Slavonians exiled from the sunflower fields of their girlhoods; Bosnian countrywomen who fed me bitter coffee and syrupy desserts; educated urbanites, whose diplomas and certificates were reduced to a fine pulp beneath the wreckage of their homes and apartment buildings.

I even visited a camp erected exclusively for children by a Japanese humanitarian organization. Each neatly constructed house sheltered several children and an adopted mother. Almost normal conditions prevailed, except that a war had taken place and, in addition to rainbows and flowers, the children there drew pictures of bombs, men wielding machine guns, and parents who were bleeding to death.

In the beginning, I had gone to the camps with questionnaires. I was ashamed of my handwriting when I sat with my subjects in their rooms or refugee-center kitchens, taking notes as they spoke. My cramped penmanship, never neat or pretty, had been the target of grammar school teachers who made me crumple up countless sheets of paper and start over, only to produce the same erratic scrawl. The women eyed my notes but said nothing.

Some of my conversations with them were superficial, and I used the questionnaires as a mat on which to place my coffee. But some women insisted that I turn on my tape recorder and write down every word. They would look anxiously over my shoulder, as if making sure that I transcribed everything correctly.

One woman from a village near Derventa told me the names of the men who had burned down her house as she stood in the front yard.

"And they were wearing uniforms."

I wrote it down.

"And they killed my son. And all of our animals."

I looked at her.

"*Write* it. I want you to put all of it in there."

THE BOOTS' PROPERTIES changed with time. In America they had been new and supple, smelling of leather and the sassafras root that perfumes the underground of mid-Atlantic woods. It was enough to smell the acrid rubber soles to remember the sweltering heat of West Virginia, where I had been working in the months following my college graduation. But in Croatia they dulled and took on the smell of the oak armoire in which I kept them. With the exception of my single visit to the children's village, which was surrounded by grass and flowering bushes, there always seemed to be an abundance of clay stuck to these boots after refugee visits. What little remained of the Virginia dirt was displaced and deposited into those vast fields of churned ground.

War had begun in Croatia following the republic's 1991 declaration of independence from Yugoslavia, when the Yugoslav People's Army (JNA) and Serb paramilitary troops responded by attacking Croatia's civilian population. The following year, war began under similar circumstances in Bosnia-Herzegovina, a country with a mixed Muslim, Serb, and Croat population. An initial united Muslim-Croat defense all but disintegrated when the two groups began fighting each other. Croats in Bosnia-Herzegovina wished to annex themselves to Croatia proper, but a Muslim-Croat cease-fire was declared in 1994. Relations between the two ethnic groups had improved, but were far from friendly. The 1995 Dayton Peace Accords effectively ended the war, dividing Bosnia-Herzegovina into two parts: a Muslim-Croat Federation and the Serb "entity" of Republika Srpska.

A year after my research in Croatia, I went to Bosnia as an archaeologist, and then the boots would take on the smell of death. Not the natural mustiness of a swept graveyard with its decomposing flower arrangements, but the stale odor of chaotic burial, the smell of the morgue with its splattered concrete floors, and the iciness of refrigerated containers that transported the bodies, like strange air-conditioned buses of death. Microscopic pieces from all those places became embedded in the soles like fossils in a strata of rock from the Pleistocene: some strands of hair, fibers from a hand-sewn shirt, powdered bone. Regardless of how much I wore the boots after that month in Bosnia, or with what force I banged them against a wall or sunbaked ground, that last assignment made the properties of these boots suddenly immutable, residue of the graves trapped in them as if in amber.

I LEFT ZAGREB on a C-130 transport plane at the beginning of July 1996 to join a Physicians for Human Rights forensic team already working in Bosnia. The sun's fiery reflection on the metal of the fuselage burned my eyes on the tarmac of Pleso Airport, and as we taxied down the runway, I pictured the wings in the cloudless blue sky that was forecast for the trip to Tuzla. I imagined the patchwork of fields and hills under the belly of the plane. From such heights it would be impossible to see the burned-out buildings or the schools that were filled with broken glass. It would be impossible to see the thousands of makeshift graveyards that dotted the landscape.

In my childhood I had traveled through Bosnia several times by car. We would make hot summertime pilgrimages to Sarajevo to visit my great-aunt Ana, but I remembered little of those trips. I could recall green, wooded hills that bore a striking resemblance to the foothills of Appalachia, and children on the roadside who sold wild strawberries on pieces of bark. After

the mountains came endless miles of farmland and then, suddenly, a sweltering city in which my elderly aunt rushed out to
meet our dust-caked car with shouts, tears, and wildly gesticu-
lating hands. She had lived in the Marin Dvor neighborhood of
Sarajevo, and I remembered a catfish that swam in a plastic tub
in her kitchen.

When I turned seven, she gave me a pair of deep purple em-
broidered slippers trimmed with sequins. They were a prize that
accompanied us back to America, packed carefully in our lug-
gage so that they would lose none of their gaudy splendor.

I thought of those slippers in the airplane on the way to
Tuzla, and I scanned the inside of the plane, seeking an example of their deep color. But the palette of drab shades surrounding me did not extend past olive and brown, and I soon gave
up. The slippers had faded over time, I remembered, losing
their brilliant color and a good many sequins as well.

I disliked flying and would have preferred going to Tuzla by
ground transport, even if that meant looking at the destruction
of places I vaguely remembered. Flying over Bosnia seemed unnatural to me, and to distract myself from the roaring sound of
the plane, I thought of how I would describe the interior to
my younger brother, Andrew. It was my first time on a non-
commercial flight, and I craned my head to examine the metal
interior with its assortment of cables and straps. The passengers
were buckled into seats along the edges, and a hatch in the rear
could open and be lowered onto the ground. Someone had explained to me that entire tanks could be transported in these
flying giants.

We landed first in Sarajevo and learned on the tarmac that
it would be ten minutes until takeoff for Tuzla, a small city lo-

cated about 80 miles north of the Bosnian capital. I unbuckled
my safety belt and looked out of the tiny circular window behind me. I recognized Sarajevo Airport, not from early childhood memory, but from seeing its skeleton on the news so often
in recent years. The buildings were pockmarked and cratered
from shelling and gunfire, and I remembered what one refugee
had told me in Croatia months before. We had been sitting in
the kitchen of a women's center, drinking coffee. In 1993 she
had attended a conference somewhere in Europe, escaping
Sarajevo by traversing a tunnel directly under the airport tarmac. The ceiling was so low that you had to walk hunched over
for hundreds of yards through the mud.

Was it possible to hear the sound of shelling, I had wondered, when you were in the subterranean passage, crouched in
the filth and cold, listening to reverberations, the wall trembling, and the rats screaming in alarm on all sides? Or was it
the silence that filled your ears, uncomfortably, trying to push
out into the darkness?

WHEN WE ARRIVED in Tuzla that evening, we held an impromptu meeting to discuss setting up the morgue in Kalesija,
about twenty miles away from our base house. A building had
been secured, and some preliminary work by engineers was already under way. The pathologists with whom I arrived were to
set up the inside of the morgue. I would stay with them for the
first few days, until transportation could be arranged to the
graves, where the anthropologists and archaeologists were
working.

A town on the edge of Bosnian Federation territory, Kalesija was just a few miles from Republika Srpska, the Serbian entity from which non-Serbs had been completely expelled. It had been under Serbian occupation until 1993, when a Bosnian Army offensive took it back. Many buildings in the town were destroyed, and those that remained were covered with holes and craters. The destruction on the road from Tuzla increases exponentially in the direction of Kalesija; the town sat squarely on what had been the front line.

The structure that had been selected for the morgue was once a garment factory. Chosen because of its inaccessibility from the road and its distance from Tuzla, it was a huge building with a guard shack and an external gate that locked. In maintaining the integrity of our investigations, we had to make sure that the "chain of evidence" was unbroken; remains would be padlocked into a freezer each evening and possessions kept under lock and key. Access to this evidence would be limited because otherwise, the strength of our case could be undermined and the guilty could go free.

Many of the mothers and wives of victims from the 1995 Srebrenica massacre were living as displaced persons in Tuzla, half an hour away by car. We expected that they would eventually come to the factory and stand at the chain-link fence, hoping to catch sight of something familiar.

OUR BASE HOUSE was not far from the center of Tuzla and had several large rooms where crew members slept. There was a living room, a terrace, and a two-tiered porch that admitted a soft breeze in the tight calm of summer.

A young dark-haired woman emerged when I arrived with

my travel companions—two pathologists, an X-ray technician, an autopsy technician, and an evidence custodian. Her name was Jadranka, and she spoke only a few words of English. Her mouth stretched into a wide grin when she realized I could understand her. She had been hired, she explained to me, to clean and cook for the crew members.

She led us upstairs, and I chose a room with a cot positioned beneath a window. I lowered my bag onto the bed and then straightened as Tim, the evidence custodian, knocked on the door. The others were behind him.

"Let's go look around," he suggested, and we made our way through the house as if we were vacationers inspecting a beachfront bungalow we might be renting.

In the bathroom, he turned the tap, but no water came out. He stared at it blankly.

"*Redukcija*," I explained to him. "The water only runs two hours out of the day." That was one of the first things Jadranka had told me, pointing into the kitchen, where dozens of plastic bottles filled with water stood like soldiers at the ready.

"Which two hours?" he asked.

"No one seems to know," I replied, making a face.

Jadranka had thrown her arms up in exasperation. "It comes and it goes," she told me. "Mostly, it doesn't even do that."

IN ADDITION TO SERVING as our living quarters, the base house would also function as a center for the database project. Survivors of the Srebrenica massacre would be interviewed about their missing family members, eventually providing DNA samples for genetic comparison with remains recovered from the mass graves, several of which were visible on satellite photographs almost immediately following the massacre.

There had been little television footage of the 1995 fall of Srebrenica, in which more than seven thousand people had disappeared. Reporters had not been able to gain access to the enclave, and the Dutch peacekeepers who guarded it had been ordered into a compound where they could hear unspecified screams and gunshots coming from the town. They had gone meekly, unable in the end even to provide testimonies regarding the fate of the town, which had been flooded with refugees in preceding months to a point well past bursting. The truth was in the ground, however, and the satellite photographs showed the scars of freshly turned earth in pastures and soccer fields.

The search for interpreters and interviewers to canvass refugee camps and centers was already under way in Tuzla. The work would be similar to my own interviews with refugee women in Croatia the year before, and I had the strange sensation that mine was a two-tiered process of discovery, before-and-after photographs that would together provide a more accurate portrait of the war than either one taken singly. There was also something oddly unsettling in the knowledge that our living quarters would also serve as this project's headquarters. The practical work of excavating the remains and autopsying them fell to the forensic team, and while we spent our days in the field, the place where we slept would be used for organizing and collecting information from survivors, and for documenting the last-known contact with the missing. It seemed as if we stood at opposite sides of a long, dark tunnel. A sad parade of mothers, wives, and daughters would provide information about their men: their age, where they were last seen, what they had been wearing. Then there was the dark, unknown transition into death. And there we were, the first to touch the bodies of their men when they emerged on the other end into the light of day, almost exactly one year later.

In the end, we did not have much contact with either the interviewers or the survivors, for which I was grateful. But their traces would be there when we returned after a day of work at the morgue: shallow coffee cups, rinsed and laid upside down on a towel to dry, and the faint smell of cigarettes in the air.

THERE IS A COMMON DENOMINATOR in refugee populations worldwide. I knew it before ever setting eyes on the women of Srebrenica that summer, not one of whom had been among the women I interviewed in Croatia the year before. In the ranks of exile, there are women who listen each evening for a telltale sound coming from the hall outside their drafty rooms that says their husbands and children have returned, Lazarus-like. These women wait first one year, then another. They grow old in their waiting, each year like a ball of noxious mercury that combines with another, so that the passage of time is fluid and indistinct. They reject conflicting reports of massacres and the conventional wisdom that all is lost.

In Croatian refugee camps, I had come to understand their need to find plausible explanations. Sometimes they held on to the belief that their husbands and sons were clinging to life in a distant prison cell or concentration camp. Was it blindness or optimism that convinced them of this? Would I hold out the same hope in their position?

One woman I knew constructed an elaborate fantasy in

which every time the phone rang and there was silence on the other side, she believed that it was her son telephoning. That he escaped periodically from his cell to call her, but could not talk into the receiver for fear of drawing the attention of the guards.

"He wants me to know that he's still alive," she insisted.

I couldn't meet her eyes. The telecommunications system in Zagreb was not the best, and dead lines were common. "What do you do when that happens?" I asked her.

"Oh, I tell him, 'Son, I know it's you. I love you. Come back to me when you can. I'm waiting for you.'"

The woman was Slavonian, but her husband, dead since the war, was from my grandmother's village in Herzegovina, and she evinced a certain affection for me. My father was born in Rakitno, I told her, but he grew up in Sarajevo and moved to America years ago. "He is well citified," I told her with a grin.

"Blood is blood," she responded with a slight shake of her head. "My husband carried the limestone dust of his childhood on his shoes until the day he died."

I was struck by the strange poetry of those words, as well as by their sad finality. I knew what she meant. My elderly aunts had lived in Zagreb for almost fifty years, but Herzegovina was evident in them from their clipped manner of speech to the tough-leafed *raštika* they ate. More than that, Herzegovina affected the way they walked through life—like warriors ready to do battle at the merest challenge.

My father never wholly lost those traits himself, and I believe that they have been passed down to me like some strange genetic coding. I told her of my theory, and she slapped the palm of her hand against her leg in agreement. Her son was the same, she said. More *Hercegovac* than was good for him.

To be *sa krša* has a specific meaning. To be *from karst* is to hail from one of the mountain regions, from an expanse of wind-scarred Dinaric stone where nothing grows.

"Don't listen to what these *Zagrepčani* tell you," she told me, wagging her finger.

Hardheaded, the city folk of Zagreb would say, joking that the heads of *Hercegovci* were shaped like square stones. From the *vukojebina*, others would state derisively, after learning our background. From where the wolves fuck.

I had learned the last phrase the day before, and loosened by the tumbler of *šljivovica* the woman had set before me, I was persuaded to repeat it, embarrassed enough that I could not look at her directly.

She grinned broadly at the vulgarity and lowered her eyes to the backs of her hands, twin constellations of liver spots and scars.

"To my son," she told me in a near whisper after a moment of silence, lifting her own glass to touch it with mine. "To my little wolf."

IN ADDITION TO MY AUNT ANA, her catfish, and the gaudy slippers I had worn even when my feet outgrew them and my heels hung from their backs, I had other memories of Bosnia. But they were so mixed up with things I had read and heard that it was hard to separate the real from the imagined. I had never before been in Tuzla, but several times that first day, I seemed to catch sight of a face or a building that was more than just fleetingly familiar.

The things I knew are gone, I mouthed in my dark room on the night of my arrival. I already knew this from five years of watching war footage, and everything I saw on that first day confirmed it: the ghost towns with their toppled minarets, the strange silence on the roads, and the old faces of the neighbor's children who had been playing in the parking spaces as we pulled up to the base house.

I reached the battleground when the war had receded to a stalemate and an uneasy peace reigned. The battle lines had been drawn with blood, melted by rain, and redrawn, and now the heavy air was completely still. I would smear the barely visible markings with my boots and bring the dead to the surface with my gloved hands. Birds would sing from trees, and the bright disk of the sun overhead would cast diagonal light through mutilated architecture. The dead left strange gouged holes in the landscape.

Some of them lay just below the surface, and in the coming weeks we were able to spy the clean whiteness of their bones in the yellow-green of a dry summer field. Other bodies hovered deeper in the dark, blood-saturated soil, and we needed heavy machinery, picks, and shovels to pull them out. Once out in the glaring sunshine, the twisted figures lay covered in plastic until we carried them up an embankment and down into the next field, where a refrigerated container admitted us into its grim, icy depths.

And all the time, whether I slept, worked, or searched for things I could remember, I was conscious of the people who were waiting for their missing. We looked not only at what the physical remains could tell us; we also scoured pockets for scraps of paper or objects that would help identify them. Such finds were rare, and it was hypothesized that the victims had been searched before execution and their possessions removed.

We paid special attention to the things we did find—hand-sewn clothing, charms, and the odd scrap of food—hoping that there would be someone left who recognized these objects.

IN THE MIDDLE of the first night, a strange wind rose from out of nowhere. When I groped my way to the blinds and opened them, I watched debris from the street blow into a skittering funnel. Somebody in another part of the house muttered in his sleep, and I could feel my heart contract. Tiny bumps rose on my forearms, and I rubbed them before returning to bed.

MY FATHER DID NOT KNOW that I had come to Bosnia, and the knowledge would have eaten away at him. I have been a largely obedient daughter, but I lied to him about my movements that summer, trying to convince myself that it would be all right in the end. Since childhood I have been accused of having an outrageous imagination and a fierce, dark temperament. It was obvious that he should expect this type of thing.

He thought I was safely ensconced in an air-conditioned office somewhere in western Slavonia, poring over topographic maps and following field developments from a distance, only venturing out occasionally from behind the armor of a large, sturdy desk.

"Be careful where you step," he told me solemnly when I'd last telephoned him from Zagreb.

Mines were still a problem in much of Croatia. After the war, families returning to their ruined homes in formerly occu-

pied areas found limited space in which they could safely maneuver. Rarely a month went by in which a child did not run
through his former hunting ground of garden, orchard, or field
and step on one of those sleeping executioners. Some houses
had even been deliberately rigged with explosives.

But Bosnia was an even more complicated patchwork of
mined areas and border crossings. Its citizens were in a tenuous
position—the right to pass between Republika Srpska and
Muslim-Croat Federation territory, which was supposedly ensured in the provision for free movement, existed in name
alone. Usually, only vehicles from SFOR (the Stabilization
Force), the UN, and international organizations made the trip
back and forth, especially into Serbian-held areas.

A number of Bosnian refugees were prevented from returning to occupied areas by ugly, gun-wielding mobs, and several
UN personnel were taken hostage that summer in Višegrad.

"I'll be careful," I had told my father, trying to reassure him.

After his escape from Yugoslavia in 1959, he had stifled nostalgia for his past. He started his new life with a sense of pride
and relief, considering his native country a closed chapter. And
yet he was unable to fully sever his ties. Each time he cut the
threads, they regrew with alarming precision. He missed his
family and his language. He would feel suddenly displaced and
long for the place of his birth. Although we visited every few
years, American passports tucked safely into my mother's purse,
my father returned like a boomerang, unavoidably attracted to
its hurler.

Those visits form a collage of my earliest memories: Walking on Zagreb's Zrinjevac Square in the evening, being forced
out of my grimy tomboy shorts and into lace-trimmed dresses,

and a cake my aunt Ljubica made for my birthday. The fat cat-fish my aunt Ana kept in a plastic tub in her Sarajevo apart-ment, and the way it swam slowly from side to side, bumping its nose with a low *tharrump* against the plastic. The sequined Turkish slippers and her tears when we left. Most of all, though, I remember our trips to the Adriatic Sea: the feel of smooth stones underfoot and the smell of pine trees; the red glass ear-rings I was allowed to select from the tables of summer markets, which would pinch my ears before I promptly lost one or both.

I AWOKE WITH A START at 6 a.m. I did not know where I was. A rooster was crowing outside my window, and sunlight bled through the window shades. I had been dreaming that I was searching feverishly for one of those earrings, scrabbling in all the crevices of the poorly lit place where I found myself. In the dream, my father sat on the empty cot across the room, watching my search and looking at me in some distress. "I left so my children could be safe," he said. When I opened my eyes, I was alone in my room in the base house in Tuzla. But the words rang in my ears after I had swung my legs over the cot's side and begun to dress.

In the bathroom, water ran from the taps in a slow trickle, and bent over the bathtub, I washed my hair. The water was ice-cold, and I shivered even as I toweled my hair dry and slipped a sweatshirt over my head. I looked in the mirror over the sink while I brushed the tangles from my hair, noting how pale I was beneath my summer skin, as if my face were on the verge of outgrowing me.

An hour later we piled into a white UN vehicle to make the

twenty-five-minute drive to the morgue. The team members were uniformly silent, looking out the windows at the passing countryside and at vegetation so wild and thick that it seemed it might overtake roofs and walls. The scarred shells of buildings, however, could not be hidden.

When I worked in West Virginia the previous summer, we battled underbrush with machetes. We found entire houses and lines of abandoned cars that had been eaten alive by ravenous green kudzu and jewelweed. I imagined how quickly those plants would cover everything, but the remnants of the ghost towns would still be there underneath, like traces of a forgotten civilization, waiting for winter to burn the coiling vines with frost. Waiting for the leaves to die in order to push their scarred faces stubbornly into the world again.

Several miles from Republika Srpska, we passed a mosque that had been mined from the inside, the minaret destroyed and tilting crazily. It looked as if it had been snapped off and then redeposited into the building like a straw, and I watched Dr. Peerwani, one of the pathologists, considering it. His assistant had told me that he was a devout Muslim. He muttered something under his breath and shook his head.

The war had meant indiscriminate destruction. Schools, hospitals, and religious structures had all been targets of shelling, bombs, and fire. Mines were placed at the four corners of a church, or explosives at the base of a minaret. In the past several years I had stood in a number of destroyed churches, always with the same feeling in my stomach, imagining the shadows of prayers that still spun in the ruined holy places. Those responsible had decided that it was not enough to remove their former neighbors through evictions and executions. They had been compelled to remove any physical reminder of them.

Some of the crew wanted photographs of the mosque, and we pulled over onto the shoulder, stones hitting the car's undercarriage like popping corn. We all got out, careful to stay on the road. I stood behind them, leaning against the door and watching the group talking and taking pictures. Pedestrians walked past with unreadable expressions, women clad in *dimije*—baggy trousers common to eastern Bosnia—with children on their hips, and men with sharply planed faces. They were accustomed to foreign faces and strangers taking photographs. They were also used to people getting back into their official vehicles and leaving without a backward glance. I was familiar with their expressions: hate sucked out into the white void, rage fed by powerlessness.

GEOFF, A BIG BEAR OF A MAN from Manchester, England, was setting up the morgue at the garment factory. He had outfitted it with electricity and arranged for the delivery of refrigerated containers for the bodies and a container with showers for our team. Hot water, I soon learned, was a godsend and an unspeakable luxury at the end of a day among decomposing bodies and clustering flies. The conditions were primitive: there were no windows in the building, and the floor was filthy cement.

An X-ray room was set up in the back of the building, where there had once been a factory mess hall. Some of us jumped over the counter and walked around the kitchen. Like children playing house.

"The cupboards are bare," someone intoned, like Mother Hubbard.

In the main hall, we set out metal examining tables, tools, and stretchers. A passageway on one side would be used as a waiting room for bodies to be autopsied. We could line the body bags up on stretchers, six at a time.

There was an inherent strangeness to those preparations. Getting ready for the dead was obscenely reminiscent of planning a child's birthday party. Everything had to be organized and readied, from the protective blue jumpsuits to the plastic jugs of soap that would be used for washing the clothes removed from the corpses. On that first day, the building was transformed from a ruined structure into a credible morgue, despite the black cables that hung from the ceiling and between exposed pipes like lifeless snakes.

Sewing machines and metal ironing boards were piled with debris in the corner of the room where autopsies would be performed. We examined everything carefully, as if we expected the cables to suddenly lower and crawl through our hair and the sewing machines to start whirring, handled by a hundred sets of ghostly hands.

That night, we explored the center of Tuzla. The cafés were crowded with people, smoking and laughing and listening to music. Many were not Bosnian, however, and I could hear snatches of French, Dutch, and German coming from tables around ours.

On the mile-long walk back to the house, I fell into conversation with Nizam Peerwani.

He tilted his head to one side. "You're Croatian?" He had heard me speaking with Jadranka earlier in the day.

I nodded. "My father is."

His sister-in-law, he told me, was a Croat from Derventa, a town in western Bosnia. She and her daughters had left just in time, in early 1992, coming to Texas as refugees. I looked at him carefully. My best friend, a nurse, had been in Derventa as it was falling. She had described the flatbed trucks that had taken some women and children out of the town. People had been crushed to death under the weight of other bodies.

There was something in the earnest way Dr. Peerwani talked about them that distinguished him from the rest of the team. For most of the others, there was no personal dimension to the work, and there were no Bosnian or Croatian team members. I had been told that several students in the field were completing graduate work in forensic anthropology.

The pathologists were slated to come in shifts to Bosnia, leaving behind their examining offices in a variety of countries, including the United States, England, and Sri Lanka. They would do shorter stints than the anthropologists, many of whom had worked all over the world: in Rwanda, Chile, Guatemala. Bosnia was just one stop along the way, and I remained quiet while listening to them describe projects in other countries.

Dr. Peerwani told me that it had been hard for his sister-in-law and her children to acclimate to America. Texas was certainly different from anything they knew. But with time, they had grown accustomed to American life, and both girls were enrolled in school.

"Do you know how lucky they are?" I blurted out, thinking of the women I had met from Derventa. My year of research had ensured that certain place-names would send chills down my back: Derventa, Brčko, Zvornik.

"Yes, I know." He looked at me suddenly. "I have to tell you that if my daughter said she wanted to do what you are going to do here, I wouldn't be happy about it. You're awfully young."

I shrugged uncomfortably, admitting after a minute of awkward silence that my father did not know where I was. I was afraid because there was a lot of media coverage of the graves, and dismayed, I had watched CNN close-ups of crew members in the days before my arrival. I could imagine him coming in from a walk with the dog, putting on his slippers, and turning on the television to see the top of my head.

Dr. Peerwani looked at me intently. "You'll have to pull your own weight and do as much as anyone else. You decided to be here, and we need the hands."

I nodded. At twenty-three, I was the youngest, and the only woman among the initial group of six. I had already fallen into the role of little sister, and I knew that the others felt protective of me. They had suggested that I stay at the base as a translator and not go out into the graves.

"But," I told them, "that's the whole reason I'm here."

"Why *is* it that you came here?" Dr. Peerwani asked, suddenly curious. We had reached the house's front steps, and the others had gone inside.

I was at a loss.

"Are you looking for something?" His eyes were still twinkling, but they did not leave my face.

"Maybe." I hesitated. I was not seeking experience or adventure. Part of me did not even know why I had come. "Maybe I came to be a witness. I spent a year documenting wives and mothers . . ."

It was the closing of the circle. I had spent so much time looking at it from the other side. Now I would see what had happened to their men.

"Do you think that if you see what became of them, it will help you to understand?"

I did not know how to answer him.

"It won't."

WHEN I ENTERED THE HOUSE, Jadranka was tidying up the kitchen. Her husband, Nedim, sat on the wall of the kitchen terrace. They were both about my age, *Tuzlani* by birth. When the war started, the university closed, and Nedim found work as a driver in one of the international humanitarian organizations that used Tuzla as a base of operations. It would be closing down shortly, however, and he was getting nervous about what he would do for money when they left town.

"Would you go back to school?" I asked.

He shrugged. It would be strange to go back to school after four difficult years, he said. He slipped his hand into Jadranka's. She had a sad smile and soft brown eyes. "I used to worry about him," she told me. "They'd send him out on errands, and shells would be falling all over the place."

Nedim shrugged again and smiled at her. "And not one of them hit. They were scared off by your worrying."

After the first few times out, he had learned to bring cassettes with him. When the shelling started, he would slip one into the tape deck and turn the volume to full blast. "It made it easier," he said with a grin. "I was a less nervous driver, and the shelling was just one more part of the general acoustics." He paused and shrugged. "It's over now. I'll tell my children about it one day."

"Do you have children?" I asked.

"No," Nedim said, suddenly shy. "Not yet."

I had met dozens of couples who had waited for the end of the war before embarking on the business of baby making.

They had delayed diapers and baby strollers in the hope of some safer time. I had met others who had refused to wait, bringing their children into an unsafe world, determining that they had no faith in a hypothetical future.

"What was the use of waiting?" a friend from Croatia had once asked me. I remembered too late that she had had a miscarriage during the war, before giving birth to a healthy daughter. "Women have babies in all sorts of impossible conditions," she told me. "The war might never have ended."

THE NEXT DAY, the bodies came.

The first black bag I unzipped was not a terrible shock, because I had been prepared by Dr. Peerwani's assistant, Ron. Still, there was an odd feeling at the pit of my stomach when I looked at the matter that had been a man almost exactly one year before. Charcoal lamps and a citronella candle were immediately lighted to keep the smell bearable and the flies away, but lamps and candles did not even partly succeed at driving off the misery of that place.

The bodies were X-rayed before examination so that the technician, Cyril, could pinpoint the location of bullets— dense spots among all that bone and soft matter. He removed them as evidence, so they would not be overlooked in the examination. Sometimes, though, the bullets had buried themselves, fusing in half-melted shapes to the white bone, and they were not easily dislodged.

When we placed a body on one of the examining tables, we removed the clothing and sent it outside to be washed. Personal effects were gathered and bagged. We reached into pockets for heels of bread, photographs, a plastic bag of coarse salt. The people who owned these objects lay quietly as we pored over them, turning them this way and that, muttering under our breath. We kept up a steady dialogue, noting each item, guessing its purpose.

The bones were then removed. Because the flesh was badly decomposed, it was in the bones that most pertinent information was stored. Removing them was like pulling sticks from wet ground, and the pathologists made sure that everything was accounted for, down to the smallest stray metacarpal bone. But the burial had been haphazard, and the bodies at the top of the grave were fully decomposed. The excavators in the field had often been unsure where one man ended and the next began.

That day, I learned preliminary ways to classify remains. It is possible to estimate age by the wear on teeth, by the degree of bone fusion at the top of the femur and humerus. Some of the teeth were new and pearly; others were worn down by years of use and yellowed from tobacco. It is also possible to detect youth in the pelvis: in young bones, the surface of one critical area is billowy, like thick, cottony clouds.

Dr. Peerwani showed me how to distinguish an entry gunshot wound from an exit wound, holding a cranium gingerly in his hand and pointing to the two holes and the distinctive beveling of their edges. He replaced the cranium on the table, and we both stood a moment looking at it. I imagined the revolution of that bullet, the moment of impact, and the point at which the bullet had pierced the rear plates of the head, ripping a hole that caused the bone sutures to come slightly apart. This had been a young man, Dr. Peerwani said, pointing to the billows of his pelvis. He had been shot from behind.

By the end of the day, I was aware that I had crossed an invisible border. As we locked the freezer and washed the equipment in soapy water, I was unsure when that moment had been. I knew that I had become suddenly quiet around midday, unable to do more than watch with large, grim eyes and follow the pathologists' instructions. I sensed that I moved very slowly, almost lumbering, as if I were walking through a viscous substance other than air.

Standing over the washtubs, I realized that I had not seen my hands since that morning. They were covered in double layers of latex gloves, and I stopped what I was doing to look at them, dumbfounded. I peeled the gloves away and held them, palms down, looking at the white half-moons of my nails as if aware of their existence for the first time.

Dr. Peerwani appeared at my side, and he too looked at my hands. He cleared his throat, and I jumped a little, making them into fists. "Why don't you go have a shower?" he suggested, and I nodded gratefully, turning away from the autopsy hall.

Ron warned me, "Start it cold. That way you wash off the mess without opening your pores. If your pores open, and the smell creeps in, it'll follow you around for days."

I had a terrible stomachache that evening. I admitted to Dr. Peerwani on the drive back to Tuzla that I had breathed through my mouth all day, afraid of letting that smell into my nose.

He shook his head. "Don't do that. You don't want that bad air going through your mouth. It'll go straight to your stomach. Just breathe normally, and you'll get used to it."

After returning from Kalesija, I collapsed on my cot. I

looked up at the ceiling, picturing the refrigerated container and its piles of bodies. I remembered the days leading up to the fall of Srebrenica—I had been in Huntington, West Virginia—and I remembered the face of a television reporter, his voice hushed as he described the buildup to the city's final defeat. He had referred to world leaders as powerless.

I had come in from surveying, hot and sunburned after a day beneath heavy West Virginia air. I had managed to put the war out of my mind for the duration of the workday, but there was something about the announcer's tone that made me drop my gear in the doorway and crawl sickly and sweaty beneath the acrylic cover on the bed. I slept an ugly sleep, and by morning Srebrenica had fallen.

Falling asleep in Tuzla, the image of the first open body bag on a gurney came into my head. Nizam Peerwani had been watching my face for a reaction, concerned and yet removed, wondering if I would be able to stand it.

After a while he had cleared his throat. "If you left this in the sun for a few days—two, maybe three—it would become earth. No more flies. No smell. Just clean earth."

My eyes had filled with tears. "Thank you," I told him.

His words helped me through the following weeks.

WE DID NOT HAVE A SUPPLY of drinking water at the morgue, and the next day an SFOR base nearby offered to give us as many bottles as we could carry. There was also a PX, which sold telephone cards. Looking at the display, I felt a sudden need to hear my parents' voices, and I bought a card, wandering outside to find a telephone.

My mother answered, her voice so soft and gentle that I felt as if my chest were a dam that suddenly cracked lengthwise. Unlike my father, she knew where I was. She lowered her voice still further to ask, "Is everything all right?"

I wanted to tell her of the threshold I had passed the day before, and the fact that nothing would ever be the same again. My mouth opened and closed like a fish's, but no sound came out.

"Love?" her English voice asked from our kitchen in Virginia.

I could look at the sky or a newspaper, but it would be different now, as if all the colors, or my perception of them, had shifted overnight. In the end, making my voice light, I said, "Everything's fine." And then I asked, "How's Dad?"

My father had been nervous when I returned to Croatia the year before, though by then the war was over.

"Be careful," he had told me at the airport as my mother hugged me good-bye. And then, "We almost lost you once."

They hadn't really, I protested on more than one occasion, but he had been adamant.

On a sunny autumn day in 1993, I was traveling to Croatia's Adriatic coast when my train was shelled from occupied "Krajina" territory. At first we could hear mortars in the distance, and then shells began to fall with roars around the train.

The train had been filled with Croatian soldiers, and they herded us to an abandoned depot. They set up a command on the first floor but ushered us into the cellar. We could hear them walking around and shouting to one another. My friend Tia and I were pushed by the throng of other passengers into a section that had once been a large coal box. It was filthy, and the entire cellar contained the strange, rank smell of fear, which nauseated me.

The electricity had gone out. After the first couple of hours I had to urinate. If I don't pee, I'll go crazy, I thought in the blackness. I repeated this aloud to Tia, who was standing next to me.

"You're out of your mind," she said. "Peeing is the last thing on my mind."

But I had to. I ran up the wooden steps, almost laughing. I was far from hysterical, though, because my need seemed to have made me human again. A woman at the top of the stairs grabbed my arms as I thundered out of the cellar, blind as a newborn kitten.

"I have to go to the bathroom," I explained, grimacing.

She laughed and pointed the way to the outhouse. I ran the ten yards, out into the gray air, out into the smell of metal, and it was relief as I'd never before known it. My abdomen shuddered; then the outhouse rocked as a shell landed nearby. I ran back to the building unburdened and strangely fearless.

One of the soldiers saw my face and smiled. "Where have you been, little one?"

I was at an uncharacteristic loss for words. Instead, I found my bag by the cellar door and brought out the food that my aunts had packed for me that morning. Country bread and butter, tomatoes sweeter than fruit. He refused the bread, but his eyes fixed on the tomatoes.

"So long since I had a tomato," he sighed, accepting one. The skin of my hand was soot-blackened from the cellar. He took the tomato in his teeth and smiled. He was from around Plitvice, he told me, where his family had owned a house with a large garden. It was under occupation now, and I could almost sense a memory unfolding in him: his mother and her vegetable garden, the house that lay in splinters.

Outside, the shelling was abating, like thunder from a receding storm, black clouds moving to terrorize another location.

The soldier wanted to know what kind of a garden my mother had in America. "Do you grow tomatoes? Do you work in the garden with your mother?"

He looked at the grit under his nails, the mica shining like a salting of stars. "Everything's fucked up, do you know that? Everything." But the tomato was wet and sweet, and he sat with me a little while longer.

A SHORT TIME after returning to the cellar, I learned that an eleven-year-old had been killed near the depot. I shuddered when this piece of information went from one person to the next in the underground space, realizing that I had, with a certainty, heard the shell that killed him. He had taken shelter under a pear tree with his family's cows and was waiting out the artillery attack.

"He could see the train," the soldiers told us when we emerged, finally, into the evening light. "He was aiming for the train from a kilometer or two away."

He? I wanted to ask. At first I thought they were talking about the boy, and then I realized they meant the person who had been firing at us. I imagined him standing on a hill, looking at us through binoculars. He smelled of brandy and had a huge scraggly beard. He was the stuff of nightmares, the killer of eleven-year-old boys.

In the weeks that followed, I found myself talking about

that day repeatedly, needing to tell my parents each new detail I remembered, craving to unload the desperation I had felt in that place. So intent was I on this unburdening that I would call them in the morning, realizing only belatedly from their groggy voices that it was the middle of the night in America. In the end, I think their trauma was greater than my own.

Now, at the SFOR base, I stood in something like a phone booth to call my parents. The door was glass, and I could see the Bosnian hills that rose behind the base, and the high barbed wire that tied it in. My mother's voice had almost made me cry, but when my father's voice came on the line, I held my emotions in check and told him rather glibly about my fictional work in western Slavonia.

When he hung up, I stayed a moment longer on the telephone, listening to the hum that still existed on the line, an entire dialogue of the unsaid.

IT WAS NOT THE IDEA OF DYING that filled me with blind panic that day in the depot's cellar, but the idea of dying *there*, of being buried alive with all those unknown people. It was the fact that my parents would not know, that it might take days for the news to reach them. I imagined an incendiary device crashing through ceiling and floor, incinerating everything in its path, and leaving not one splinter of evidence behind. They might never learn what had truly happened to me. I could imagine them searching hospital wards and mental asylums, wondering what had become of me, inventing realities in which I somehow thrived but was prevented from returning to them by an amnesiac state.

They would not even be certain under which name to look,

if a name could miraculously survive. Names seem to be among the first casualties of war. The year before, I had started going by my middle name, Angela. My aunts always considered my first name an impossible act of verbal acrobatics, and so I had switched. I had been given the name for my grandmother, Anđelka. And all the time they worried about which name to look for, I would be a sooty stain in the wreck of an abandoned railway building.

My father had been troubled when I started responding to the name Angela. I think it seemed to him a rejection of the safe life he had created for us in America. "She had such a hard life, your grandmother," he had told me tightly.

When we were evacuated from that train, I had grabbed a book from my backpack for some reason. In the cellar, I tore out a page at the end and filled it with a letter to my parents and my brother, apologizing for this predicament. When the shelling seemed to abate suddenly in the early afternoon, I rolled it into a thin cigarette and rushed outside to stick it in a crack of the building's exterior wall.

Why I thought a piece of flammable paper would survive what my teeth would not, I am unsure. I only know that I retreated into the cellar again, satisfied. When the shelling stopped, I covertly removed the scrap of paper and destroyed it.

I had signed it "Courtney Angela." In case one name was burned away, the other might survive.

HERZEGOVINA

1918–1931

Several windows, white and luminous, behold me from
   out of the gloom:
like the handful of shining and joyful moments
from the dark lives of men

   —A. B. Šimić, from "Herzegovina"

CHILDHOOD WAS a collection of Herzegovina's rough textures, and from an early age Anđelka learned to identify them all. There was the feel of night, the clear sky that made the stars so bright it ached to look at them directly, and the sound of the village stirring when morning came. She would lie awake in the bed she shared with her younger sisters, watching darkness recede from between the curtains as if it were a black cloth steadily unraveling in someone's hands.

There were the harsh limestone hills around their village of Posušje, the fields of rough ground and sunken spaces that trapped an underground labyrinth of rivers. The water hummed through rock so far beneath the surface that digging wells was futile, and people collected scant drops in *čatrnje*, rainwater cisterns. And there were the hills on whose stone sides thirsty brush desperately clung.

"Are we like roses?" her younger sister Ljubica had once asked their mother fancifully, looking at the delicate design of one of their few china cups. She had been sitting cross-legged on the floor, trying to coax imaginary liquids into her cloth doll. "Or are we as pretty as violets?"

"Neither," was the response, so abrupt that even the twins, who were not yet out of diapers, looked up in surprise. Their mother had grown ill that year, and her eyes were ominously bright. She strode to the door and flung it open, pointing to the dry yellow fields behind the house and to the hills in the distance. "We're the brush that clings to the rocky ground," she told them as they crowded in the doorway behind her. "That's better than roses or violets."

In Posušje's church, Anđelka had heard the Franciscan priest explaining the parable of the seed. Where seeds—God's word—fell upon fertile soil, entire fields sprang up. When the seeds fell on barren ground, like God's word on deaf ears, nothing grew.

There was little fertile land around their village, and nothing should have grown from it. It was backbreaking work to coax out a handful of tough-stalked tobacco fields, and the men who farmed them had craggy faces etched by sun and rain. They spent their lives planting, harvesting, and drying the "yellow gold," until coming to rest, gaunt and unadorned, in that same ground. Or they went *trbuhom za kruhom*, following their stomachs in search of bread, and worked as manual laborers in mills and mines in strange countries where they died alone.

In Posušje there were few gardens, even fewer flowering bushes, and their mother grabbed the rosebud cup from Ljubica's hands, placing it back in the cupboard.

In the ensuing months, the sisters drew pictures on white butcher's shop paper—stained here and there with flecks of rust-colored blood—of rocks from which entire fields of flowers grew. In Herzegovina, they bloomed in spite of barren ground.

ROUGH DUST ROSE on the daylong journey to Mostar, where Anđelka was sent to a parochial school for girls. The dust rose in wreaths from beneath the wagon wheels and clung to her in a haze during the entire trip. Even when she reached the girls' dormitory, unpacked her few possessions, and washed the dust from her skin and hair, she could picture it billowing up from the ground.

When she began her lessons, she was in fact more interested in the elements of her landscape than in the minutiae of daily religious and domestic instruction. She was fascinated by Mostar's white slabs of city stone and arbors, and by the vendors who hawked their wares in the city's market.

When she could, she stole away to the bridge and stood at its peaked center, watching the intense green of the Neretva River flowing beneath her feet. She had learned that the river spread into a delta before it reached the coast, miles away. The soil there was reputed to be black and rich, yielding every variety of fruit. She had seen the proof in the marketplace: baskets of giant peaches with blood-red pits brought overland from Metković.

From the bridge she could see women washing clothes in the shallows downstream, skirts lifted above their knees. They beat fabric against rocks rhythmically, and she imagined the water leaching the cloth of its fibers, removing dust from the rocks on which they stood, depositing these materials far down-stream. No wonder Herzegovina was bare, she thought; every bit of softness and silt had been carried out of it. And she imag-ined herself floating downriver, rushing out on a flood of azure water into the sea she had never seen.

It was in Mostar that she first heard *sevdalinke*, the romantic and mournful ballads the city was famous for. In the evening she would sit in the stone window of her dormitory and listen to the music rising from the town. She and the other girls were not allowed into the town at night. They were expected to concentrate on their devotions or study their books and were thus shielded from the very strange world of men that existed outside the school walls. Anđelka yearned for the freedom to observe that world, so different from Posušje, where she seemed to know every stone of every house, and every tree in every parched garden.

The *sevdalinke* were different from the *ganga* songs of Herze-govina's highlands. *Ganga* sounded mournful in the mouths of women. When men sang it, however, the tones were powerful and feral, the best *ganga* singers able to use their bodies like gi-ant vibrating instruments. The songs were often about *bećari*, rakish men whose twin passions were carousing and seducing women. The songs had begun, her own mother had told her once, in answer to the vast silence of the mountainsides. Shep-herds, alone or with their comrades, had used the songs to fill up all that space.

Anđelka had never given those songs much thought, but in Mostar she began to realize the sheer force of the *ganga*. Men and women sang hymns together in church, but *ganga* was a segregated practice, and she spent weeks imagining that they were the war cries of opposing armies.

Truth be told, she preferred the harmony of the *sevdalinke*. She liked listening to the stories they told of jasmine gardens and lost love, and on many nights she fell asleep listening to a guitar that she imagined played its tender notes for her alone.

LATER THERE WERE THE DUST CLOUDS of her return trip and the waxen texture of her brother's skin, as women in the main room readied Franjo's small body for burial. They shooed the other children out of the room, but Anđelka had been allowed to remain. She shifted silently from foot to foot as they wiped him clean with a cloth and wrapped him in a sheet her mother had taken from her dowry chest.

Before they placed him in the simple wooden box, Anđelka thought she saw her mother mouth a quick prayer as she bent to kiss him. She moved closer, watching her mother's lips as she repeated one word over and over. *Sleep*, she thought her mother was telling him.

Later still, there was the feel of her own dowry chest, with its elaborate carvings of vines and flowers. Making it was one of the last tasks her father completed before he joined their mother in the cemetery's rocky soil during an epidemic of Spanish influenza. When Anđelka was left suddenly alone at the age of fourteen, the eldest of five living sisters, she had possessed little other than the rectangular box of sweet-smelling wood, half empty of the things a dowry should contain. And when her sweetheart explained his mother's sudden opposition to their match, alluding to her four younger sisters along with their four hungry mouths, Anđelka had closed its lid carefully and concluded that the kind optimism with which her father made it had been in vain.

But Herzegovina's pure light shone through all her childhood days, and it was what she would remember most clearly
about her native region. It made the rocky ground blinding in
summertime, and the roofs of the stone houses stand crisply
against a January sky. In winter the wind howled around those
houses while the villagers wrapped themselves in woolen layers
to stay the cold. They muttered that the wind boded no good,
that its howling at night made the animals nervous. But
Anđelka liked it. She drew her coat tightly around her shoulders and struck off down country roads amid the puzzled stares
of neighbors. When she was a safe distance from the village,
she found that she could face down the stinging wind by
screaming, and the wind would steal her voice across fields of
ice and white stone. And she would think without rancor, At
least my voice can escape.

In her sixteenth year, when Marijan, the neighbor's son, returned from teachers' college in Derventa on just such a day of
curious, gusting light, she took it as an omen and chose him for
her husband.

ALTHOUGH HE HAD BEEN BORN in Posušje, Marijan Brkić
did not qualify as a native of Herzegovina. His mother was from
Imotski, twelve miles away and across the border in Dalmatia,
the strip of Croatian land on the Adriatic Sea.

When he and Anđelka announced their wedding, the entire
village looked at her suspiciously, trying to remember how flat
her belly had been before the news. But their opinions did not
matter to her, and when her former sweetheart tried reasoning

with her, saying that he had only meant they should wait awhile before marriage, pride made her ignore his imploring eyes. She had reached her decision, she told him obstinately, and would not change her mind.

Marijan's hair was coal black and startling against his pale skin. He loved musical instruments, the pads of his fingers coaxing out songs and his voice finding their edges. The villagers shook their heads in amazement as he took up one instrument after another, immediately proficient. Percussion, strings, it did not matter.

He painted, still lifes and nudes on huge canvases. He was fond of bright and bold colors, and the smoothness of the oil shone in the light his mother extinguished benevolently when he fell asleep after a long night of carousing.

A typical *bećar*, he loved to drink, his head thrown back and his white teeth slicing through the air. And he loved to argue, driving other men to distraction, so that they wanted to wrap their hands around his throat and squeeze. But he did not like to fight, and he was famous for starting arguments, then leaning back in amusement as others took them up.

Although Andelka knew all these things, she was determined to get along as other wives did.

But it was the politics of men she hated. *"Politika je kurva,"* she would learn to say. Politics is a whore. And once she was married, she had no patience when her husband invited people into their home to sit at the table and debate the intricacies of this or that political maneuver. Like other generations of women, she stood in the background of their polemics. She set out the glasses and the bottle of clear *rakija* and left them to their discussions.

So it was especially crushing to her when Stjepan Radić was murdered in Belgrade in 1928. She knew who he was, more or less. He was the great Croatian statesman, and Marijan was his ardent supporter. When Radić was murdered and reprisals took effect against his followers, Anđelka and her husband were sent nine miles away into "internal" exile by the Kingdom of Yugoslavia to the backwater of Rakitno, a hamlet with a few houses and a church. Marijan was to be the schoolteacher, and Anđelka blamed him for their punishment.

On the day they arrived in Rakitno, she stood on the stone threshold of their new home, the village schoolhouse. They would live in the adjoining rooms. Behind her were the floors that she would wash a thousand times in the months to come, the stove whose belly she would fill with wood so she could cook their meals, and the kitchen table on whose surface she would eventually bear two sons, her first surviving children.

But she knew none of this as she stood there with her back turned on the kitchen and its possibilities. She chose to look out into the daylight, out across the rocky ground that inched up to the house. The sun was so bright that she could barely look at the scorched stones. Beyond them was the brown of fields and the pale green and yellow of dry summer grass. She wistfully recalled the green Neretva rushing beneath Mostar's stone bridge.

Her dress and shoes were gray with dust from the trip, and she bit back tears. There were no shops here; nor were there sisters or friends whom she could visit. The women of Rakitno had tired, hungry eyes. Their spindly-legged children would come to classes barefoot. Posušje was small and poor, but Rakitno was tiny and starving.

Her husband walked past her, his guitar slung across his

back. He set it down on the table and took her hand, spinning her away from the outside, away from the threshold. He twirled her around and around, and she was too tired to protest. In the end he won a small smile from her.

"You are not as annoyed with me as you think," he tried.

She batted him with the palm of her hand. It could have been worse. Ljubica and her husband, Ante, had also been sent into exile, but hundreds of miles away, to an even smaller village in Macedonia. They had cried when they parted, Ljubica and Ante eastward, Anđelka and Marijan to Rakitno, while the three youngest sisters stayed with an aunt in Posušje. Anđelka had to be honest with herself, though. She also felt a sense of relief in leaving. "I think I would love my sisters best at a distance," she had once confessed to Marijan.

He had used this as artillery when he told her of the impending move. "Your sisters are a nuisance. They have their aunt to take care of them." He had been white-lipped, having just heard the news himself.

It was true. Besides, what use was it to be the branch that stood stiffly in the wind, wearing and tearing and scattering splinters? It was better to bend, quietly. She moved away from him and started unpacking their belongings.

SEVEN MONTHS after their banishment, there was a strange heaviness in her belly, and then the sickness that heralded a pregnancy. Will this one die like the others? she wondered. The first baby, Zlatko, had died just hours after his birth. The labor had been a battle, leaving her exhausted, pale, and bathed in blood and sweat. The baby had not cried, and they knew immediately that something was wrong. The other one had been fiercer. A little girl named Katja, she had hung on almost a month before starting to fade. She became quieter, smaller, slept more. Her skin grew translucent, like transparent marble, as if she were disintegrating little by little from the inside. A match held behind her would have shone through her as through a glass.

"Will this one die?" Anđelka asked God the question while she cleaned the house, while she listened to the sound of her husband's pupils in the other room, and at night, while the winter moon pierced the white of the curtains and her husband stirred in the bed next to her.

There was a reason her mother had let her stay in the room when they washed her brother's body. She understood it as soon as she began burying her own children.

"*Spavaj*," Anđelka had whispered to each one before they were placed in the ground. "Sleep."

Once the pregnancy began to show, the old women in the village were full of advice. Anđelka listened patiently while they leaned their black-kerchiefed heads close to hers, waving their hands about. There were a hundred remedies, many of them contradictory. This root and that leaf, and timing was the most important. They took her wedding ring and spun it above her belly on a string. It would be a boy, they told her. She listened, thinking of other things.

Sitting on the swept threshold, she watched the fields, her hand on her belly. "You must live," she told him fervently. "You must."

THAT IS HOW she came to plant her garden on a particularly harsh section of that rocky earth called Herzegovina. But she planted it in shallow ground, and each plant had two kinds of roots. The first were adaptable and mobile, able to be replanted and still ensure the plant's survival. The second were deeper roots, which broke off and remained cradled in a sheath of stone. Calcified remains, they became artifacts, and later she recognized this attribute of Herzegovina as well.

He would survive, a tiny and frail baby with olive skin inherited from his father's mother. Anđelka thought up a thousand ways to make him strong, to make the milk come, and to entice him to eat more. "I will make you fat," she whispered to him as she fed him.

She did not leave his side for a second and would not allow him to be cared for by others. She trusted him with no one. Her husband was baffled, and the women in the village felt snubbed by her when she turned down their offers of help. But even as they retreated, they recognized this stubbornness.

At night she pulled the cradle within reach of the bed, and she slept fitfully, awakening whenever she felt him stir and when the milk came, when she imagined that he had cried out, or when her heart thundered after dreaming that something soft, black, and infinitely evil had entered their room and crawled in beside him. Her husband snored softly through all of it.

Villagers had made their predictions, however. The older women shook their heads. They were surprised when the baby grew stronger and larger. His living did not disappoint them, but it confused them. It threw the order of the world into doubt, because it was much easier to predict a baby's death than its survival.

They named him Berislav, after no one. It was a name cut out and made for him so he would not grow up in another's shadow, but they shortened it and nicknamed him Bero. One woman from the village suggested putting a pinecone in the cradle with him so he would get used to a little discomfort. Anđelka listened without comment.

"*U životu nije sve glatko,*" the old woman insisted. "It's not all sweetness in life. Make him tough, and he will weather it all better." Anđelka smiled tightly and thanked her for the advice. With pursed lips, the woman watched her go, and Anđelka could imagine what the woman would say to others: *The schoolteacher is an upstanding young man, but his wife is headstrong and will not listen to reason.*

That night when she bathed him and sang him to sleep, she squeezed his foot. *A little discomfort,* she remembered, and shook her head. He stirred in his sleep, his head finding the hollow between breast and arm. "Nasty old woman," she murmured to him. "As if we don't already know that for ourselves."

SHE SANG TO HIM. Songs she remembered from childhood, which was not that long ago, because she was then only nineteen. Some of the songs had no names, and some did not even have words, but she hummed them to him under her breath. And there were new songs that she made up, pulling their invisible threads from the air. Songs about warm suns and pinewoods, grapes and the sea. Songs about places she had only known in stories, and she braided them together and wrapped them around her sleeping child.

Standing in the kitchen in her shift, she washed her hair with water she had brought in from the well, the baby in a wooden cradle she dragged from room to room. He lay on his back, watching the ceiling in amazement, as if there were colors floating in the air that none of the rest of them could see. He listened to the sound of the pouring water and the sound of her hands as she rubbed soap into her hair. He listened to her humming.

She rinsed the bubbles away and stood up. The water had made little highways across her back, and her shift stuck to her skin. Though it was September, it was still hot. Not the angry, thick heat of full summer, but a radiating heat. She took the baby in her arms and went out into the sun to dry her hair. He fell asleep smelling the clean smell of her, and she held him tightly with a slow, sure smile of satisfaction. Two months had gone by, and he was still alive.

AFTER HIS FIRST BIRTHDAY she felt as if a burden had been taken from her. An old woman had told her that this milestone was a mountain summit, and once you had reached it, the way down was much easier. He was still thin and often sick, but he had wrapped tremulous fingers around the edges of his crib and held himself up on wobbling legs.

What would happen to Bero if she got sick? She promised herself that she would sleep, and she sank into the white linen of the bedsheets. The baby was talking to himself in the cradle. He laughed, watching all the baby colors that were invisible to her. She closed her eyes and dreamed. In the dream she was pregnant again. She looked down at her belly and held it on both sides with her hands. She smiled in her sleep, and the baby kicked. When her eyes flickered open, the room was in black shadow. Bero was breathing shallowly in the cradle, and she stuck her leg out from underneath the bedsheets to touch the smooth wood of the side with her toe. She wondered where

Marijan was. He had gone to another village, but he should have been home by dark. Sometimes, when he went hunting for days at a time, she taught his classes while the baby slept in his crib. Although Marijan always managed to bring home something—a bird or a brace of rabbits—she knew that the trips had more to do with drinking and telling ribald stories than with hunting.

When she fell back to sleep, she dreamed that she was sitting at the kitchen table, a shallow cup of coffee in front of her. For amusement Anđelka would tell people's fortunes from the patterns the dried grounds made on the inside of cups. It had started innocently enough, a game in which she did not believe.

In the dream, she was studying the sugary grounds. There were loud thunderclaps and the bodies of men without eyes, without heads. Her children were hungry and chattering excitedly about bread, eyes wide and sunken in their faces. There were barking dogs and men who came and beat down her door, dragging her out into the night. She opened her eyes slowly in the darkness. Her heart was in her mouth.

Outside in the yard, Marijan was calling her name. He sounded happy and a little drunk, his voice rising through the windows.

She sighed, put a hand on her stomach, then got out of bed to light the lamp.

THE NEXT BABY, also a son, had sky-blue eyes. He was even smaller and weaker than Bero had been. His skin was pale, and she wrapped him in blankets to keep the sun's rays off his whiteness. They named him Zoran, from the word for *dawn*.

Typhoid had struck the surrounding towns around the time Zoran was baptized. Anđelka, cradling the baby as Bero held on to her legs, heard the whispered conversations.

When she became ill, she shook with the fever, and they had to pry her fingers loose from the baby. They put her to bed, and a woman from the village sat at her bedside the first night. The woman brought brackish water in a basin and bathed her forehead with a rag. Anđelka shivered so violently that her teeth rattled, and the old woman was afraid that she would bite off her tongue. She tossed from side to side, muttering in her sleep. Marijan grasped her hands. Her eyes fluttered, and she muttered unintelligibly.

Marijan was uncommonly pale, and his hands shook. "We have to get her to a doctor," he announced tersely.

They fashioned a stretcher from a door, and they wrapped her with blankets. There was no road from Rakitno, just a rutted track for donkeys and tired pedestrians, but the villagers hoisted the door onto their shoulders and started walking. At some point she opened her eyes. A thousand stars looked down at her, and when she turned her head, she saw the heads of men from the village, fathers of her husband's pupils. She knew them but could not remember any of their names. Their faces blurred, but before she lost consciousness, she tried to ask them if she had died and they were taking her to the cemetery.

When they reached Posušje, the closest town, they tracked down a friend with a car. People on the street stopped to watch the procession: villagers in coarse clothing carrying a woman on a door.

They transferred her carefully to the car and drove the distance to Mostar hospital, where the night-ward sisters took over. Anđelka was folded into their waiting hands, and Marijan stood to the side, turning his hat round and round in his hands. A warmth had started creeping into his legs. His eyes were like pieces of black glass, and the man who had driven him drew instinctively away with a barely perceptible motion. Marijan realized that the nurse had been speaking to him for some time, and he concentrated on her mouth, trying to combine the sounds so that they made words and the words so that they made sentences.

The nurse moved toward him, placing a hand on his forehead. He took a step backward and smiled, but shook his head. The heat was threatening to creep into his rib cage, and he knew he must leave before it reached his head. He foresaw his death in that hospital. He caught sight of his wife covered in white. Like an angel, he thought, not realizing that he was looking at the bedsheets.

"She will survive?"

The nurse was chattering to him and nodding. Marijan could not make any sense of it. He had to leave. He thought of his aunt's house in Imotski, several hours away, where he had spent many childhood days, and he decided to go there. He had to leave soon, afraid that otherwise he would not find the house upon his arrival. He thundered blindly down the steps into the deserted night. The nurse called after him.

He traveled hours to his aunt's house, shaking himself and trying to dislodge the sickness. But it stuck to him like soot from a chimney. When he arrived, he pounded on her door and collapsed on her front step. "Djinko?" she called him by his nickname. "Djinko, what's wrong?"

He could not speak, and just smiled at her. She led him into the house and seated him at the table. She brought him *rakija*, and he drank it back. The heat receded for an instant, and he became aware of his surroundings. He saw his aunt seated across from him, her face flushed with worry. He saw the lamp she had lighted. The oil was making the air pungent, and he realized that the chair he was sitting on was wooden and had no cushion. He shifted, feeling the pain in his joints. There was a bowl of red apples on the table. They looked crisp and tart. When he was a child, he used to steal apples from fruit trees with his brothers. They always got caught, but he never did. Years later he had been riding by an orchard on horseback, and he leaned over to pick one from a tree. The farmer had caught him and, waving a gun in the air, threatened to shoot him. But he extricated himself the way he always did, with an easy smile and a quick tongue, and they had ended up sitting beneath the apple trees drinking *loza* together.

He pulled the wooden bowl toward him and listened to the scraping sound it made. The apples were huge, and he took one in his hand.

ANĐELKA WAS ONLY HALF CONSCIOUS, but she could hear the ward sisters speaking. "Her husband is dead." The words hovered in the darkness beyond her. It was an odd darkness, and it smelled of antiseptic and burning charcoal.

"The one that wouldn't stay? Poor fool." It was a young voice. The nurses were bathing her. She shuddered, wondering whose husband had died. *Where are my children?* she tried to ask the nurses. *Where are my boys?* But the air was so heavy. It pinned her mouth shut and her eyes closed.

SO SHE RETURNED to Rakitno a widow. She took only a day to pack their things and arrange for them to be transported to Posušje. Her younger sister Iva had come to help her with the children, and Anđelka gathered the last of their possessions while Iva swept the steps outside. Her sister's tidying seemed pointless, but Anđelka's body was weak, and she lacked the energy to say so. She felt like a shell.

She looked down at her hands and inspected her smooth palms. She turned them over. They were strong hands, although they did not look like the hands of a twenty-one-year-old woman.

"Fool," she told the air softly, lowering her hands in disgust. "Fool for not staying at the hospital," she told him as he seemed to skirt the edges of the room. "Fool for eating apples and dying." They had torn his stomach apart, his aunt had told her, and he had died in agony. Everyone knew better than to eat when sick with stomach typhoid, but Marijan had always felt untouchable.

She bent to collect the last of their things. She could hear Zoran crying outside, and Bero was running in unsteady circles in the yard.

"Careful!" she called through the open door. "Don't fall."

But Bero threw his arms into the air, as if flapping wings. "Ma-ma-ma-ma-ma," his voice called out to her, louder when he neared the door and fading as he ran away. "Ma-ma-ma-ma."

The curtains she had made still hung at the windows. They were drawn, but the open door cast a river of light across the plank floor. Each time Bero neared the doorway, his shadow darted across that field of light, and she could not help but smile, watching its clean edges move over the already dusty floor. By tomorrow morning, she thought, they would be long gone, and her son's shadow would never again move across it.

She closed the door behind her and descended the two steps into the yard. Her sister handed her the baby, and Bero grinned and ran to her, arms flung wide.

AFTER THEIR PARENTS' DEATHS, the three youngest Jukić sisters who had remained in Posušje looked after themselves with the aid of cousins and their aunt, Ujna. Thanks to epidemics of tuberculosis, influenza, and typhoid fever that tore regularly through the mountains, children without parents were no rarity. They formed marooned populations, the fortunate ones assimilated into existing family structures, expected at mealtimes and in the same pew at mass, albeit sometimes grudgingly.

Herzegovina's situation had worsened with the advent of the Kingdom of Serbs, Croats, and Slovenes after the defeat of the Austrian Empire in the First World War. Croatians and other groups realized belatedly that Serbs did not consider the kingdom an equal partnership of Southern Slavs. Instead, Serbs were aggressively dominating the union and felt entitled to exploit it. Among other justifications, the Serbs cited the fact that Serbia had been independent of the Ottoman Empire since 1878, whereas other groups had served foreign masters until just a few years before.

Tensions were on the rise in the kingdom, and the standard

of living had fallen sharply. Without the Austro-Hungarian in-frastructure to employ men in the hungrier regions, fathers were a scant resource even in families unscathed by disease. The long-entrenched tradition of going "out" for work—to Germany, Austria, and even America—became increasingly frequent. By sending back portions of their wages, these men managed, just barely, to keep their families in Herzegovina from starving.

In the villages, women endured a lifetime of their men's ab-sence. There were sporadic visits home, frequently resulting in pregnancies, and wives were left to raise the children as best they could. They followed a cycle of childbirth and death, fast-ing and holy days, and the women grew bent as they tilled the dry dirt of their fields alone. They were fiercely Catholic, and their belief was the balm that soothed the wounds of this life, promising an end to hardship in the life to come.

At the end of their careers as laborers, the men returned, looking old beyond their years. They entered their houses or stood calling up from their courtyards, and they were greeted with curiosity and surprise, so wholly unrecognizable were they to their families. And no sooner were they welcomed home than their sons would depart, amid the bitter tears of wives and mothers, so that in many families the population of men was in perpetual rotation.

Sometimes the men did not return, but died in accidents. If a man had worked with brothers, cousins, or others from his town, word would reach home in the course of weeks or months. If he had worked alone, news might come years later or not at all. It was not uncommon for a man to disappear, the delivery of money stopping abruptly.

Widows were expected to remain faithful to a dead or missing spouse and not remarry. The handful of women who did not
follow this social code were ostracized and regarded with suspi-
cion. "*Kurva*," other women would comment to one another.
Whore. "That she should dishonor her husband's memory." Frequently widows themselves, they would draw their black shawls
around their shoulders and join together in an offended but
united front.

KATJA AND IVA JUKIĆ were twins, as dissimilar from each
other as night and day. Katja was a tall, ruddy girl, always quick
with a joke. She had lively eyes and could be merciless in her
teasing. Her wit promised that she would be a rarity in Herzegovina—a woman able to hold her own among men, even in
conversations that most women would not dare join.

Tiny Iva was renowned for her humility and quiet obstinacy.
At the age of twelve she had been warned against singing a
hymn that was banned in the Kingdom—"Virgin of Paradise,
Queen of Croats." Despite her sisters' pleas, she had joined a
group of women and children in the church who raised their
voices in the hymn, and although still a child, she was briefly
jailed for her efforts.

Iva was shy and resolute. She lacked Anđelka's beauty and
Katja's outgoing temperament, but she possessed a serene nature uncommon to teenage girls. And although this did not in-
crease her beauty or make her the subject of amorous pursuit,
her humility and unerring virtue were the source of some pride
in the town.

Iva hoped one day to go on a pilgrimage to the tomb of Diva

Grabovčeva, which lay beside a lake in the region of Rama, north of Posušje. The story, part fact and part legend, tells of a beautiful young martyr who chose to die rather than satisfy the lustful advances of an Ottoman nobleman. Pilgrimages of pious young women went frequently to the tomb.

The tales of Herzegovina were rife with the presence of martyred virgins, many of them slain centuries ago. By dying rather than acquiescing to the brutal demands of men, they protected the pillars of their faith against attacks by jaded noblemen or marauders, and their tombs peppered the countryside. The stories, embellished with each retelling, became fables of decency and honor. In choosing death, young women were counseled, a girl chooses freedom.

While all the Jukić girls were relatively virtuous, Iva was the one village mothers pointed to approvingly. They lectured their own daughters, holding her up as an example: "She's no beauty, that one, but her virtue increases her worth more than beauty could ever do."

A local poet was so taken by Iva's piety that he pined for her, until being silently rebuffed, and he wrote many verses dedicated to her quiet eyes and softly recited Our Fathers.

DRAGA, THE MIDDLE SISTER, was the most tempestuous by far. She had a sharp tongue and piercing green eyes. When she heard that Iva would be the only sister officially adopted by childless Ujna, whose husband, Steve, was working in America, Draga ran from the house in tears.

"You see?" Anđelka called after her, wagging a cautionary finger. "Iva should be an example to you. She doesn't have a bad word for anyone."

Draga had promptly stuck out her tongue and run up the road to the church, where she flung herself into a pew and cried in great heaving gulps. When the deluge of tears had quieted to an occasional hiccup, she looked up at the paintings of the Virgin and the saints. Iva, she decided in a moment of pique, had just such an imbecilic expression of piety, and she spent several moments imitating it before breaking into fits of giggles and rising to her feet. Then and there she decided that she was done with church, and masses, and all the saints. *I'm no saint*, she thought with satisfaction, and she imagined the shock with which Iva would receive the news. She returned home relatively calm and was greeted by her sisters' suspicious gazes.

Ljubica, the second eldest, returned only rarely from Macedonia with her husband, Ante. They would come by motorcycle and sidecar, making the trek once a year and arriving coated in dust that seemed inches thick.

"What are the people there like?" Draga would pester Ljubica. "Do they speak our language?"

And Ljubica would shake her head in disgust. "Something similar, but you can't understand a word of it."

Each time she returned home, Ljubica appeared more drawn, and each time, her sisters waited hopefully for an announcement of a coming baby. But the news never came, and Draga would finally ask in some impatience, "Well, when is he going to put a baby in your stomach?" The other sisters shushed her with reproving looks, and Ljubica pressed her lips whitely together and left the room abruptly.

When Marijan died, Anđelka and her sons came back to Posušje. She was pale and thin, and her aunt had clucked her tongue. "A good wind would carry you away, girl," she told her.

When a benevolent family in town offered to take Anđelka with them to the Adriatic Sea for several weeks of recuperation, her sisters urged her to go, promising to take care of the boys in her absence. The sea air helped her to shake off the last vestiges of her illness, and she returned with a fresh face and fewer shadows beneath her eyes.

Ljubica, who had grown attached to the children in the interim, suggested that she and Ante adopt the baby, Zoran. But Anđelka was shocked by the idea.

"You can't take care of both of them, *seka*," Ljubica insisted officiously. "You're being selfish."

But Anđelka cut her off with a firm gesture. "No."

And Ljubica stifled bitter tears.

IN THE YEARS that she had been away, Anđelka had lost her child's face. It had planes and valleys now, and her jawline was as pronounced as stone. She had married at sixteen and been pregnant through most of the succeeding five years. Only two of four children had survived, and she clung fiercely to those two.

"Two children," Ljubica told her wistfully before returning to Macedonia. "And both of them sons."

Anđelka folded her arms and told her evenly, "Not to mention a dead husband. Be careful what you wish for, sister."

At night she would lie in her bed between Bero and Zoran, her thoughts racing. The idea of staying in Posušje was unpleasant. At the age of twenty-one, the life of a respectable village widow seemed too grim a future for her to consider. The alternative, however, could be even worse. She could imagine the less honorable men in the village believing that a pauper widow with two small children would be happy for any scrap or morsel they would throw her way.

Even one of Marijan's younger brothers tried to approach her once, although his clumsy effort drew only her contempt. On an evening when Anđelka had taken her sons to visit Marijan's father, Tomislav crept lumberingly into bed beside her when he thought she was sleeping. He huddled under the covers and went completely still, like a dog playing dead. Tomislav had a wide, dumb mouth, and his own sister, Ana, had remorselessly nicknamed him Snout.

Anđelka had been awake and not in the least amused. "What do you think you're doing?" she asked in quiet rage.

"I—I thought you might be lonely," he stammered.

She unleashed a tirade so cutting that she had not needed to raise her voice past a whisper to convey her meaning, and he had slunk away in shame.

"Snout," she muttered after him, and he was unable to meet her eyes for weeks afterward.

Listening to the breathing of her sleeping children, she decided that she was tired of villages. She was tired of the hunger and poverty and of the black-clad women who worked like animals. They strained over one child and then the next, bringing them into these sad spaces. She was fast approaching their ranks, and it frightened her.

Increasingly she thought of moving to Sarajevo. Marijan's eldest brother, Ivan, was there. She had always liked his gentle ways and quick intelligence, and she was sure he would help them get started.

The rocky soil of Herzegovina had worked its way into the

undersides of her feet and risen vertically through her blood. It lay against her heart, so that it stabbed when she turned. A splinter of tough stone, she noted with grim satisfaction, which all her blood and tears would not dissolve, nor all the years erode a single edge of it.

IN THE FIELD

1996

I fell silent. Death's chill sat upon my back,
   Upon my limbs, and I was alone
Among the frozen corpses. In the coldness of death,
   I thirst for fire to warm my mouth and throat.
The ice of death is silent. Hell burns inside of it.
There are no screams and loneliness resounds.

—*Ivan Goran Kovačić*, The Pit, *Stanza VII*

I N EASTERN BOSNIA, the Bosnian Serb Army and paramilitary troops besieged the Muslim town of Srebrenica for three years.

What can be said of lives lived in postponement? Of a vortex in which thousands of days are lost, and children age prematurely? No reparations can recover the dead, or the lost years.

By July 1995, refugees had swelled the town's population by eighty percent, and sanitary conditions were abysmal. Reports reaching the outside told of starvation, surgery conducted without benefit of anesthesia, and rampant dysentery—all easy to remedy had food, medicines, and clean water been allowed in. They were not, and people were starving. They were eating grass.

The town began to fall, as if in slow motion but relentlessly, and everyone knew it: the terrified people trapped inside; the world that listened to reports of impending mass execution; the men who had besieged the city, who bided their time by carefully plotting their advance and further constricting their lines to the point of redundancy.

The Romans had named it Argentium for the silver mines nearby. Later the Slavs followed the same logic and called it Srebrenica. The Silver Place. To the uninitiated, the name could evoke a sense of ethereal beauty. It was a whisper, a dream.

After several months of intense bombardment, Srebrenica had been declared a UN safe area in 1993. Its Muslim defenders had run out of ammunition and could hold out no longer. But reports of Serbian atrocities in other parts of Bosnia, as well as the Muslims' own dealings with the Bosnian Serb Army, made them loath to lay down arms for their attackers. They knew that if the town fell to the Serbs, many inhabitants would be liquidated.

The compromise brokered by the UN lacked logic and sense, but it postponed a massacre: The Muslims would surrender their arms, and the Serbs would remain at their positions without overtaking the city. It was up to the UN to observe this civilized agreement, but there was reason to doubt Western efficacy.

In 1991, two years before, the eastern Croatian town of Vukovar had fallen to the JNA and paramilitary formations following an intense three-month siege. Summary executions, abductions, and deportations began immediately. Many inhabitants were sent to prisons and concentration camps in Serbia proper. In addition to the thousands who were killed during the siege, two hundred ninety-five people—wounded soldiers, civilians, and hospital staff—were taken by the JNA from Vukovar

Hospital in the presence of International Red Cross representatives. Over a space of hours they were taunted, beaten, and finally executed at Ovčara farm.

Vukovar was filmed after it fell, and the footage must have aired in parts of what then remained of Yugoslavia. It must have reached Bosnia, where an uneasy population had already begun to ponder the possibility of war spreading eastward. The newsreels show civilians clasping plastic bags. The scant possessions inside them would have to suffice for remembering the dead and the missing, and for recalling the lives Vukovar's residents had led. You could see plumes of slate-colored smoke rising in the sky behind them. There were people in the exodus who said they had been forcibly separated from their sons, from their husbands. The footage also shows Serb paramilitary troops giving victorious three-finger salutes behind long columns of women, elderly, and children. Some residents wept; others turned away their exhausted faces. Though I did not know it at the time, I had cousins in those columns.

Journalists stopped one young Croatian woman on the road out. She was clasping a plastic bag, tears streaming down a face frozen in disbelief. Her voice was bewildered. "But we still don't hate," she told the journalist in English. "We still don't hate."

It was there that Belgrade gauged the West's reaction to the killing of civilians and assessed the degree to which they could successfully "cleanse" regions in the future. The fall of Vukovar was a phenomenon that spread outward to other parts of Croatia, to Bosnia and to Kosovo.

By the time Srebrenica was on the verge of falling, in 1995, Vukovar's surviving residents had been living as refugees for nearly four years. I wondered what they thought of the utter senselessness of history repeated. And what must they have thought when they heard reports about the increasingly desperate situation inside the city, or when they saw footage of the army and paramilitary troops delivering glib promises of gentlemanly conduct?

I believe they saw these men for what they were: butchers who sharpened their knives industriously and waited. Jackals at feeding time, outside the gates of hell.

ON JULY 6, 1995, the Dutch battalion stationed in Srebrenica asked the UN High Command in Sarajevo for air support, but their requests, which made it all the way to Lieutenant General Bernard Janvier and Yasushi Akashi, the highest-ranking UN personnel in the former Yugoslavia, were denied. The battalion stood by and watched the Bosnian Serb Army overrun the town, separating men from women, sending the women away on buses. The Dutch soldiers were ordered onto their own compound, and they complied.

A few months later I heard psychologists on television discussing the ramifications of this experience on the psyches of the Dutch soldiers. "Many of them will suffer from post–traumatic stress syndrome," one expert stated. "These men are under severe emotional duress."

More than seven thousand people disappeared from Srebrenica, and I am sure their families would not miss the irony of that psychologist's words. Wives, mothers, and children had embraced their husbands, fathers, and sons before being separated. Kisses were planted on foreheads and cheeks. How many knew they would not see each other again?

Men and boys were not the only ones to die. The soldiers who accompanied Ratko Mladić as he inspected convoys leaving Srebrenica are said to have removed elderly people from the trucks and slit their necks.

And while the roadside executions took place in plain view, witnesses say that Mladić murmured, "Don't touch them." Smiling, he spread death like a wake behind him. While his soldiers murdered people, he passed out chocolate bars to their children.

"No one will touch you." That is what other witnesses at Konjević Polje remember him announcing. And then the executions began. Women were raped and killed. Even many who managed to escape with their lives did not ultimately survive. One left her children on the road, walked into a wood, and hanged herself from a tree in a now famous photograph. Female detainees at the Potočari factory complex were removed at night and never seen again. Teenagers, mothers, old women.

Some men fled into the wilderness, struggling to reach free territory. Many—four thousand, according to some estimates— were haphazardly tracked and hunted, their bodies left out in the open. Others were rounded up and taken to impromptu execution grounds, *gdje se gubi svaki trag*—where all trace of them is lost.

Many of the women had known, I was sure, as their buses rolled away. Just as the women I had met from Vukovar had known when their sons and husbands were removed from the columns fleeing the smoking city.

Srebrenica's men must also have sensed something as they watched the buses depart with their families, and I imagined a heavy silence descending upon them, filling their ears and swimming in front of their eyes.

One year later I held what was left of them.

• • •

MY FIRST MEETING with Bill Haglund, the Physicians for Human Rights official running the exhumations, was not auspicious. A wiry man in his fifties, he had graying brown hair that stuck out in tufts from beneath the Indiana Jones–type hat that he wore at all hours of the day. I endeared myself to him after returning to the field house, tired and sweaty from a day at the morgue. We had been in Tuzla almost a week.

Although I had seen television interviews with Bill Haglund, I did not recognize the man standing in the living room. We shook hands, and he looked at me expectantly. There was an awkward silence. "I'm sorry, I didn't catch your name . . ." I stammered.

I had been impressed by the interviews he had given, especially the one in which he had debunked propaganda that the graves were of combatants killed in action. "I don't know how many soldiers fight with their hands tied behind them," he had told journalists wryly.

After he learned I was an archaeologist, he looked at me skeptically. "In my experience, archaeologists are not used to bones coming with decomposed flesh on them." He turned to speak with the pathologists, and I felt dismissed.

His words had stung me, although later someone told me with a shrug, "That's Bill. He's gruff. Don't take it too much to heart." I smiled uncomfortably and walked onto the porch. A short time later I was told to pack my gear. The next morning I would be leaving with Haglund and a UN investigator for the SFOR compound where the excavators were being housed.

• • •

WHILE I MOVED to Republika Srpska, the Serb-controlled area where the graves were located, Dr. Peerwani and the other team members with whom I had come to Bosnia would be taking a day off to visit Sarajevo, the city of my father's childhood.

We said our good-byes the night before.

"You could have come with us if you weren't in such a hurry to get out to the field," Dr. Peerwani said.

Ever since reaching Bosnia, I had been thirsty to see the place I remembered only vaguely from childhood. It was the city of my own father's childhood, the place where my widowed grandmother had settled with her two young sons. Sarajevo would wait, I thought. I was anxious to reach the exhumations, where my experience would be useful and where I envisioned wiping away the near ineptitude I had felt in the morgue.

When our group had arrived in Bosnia, none of us knew what to expect. We entered a chaotic situation, but we quickly and capably organized ourselves. I had been the youngest and the least experienced of the group, but I paid close attention to Dr. Peerwani's directives and withstood that overwhelming first week.

I had been hired as an archaeologist, primarily, and because I could translate. The morgue had never ceased to be a foreign environment to me. Filling gaps was what the work, so far, had entailed: assisting in examinations, washing bones, and hanging clothing to dry. While I spread the clothes on racks, tagging each article with a corresponding number, I tried not to think of other women who had, at another time, hung the same freshly washed articles to dry.

"Anytime you want a job as a pathology assistant in my morgue, young lady," the other pathologist had told me, only half joking, "just let me know."

Dr. Peerwani, on the other hand, had sensed that I could not wait to put the morgue behind me. But the field represented forbidding territory as well. I had not yet met the other excavators, but their fatigue had already been communicated to those of us in the morgue. They had been in Bosnia much longer than we had, and they worked days on end without a break. The recently excavated site had been especially difficult because of its location on a steep slope, and the weather was blisteringly hot. Nerves were getting frayed, we were told, and tempers were flaring.

Most of all, I admitted to Dr. Peerwani, I was anxious about working in Serb-occupied territory, even with the war over. Slowly, I was losing my nerve.

"Maybe I'm just being silly," I said.

Dr. Peerwani, who had a deeper understanding of what the war and its resulting geographical divisions meant, raised his eyebrows. "No. I don't think so."

I had been in Republika Srpska only once before, with my friends Judita and Belkisa, a Muslim refugee living in Croatia. Belkisa had wanted us to meet her family in Orašje and Gradačac, and we had taken a bus through a corridor in the Serb-controlled section of Bosnia. Her own home was in Bosanski Šamac, which was under occupation. She had nevertheless returned weeks before our visit to inspect it. She was warned repeatedly against making such a trip. One of her neighbors had gone a few months before and had not been seen or heard from since. But Belkisa, a sturdy middle-aged woman with a wicked tongue, had taken a little-traveled road and walked calmly up to her damaged house. After silently lugging the rugs, which had been part of her dowry, into the yard, her former neighbors approached, tentatively at first. One of them mustered the boldness to kiss her three times.

The town's Muslims had been forced to flee by their Serb neighbors and imported Serb paramilitary troops. Some particularly nasty concentration camps were operating before the town was fully cleansed, and residents of Slavonski Šamac, the Croatian town directly across the river, had spent many nights listening to screams coming from the Bosnian side.

Belkisa's eyes had been unreadable when she told us this story. *"Pička im materina,"* she had said succinctly, cursing their mothers' anatomies and pointing to the rolled and tattered shapes of the carpets now in her sister's hallway. I remember that they had looked like bodies casually tossed on the tile floor.

"I would have liked to visit Sarajevo with all of you," I told Dr. Peerwani finally. "But it's time for me to earn my keep."

Tim Curran, the evidence technician who had been listening to us, excused himself and returned a moment later with a bulky black object.

"Take this," he told me. He placed the Kevlar vest in my arms. It had the weight of a small child.

I slipped my arms through the holes, and we all began to laugh. It covered me from my neck to my knees. I looked ridiculous and started immediately to sweat.

I took it off and put it back in Tim's reluctant hands.

• • •

WHEN WE PASSED into Republika Srpska the next morning, in a white UN jeep, I had the sensation that I was falling. My every experience classified that border as the one between hunter and prey. On the other side of it, law ceased to exist. It was a place filled with people who hated Muslims and Croats. And, therefore, me. I looked out the windows at the ruined houses and destroyed mosques. I studied the faces of the people we passed, wondering what crimes had been committed on the ground they now walked on, swaggering nonchalantly and spitting into the dirt after our jeep, which sped along in a cloud of dust over the damaged roads. Some raised their fists; others did not bother looking up as we passed.

I learned that some had themselves been displaced from the suburbs around Sarajevo, which the Bosnian Army had liberated the year before. They came from Grbavica and Ilidža, districts they had wiped almost entirely clean of other ethnicities three years before. When they left, they dug up their dead from cemeteries and brought them along. "*Gde je pokopan i jedan Srbin tu je srpska zemlja*," nationalist politician Vuk Draškovic had said. Everywhere a Serb is buried is Serbia. So they disinterred remembrance itself.

MEMORY IS A MYTHOLOGICAL QUARRY that flees from you through the forest of the Balkans. It is Baba Roga, the Slavic witch of legend, in her cave. There are a few signs to suggest its existence, yet one can never be sure. History is written, then rewritten and heavily edited. There is the official version, the new official version, and the newly improved official version. Accurate memory can be a casualty, but it is also the last defense of any logical mind.

Revision of memory is, among other things, what my father had fled when he left Yugoslavia in 1959. While working for Radio Zagreb, he broadcast an interview with a former Partisan general whom he had met on a train. The man, a disgruntled hero of the Second World War, had deplored how low "brotherhood and unity" had sunk. Police informers, gulags, and greed had shattered his dream of Yugoslavia.

And memory is what led me back, away from a comfortable American life. In 1992 my father made preparations to attend a literary conference in Zagreb. It was a year into the war, and fighting still raged in other parts of Croatia, but the capital was relatively safe, and I begged to accompany him.

"Why?" my father had asked.

I knew that everything hinged upon my response. "I'm beginning to forget things," I told him finally.

But my great-uncle Mile had awakened a few nights before our slated arrival, feeling tightness like a vise in his chest, and an ambulance had borne him through the wet autumn streets of Zagreb. He died before ever reaching the hospital, and my father's aunts had telephoned America with the news. Aunt Katja's wails climbed their way to orbiting satellites and delivered themselves, bewildered and of startling pitch, on the telephone in my parents' kitchen.

My father telephoned me in Madrid, where I was studying in 1992, the news cutting its way back across the Atlantic Ocean.

"I'm sorry," I told him, placing a hand against the phone booth's smeared glass.

In the preceding months my father had been listening to reports of the war on a shortwave radio. He had become fanatical about this evening ritual, following one town after another as they came under siege and were bombed, overrun, and buried.

"Do you remember that place?" he would ask me. "We drove through it so many times."

But the past was a territory of ghost towns whose unmarked faces existed only in family photographs and footage my father had shot while making a documentary film years before. And while I struggled to remember them, I am ashamed to admit that I did not.

"I'm sorry," I had told my father when Dubrovnik was bombarded and snipers in Sarajevo were picking off civilians like bottles. It felt as if the places themselves were family friends who had died.

By the time Srebrenica fell, it was shocking only in its scope. The war had devolved into numbing repetitions.

"They're trying to erase the past," my father would say, enraged. And I imagined a wall of fog dropping on one town after the next, moving to encompass fields, mosques, and graveyards.

And then there were our family and friends, the people we called when lines permitted, for whom we lit candles. Uncle Mile and my aunts had descended into the cellar of their Zagreb apartment building during Yugoslav Air Force bombardments in 1991. Only Aunt Ljubica had refused to go down into the shelter, and no amount of coaxing on her sisters' part could convince her. "She was always stubborn," my father said by way of explanation.

The sounds of those planes intruded on their dreams and, in a strange transference, on our own.

In America we were safe, but we thought about them in the darkness. Their letters were frightened and scribbled. On our television screens, we watched towns falling like dominoes, and streams of civilians who were forced to flee them. My father, seated in our living room, sometimes recognized people in the columns.

The children of friends went off to war and died, or came back with the faces of old men.

The night my father told me of Mile's death, he sighed. "It's ironic, to die of natural causes in the middle of a war."

It was not what my father said that made tears run down my face, its reflection frozen in the glass of the Spanish phone box. It was his even tone.

"He's dead," he said. "He'll be buried at Mirogoj with your grandmother." But across the telephone wires I heard something else completely in his words. Some shadow of our conversation. *Memory dies more each year.*

I walked back to the room I rented in Madrid and started making mental notes for my trip to Zagreb. When I entered the apartment, I could hear my landlady watching television in her living room. I listened for a moment to a news clip on *la antigua Yugoslavia* and shuffled along the hallway until I could see the television. The location was a shelter somewhere in Bosnia, and the correspondent on the screen wore a flak jacket. His thick Madrid accent seemed strange against the background of the shelter.

Behind him, people sat on cushions and chairs. Women leaned their heads close to one another, speaking about matters of greater importance than the appearance of another foreign reporter in their midst. In one corner, two men sat playing chess, a tray with Turkish coffee at their side. There was a sudden thud, and the lightbulb that washed out their skin like bleach swayed overhead. The reporter continued talking, but raised his eyes to the bulb. In the next breath the light was extinguished, and frantic Spanish voices from the crew were quieted only when a giant camera light was turned on. It shone like a powerful candle through the underground room, illuminating the figures of the women, who kept talking, and the men, who continued to pore over the chessboard, not even raising their heads, as if, after so many nights spent in the dark, they could see quite well without light. Only the children looked at the reporter, their eyes huge in their sunken faces. As if he were some invisible being that only they could see.

I traveled overnight by train, then met my father in Austria to drive across the border. The man in the car-rental agency had looked at my father's last name suspiciously. "You are not permitted to take this car over the border into Yugoslavia," he said severely. "Because of the war."

My father looked at him innocently. "I have no intention of going to Yugoslavia!" he declared, as if he found the very idea preposterous.

Outside the agency, he looked at me with a sly grin. "People should learn their geography," he told me. "And the fact that the war isn't actually happening in Yugoslavia." Although Croatian and Bosnian independence had been internationally recognized, most people had been slow to recognize that fact.

In Zagreb my uncle's obituary in the newspaper was surrounded with the faces of young men, some younger than my own twenty years. My aunts cut the announcements of his death from city newspapers and presented them to my father, but pictures of dead teenagers were also on the reverse of the newsprint.

Air attacks on Zagreb had stopped after the first few months of the war, and shelling was largely confined to towns to the south and east. Each evening, as people settled down to watch the news or imported American sitcoms, the words *opća opasnost*—general alert—would flash across their television screens, along with a list of towns being shelled. Karlovac, Ogulin, Pakrac, Šibenik, Zadar, Dubrovnik.

Zagreb was flooded with refugees and displaced persons from other parts of Croatia and, increasingly, from Bosnia, but its treelined parks and Baroque buildings presented a relatively tranquil face. Looking up at the lamps on Ban Jelačić Square in the evening, with the background noise of young people meeting in front of the Znanje bookstore and the smell of chestnuts roasting, you could almost believe that war was nothing more than a rumor. But when you lowered your gaze, it fell on the worn and tired faces of refugees who stood around the square's corners, some with a collection of dirty canvas and plastic bags at their feet. It fell, also, on a sea of camouflage, and in the city you learned to make the distinctions drawn in battle. There were tough and tired-looking men whose skin had weathered a year or more on front lines. There were women as well, with somber faces and hair tucked into caps. And then there were new conscripts, their faces baby-soft and pale as newborn mice. You could tell how long each soldier had been in the war by how much the camouflage had softened and the colors faded. The newer soldiers sported fresher camouflage, stiff and uncomfortable looking. But it was always enough to look at their faces.

The night before I left Zagreb to return to Madrid, my father and I ran into an old school friend of his in front of the Hotel Dubrovnik, and I stood slightly to the side as they spoke.

It was bitter cold, and I shoved my hands into the pockets of my black coat.

On the other side of the streetcar tracks, a man my age stood watching me. He grinned, folding his arms in front of his chest, and pretended to shiver. I smiled and looked away. My father was still deep in conversation. When I looked back, the man had lit a cigarette and was looking up the tracks for his streetcar. There was something familiar about his lanky height and the easy way he held himself. He shot me a quick, wry smile before his streetcar slid between us. My father finished the conversation and put a hand to my elbow, ready to walk back to my aunts' apartment, and I turned and watched the back of the streetcar disappear down Ilica Street.

The young man's fatigues had been thin, the material washed so many times that it had lost its resilience altogether. The dark brown and green colors intended to make a chameleon of a man in wooded areas had faded into a worn dullness. In the weeks and months that followed my return to Spain, I looked for his face in all the footage and newspaper photographs from El País's war correspondents.

Months later my father mentioned him. "The one on the square," he said. "Do you remember? He was so like your brother." And I had shivered, wondering how many times my father had seen his American son in the faces of the soldiers.

Such is our nature, he told me later. We see our living among the dead everywhere.

IN THE UN TRUCK, I leaned my head against the back of the seat and closed my eyes. Bill Haglund and the investigator were talking about the SFOR camp where the excavators were staying. One of them flipped on the radio and turned the dial distractedly. There were news reports, a phone caller shouting about politics, and a woman singing a warbling song about her beloved. The radio was switched off again, and the two men fell silent. The sun was just rising, and I felt the hesitant warmth on my face as I pretended to sleep.

I forced myself to think in terms of stratigraphy. Of the law of crosscutting relationships. *The morgue was messy, the field will be, too, but I know how to triangulate, for God's sake.* I knew how to make a perfect square meter with two tape measures, four nails, a line level, and some string. I imagined that I could get lost in the familiar work and that comforting rules would once more apply. I imagined a studiously mapped field, earth broken down into a neat grid.

I did have some experience excavating burials. Only the year before, I had spent two wintry spring months on the Eastern Shore of Maryland, excavating a colonial Dutch house. We found a mother and child nearby, their white bones like porous shell in the acidic soil. We spent hours uncovering them, and I was given the task of sketching their positions in the ground. Seated on plastic sheeting, which offered little protection against the almost frozen ground, I blew on my cramped fingers, but they were so stiff with cold that I could produce only a crude, hasty sketch. I tore off the piece of paper, crumpled it into a ball, and started again.

"What's wrong?" a colleague had asked as he removed soil from the crushed ribs with a trowel.

"It's no good," I sighed.

"It doesn't have to be perfect," he said with a laugh. But there was something about the tiny, nearly dissolved bones that begged for a more exact rendering.

The grave had been hundreds of years old, though, and even as I remembered it on my way to Srebrenica, I realized how ridiculous was the comparison with the work I would be doing in the days to come.

Still, I tried to remind myself of the dry rules of excavation. I attempted to recall entire Munsell pages—charts that identify different types of soil through color and consistency. I visualized the red clay of Virginia's Piedmont. But it was useless. Stratigraphy can't save you now, I told myself.

Nor had any attempt at a clinical approach in the morgue prevented me from seeing the living in the dead, just as my father had said. I saw my brother in the faces of strangers on the road. In bones left to dry on tables in the sun, specifically in the sharpness of a zygomatic arch, a ridge below the orbit, which indicates high, angled cheekbones. I saw his features in the Bosnian policeman who guarded the factory's front gates. This guard had wanted to know where we discarded the buckets of dirty water in which we washed clothes from the corpses. With hurt brown eyes he asked if we dumped them down the drains in the factory. The gutters led to a nearby stream, he explained in some agitation. He knew children that swam in that stream, and he was dismayed by the idea of the putrid water touching them.

Unlike Sarajevo and Mostar, which I remembered from before the war, I had never before been in eastern Bosnia. Our truck skirted towns whose recent histories I knew by dint of the murders and expulsions that had taken place in them. I opened my eyes just as we passed a sign for Zvornik, a town on the Drina River. Zvornik had been sixty percent Muslim before the war. Now that community was gone.

I had read testimonies from Zvornik refugees, and they played out in my mind like horror films. I remembered the face of a child, barely a teenager, with the flat eyes of a cancer patient. She had haunted me for months. Her older cousin had brushed away tears when we were alone. The girl would never know love her first time, would never open her arms wide to someone without a sense of fear. It was not the loss of innocence that haunted her cousin, but the cementing of an act in a child's mind without tenderness, without security and love.

The older cousin, who was about my age, had looked at me dully through a haze of cigarette smoke. Maybe the younger girl would never marry. So many of the boys had died anyway. They were all pushing on through the grimness of unfolding days, suffering each one. Life was that thing to be withstood. Memory was a vision of the irretrievable, and a cruelty to be avoided at all costs.

I straightened in the backseat. The investigator, who was driving, looked at me in the rearview mirror and grinned. He offered me a stick of gum. I unwrapped it and then folded the foil into a perfect, tiny square.

ALL THE SFOR BASES in Bosnia had been given women's names. A twisting road led to Camp Lisa, where the excavators were staying. It snaked around a small hill, at the top of which the camp was built. People slept in identical shipping containers, each with a handful of windows. From a distance they looked like a collection of enameled tin coffins, or a shipyard stranded far from the sea.

Wood-planked walkways connected them and were suspended a few feet above the dirt. They led from the containers to buildings of other dimensions but similar construction: showers, offices, a mess hall. It was like a small town—independent, manufactured, and ringed with razor wire. It was clearly possible to exist there, navigating the neat wooden planks, without ever standing on Bosnian ground.

We arrived at the base at seven in the morning, meeting the other archaeologists and anthropologists at breakfast in the mess hall. There were three American women, three Latin American men, and a policeman from the Netherlands. I was suddenly nervous and shy. Bill Haglund sat across from me.

"Archaeologists," he said, repeating his pronouncement of the day before, "tend not to believe bodies have flesh on them." Then, after a moment's thought, "Don't eat much."

I looked down at the slice of bread and jam on the plate in front of me. I had spent a week working in the morgue, I wanted to tell him. No matter how bad the field was, I would be outside.

The others at the table rolled their eyes. One of the Americans, a woman with friendly brown eyes, grinned at me and whispered, "Don't listen to him. You'll be fine."

A man from Peru looked from the girl to me over the rim of his glass. "Just don't concentrate on faces and hands. Those are the hardest. The faces and hands."

BECAUSE TIME WAS OF THE ESSENCE, the extensive grid systems of conventional archaeological digs were superfluous. But the team shot coordinates with a transit, recording each body's location in the ground, noting its position in relation to the other bodies as well as physical details such as the degree of decomposition.

That morning I was given a single grave to excavate. It was located some twenty feet from one of two larger graves. Their edges had been determined with a T-bar, a handheld core that revealed samples that smelled of decomposition.

The single grave was shallow, discovered because a piece of bone had protruded from the soil and grass. The grave was, in fact, so shallow that the remains were fully decomposed and clean. White bone and clothing were all that were left. After the first hour it occurred to me that I had been given the grave as a way of easing me into the work. I had not yet ventured into the pit, where the intertwined bodies were buried deeper and the work was far less pleasant.

For the entire morning I contented myself with digging around the body, opening the grave completely so that the clothed remains were nicely pedestaled on a bed of earth. Becky, an archaeologist from New Orleans, came to stand beside me when I had finished. She had a bemused expression on her face.

"Here, you can't dig like you would on a regular archaeological excavation," she explained. "We've got to do it carefully but quickly."

I faltered for a moment, feeling foolish. I looked at the grave I'd just uncovered and realized that it resembled something a team of classical archaeologists, obsessed with the fragility of bones that were thousands of years old, would take days to uncover. I touched the bone with my trowel. It was fully intact, and I realized sheepishly that I could have done the job in half the time.

Becky grinned at me. "Don't worry. You'll get the hang of it." She helped me map the grave, and then she photographed it. She showed me how to write my notes, and together we "pulled" the body and placed it in a body bag. The clothing helped keep everything in place as we lifted it onto the black plastic. The man must have been quite tall, judging by the length of his trousers, but his bones were very light.

After we carried the stretcher to the refrigerated container in the next field, we broke for lunch. That morning at the mess hall, someone had told me to pack a meal and had pointed to a table where MREs—meals ready to eat—stood in identical brown cardboard packaging. Now I removed the boxes and examined their contents. There was a diagram demonstrating how to add water and set up a solar-heating system to warm the resulting paste. Most of the anthropologists did not bother and ate the contents cold. I followed suit, but I put the envelope down after a few bites.

Clea, the woman who had spoken with me that morning at breakfast, saw me grimace, and she winked.

"During the war," I told her, "they used to air-drop these to the starving population. People didn't believe you could actually eat them." They had burned them for warmth instead.

She laughed and pulled out some crackers and peanut butter, which she shared with me. "These are a lot safer."

It was sweltering, and we sat on the grass in the shade the trucks provided. We fell into conversation, and she told me that she had recently worked in Rwanda. "This is hot," she said, "but that was really hot." She had excavated graves with hundreds and hundreds of bodies in them. "How are you doing?" she asked me finally.

"I think I prefer it to the morgue." I looked at my half-eaten cracker. "I don't think I was really prepared for that."

She tilted her head to one side. "I don't think you're ever prepared."

I shifted, feeling the blue jumpsuit stick to me in slicks of sweat. The shorts and T-shirt underneath it were soaked through. "And I think these clothes might get up and walk away on their own after this," I told her with a smile.

She told me that in Rwanda she had chosen one bra to sacrifice to excavating. After months and months it had smelled so strongly of death that no amount of laundering could remove the stench.

We finished lunch and gathered our litter of napkins and empty cardboard boxes.

"What did you do when you were finished there?" I asked as we turned to walk back to the graves. "With the bra?"

"Burned it," she said with suddenly serious eyes. "The smell only got stronger as it burned."

AFTER LUNCH I joined the excavation of the larger grave, lowering myself into the ground beside the other excavators. The heavy work had been done for us by a backhoe operated by a smiling man from the Philippines, so we were spared from moving tons of earth.

The difficulty, I quickly realized, was in knowing where to sit or stand. The bodies were so enmeshed that it was hard to see which extremity belonged to which corpse. The Peruvian, José Pablo, had been right. The faces and the hands were by far the most difficult, perhaps because clothing covered everything else.

Toward the top of the grave, where the remains were fully skeletal, it was easy to avoid considering them. But as we got deeper, they took on the appearance of life. At one point I realized that my gloved left hand rested neatly atop a hand from one of the corpses as I troweled with my right. When I looked down, our hands seemed clasped, and I jerked mine away as if I had been burned.

IN TRUTH, there was an odd normalcy to the whole affair, to the routine.

Each morning we were accompanied by an American SFOR contingent of Humvees. They rolled in front of our cars and brought up the rear in a tough-looking procession. The weather was hot and humid, and while we worked at the site, the SFOR soldiers sat sweltering inside the bellies of the metal monsters.

SFOR had agreed to house the excavators and provide for their safety by escorting them to and from the graves, but they did not want to give any other assistance. It was an unorthodox alliance, and we were regarded with a mixture of fascination and exasperation at Camp Lisa.

There was also a contingent of journalists who kept to the road, beyond cordons connecting the two sites where we were working. They milled around, hoping to catch sight of something, but they were not allowed to enter the general area of the graves. A somewhat freakish atmosphere existed as we carried covered stretchers up the steep slope between the farther grave and the throng of reporters who talked on their cellular phones and pounded out stories on their laptops.

The press were growing frustrated, we learned, with the

amount of information being given them. Haglund called sporadic press briefings, but the flow of information seemed somewhat haphazardly managed.

"He likes being in charge," one of them told me a little bitterly. "He likes having power over the information and standing in front of our microphones."

But in those first days it was not the graves or reporters or crew politics that unsettled me, but the local Serbian workers who had been hired for heavy labor and to remove excess dirt the backhoe could not reach. Some claimed to have been expelled from Ilidža at the time the Bosnian Army retook it. From the moment I set foot among them, I tucked my identification card into my T-shirt, making sure that each time I bent to scrape at the earth, it did not slip out.

I learned that they were the second group of laborers. The first group had allegedly been scared off by Serb authorities. I got a sick feeling in my stomach when I heard this, because the second group seemed rather unconcerned.

"Did you wonder why these guys weren't scared off as well?" I asked Haglund and two UN investigators.

They had stared at me in surprise. "No, not really."

There was a pecking order among these workers that unnerved me. Perhaps I had spent too many nights reading case files and spoken to too many victims of paramilitary groups. I tried hard not to think of it as a command structure, but it was obvious that when the two in charge gave orders, the others jumped. One of them was nearly six and a half feet tall, with curly black hair and a thick, matted beard. The other had dirty-blond hair, a thinner, scraggly beard, and a very bad temper. The rest were men in their early twenties who spent most of the day in the tree shade, taking swigs from a bottle of *šljivovica*, watching the excavators, and occasionally jumping when barked at by one of the foremen. One of the men, Aleksa, seemed to fall outside the scope of the group. He was also the only one who worked.

When I first signed on in Zagreb, I had met with an American in the International War Crimes Tribunal office. "There are local workers on the site, and you may not want to let them know your ethnicity," the man had told me. I nodded, pushing past a slight feeling of vertigo.

I had agreed that it would be best to keep my identity card tucked inside my shirt in the presence of the workers so that they would not see my name. But that information had not made it to the field, and on the very first day I arrived, I was asked to deliver some directives to the workers.

I hesitated, but they had already been told that I would be able to communicate with them and that I could understand them. Nervously, I looked from my colleagues to the group.

The workers waited expectantly. In the end I spoke with them haltingly, hoping they would conclude that I had picked up some words working for the UN. It was an idiotic choice, I realized immediately, ensuring that I would get the worst of both worlds. On the one hand, they were suspicious; on the other, they felt at liberty to openly discuss my anatomy within earshot, using colorful words that someone with a passing knowledge of their language would be hard-pressed to understand.

THE NEXT DAY, Aleksa began quizzing me.

"No," I lied to him with a winning smile. "My family is Italian. I just speak a couple of words of your language." I bent to pick up a rock and tossed it onto the dirt pile.

Aleksa, who it turned out spoke some English—thereby making my role of interpreter doubly idiotic—started speaking about a translator accompanying one of the American journalists. He pointed her out, standing on the road above us. "She shouldn't be here," he told me. "She's going to be sorry she came."

I looked up sharply.

"She's a Muslim," he explained matter-of-factly. "She doesn't belong here."

I raised my eyebrows. *Less human?* I was tempted to ask. Some devil made me suggest, "Maybe she's a Croat?"

"No." He shook his head. "And they don't belong here either."

I let this piece of information work its way into my brain as I removed the dirt beside a dead man's cheek.

For these workers, the excavation became a game of sorts. When we had started to uncover the single grave on the first day, one of them shrugged. "A cow?" The others laughed.

Becky made a face and kicked softly at the dirt. "I don't know. I don't know how many cows wear tennis shoes." She tapped a piece of rubber with her foot.

"A Serb victim," suggested one.

"A body from World War II," said another.

Most of the time I wished that I did not understand. I tried to block out the things they said—about the bodies and the stench, about me and the other women who were digging in the dirt in front of them, struggling with body bags and stretchers. When we disappeared behind the bushes, they would laugh and make ugly remarks. I stopped drinking water in the field so that I would not have to urinate in their proximity. But the days were beastly hot, and I returned to the base most evenings with a headache that ran like a poker through the center of my forehead.

At one point, as I sat on the edge of the grave, sweating in the heat, I could hear the commentary behind me, something about grown men and fear. I tried to shut it out and examined my trowel. It was not a Marshalltown—the best trowel by archaeological standards—but it had been all I could find before I left Zagreb. A plumber in Tuzla had honed it for me good-naturedly with a piece of cinder block. The edges were sharp, and I could feel their bite through my field gloves and the surgical gloves beneath. I rose, stepping down into the grave to begin work again.

I saw Aleksa approaching. He looked intent and began to help me dig around the patch of ground on which I was working. After a while he struck up a conversation, asking me about America, about films. He fell silent. Could he see my tags? he wanted to know. He had never seen UN identity tags before and was wondering what they looked like. I pretended not to understand him, and turned my back.

A FEW DAYS LATER a group of former French Foreign Legionnaires were hired to protect the site at night. They were housed on the same base as the excavators, and we looked at each other somewhat dubiously.

"Mercenaries," one of the Latin Americans had said in disgust.

But they were deemed a necessary addition to the team.

There were fears of site tampering in the hours after we left the field. Some of the investigators had already spent the night there in sleeping bags, huddled together beside the grave some distance from the road. "Unpleasant," had been their curt pronouncement the next morning.

The legionnaires were also soberly fascinating. None spoke English well, and they looked at our crew as if we were a group of children scraping in the dirt.

One had brought his dog, and he allowed some of us to pet it.

"No touch when I gone," he ordered us sternly. "*Comprenez-vous?*"

We nodded, looking a little more hesitantly at the dog. It had the wide, serious eyes and powerful jaw of an attack dog, and it spent those first days tied to the tent where the mercenaries were staying. One American GI on the base had approached the dog to pet him, nearly getting his hand bitten off in the process.

A lot of the crew, especially the Latin Americans, viewed the legionnaires with specific distaste. Theirs was a scorn reserved for all uniforms, based on bitter experience from their own countries. Some saw the war as one waged by armies in which every soldier, on every side, bore equal guilt. They did not see it as one group's attempt to assert itself over other groups by wiping them off the landscape.

I did not think all sides bore equal guilt, and I said so. That was a figment of the international imagination, I told them, and an excuse to stay uninvolved. Besides, the adage that *it takes two to fight* did not hold water there. One army could wage war all by itself, and had done so rather successfully.

John, one of the UN investigators, had turned to me abruptly one day in the field during a conversation. "I've been at graves where the victims were Muslims, graves where they were Croats, and graves where they were Serbs. It happened on all sides."

I digested this for a moment, shocked that he might think I doubted it. "Of course it did," I told him carefully. "Anybody who thinks that any side is completely blameless is ridiculous."

He looked away.

"But there are degrees," I told him, "of how much the killing of civilians was a part of official policy."

Some members of the crew looked away from me during such conversations, and I felt my stomach flip-flop. I had met an Italian on a train once. "They're all insane," he had told me rather knowledgeably, "like crazy animals." I discerned a similar sentiment in the faces around me.

And you're one of them, their eyes said.

I WAS ONE OF THEM, and I was not.

After leaving Madrid, I had decided to take time off from my studies. I lived in Zagreb with my aunts for several months in 1993, during the war. They were good cooks, and their kitchen produced hearty meals whose fragrance swept the hallways of their building on Trpimirova Street. Their soups were warm and nourishing, and their compotes cool and sweet.

My favorite meat is lamb. It is a preference imprinted in our Dinaric mountain genes, so that my brother and I, bred in America, asked for it excitedly on our visits, and dreamed of it in between. The best lamb spends a lifetime grazing on chamomile. The yellow, fragrant hearts of the plant scent the fat. Baked and moist, the meat carries the memory of mountain fields, of Herzegovina. Lamb is roasted for weddings, festivals and birthdays, Easters and baptisms. More urbane classes enjoy looking down upon such greasy pleasures, but I had no such aversion.

Bread is the necessary accompaniment to any Croatian meal. Aunt Iva, especially, had a knack for making bread, and her loaves were light and airy. When she baked, the entire kitchen smelled of yeast and warmth.

My father bakes bread as well. As a child, I thought there was something magical in bread, in its rising in the silence of a warm kitchen, my father's black head bent in concentration as he kneaded it, and the flour making the olive of his hands ghostly. My brother and I would attack the bread when he left the kitchen. Our father considered it unhealthy to eat it hot, so we would sneak into the kitchen and dig craters from the center, stuffing the warm stolen flesh quickly into our mouths. With time, we learned subtler measures—warm bread can be peeled ever so slightly from the soft center of split loaves—but we were almost always found out.

"You don't respect the bread," my father told me several times, mournfully. "You massacre the bread."

I did not understand what he meant. Although our father's English was good, he occasionally transposed Croatian phrases into English.

"How can you respect bread?" I would ask him. "Bread is bread."

He would look at me gravely. "Bread is life. You eat bread. If you don't eat, you die."

I would shrug, knowing nothing of hunger, somewhat

amused by this earthy wisdom. Later, my aunts would shake their heads, watching me slice bread with a metal serrated knife in their kitchen. They cringed at the folded, shrunken pieces I produced and, in the future, assigned me other tasks. I told my aunts about the business of respecting the bread.

"Yes," they told me sagely. "He's right." And they looked at one another. "How could you know when you've never known hunger?"

I did not know what it meant to be hungry, but I knew plenty about *čežnja*—longing. My father longed for the place he came from, and he instilled this longing in me. And although Zagreb was Croatian, and he had spent years studying and working there, it was not where he was from. In coming to Zagreb, I felt that I had come only partway, unsure where I needed to go. I did not want to go to Sarajevo, which was under siege. If I did not die there, I would die when my father caught up with me and tore me limb from limb. I did not want to go to Herzegovina, hours away, where I remembered the seasons went from one extreme of discomfort to the other. Instead, I dreamed of the sea.

But we were not from the sea. We were from the hills behind the sea. Still, my *čežnja* was there. I wanted to leave the strange suspension of Zagreb behind and recapture those landscapes of my childhood summers.

I was sure that Zagreb's rain had soaked me through and left behind certain trace elements: dust from smokestacks and soot from exhaust pipes. Even after I washed my hair and lay reading in bed, the television in the next room showing news about the war, I could still smell the grime.

In the end, I decided that the sea was the only substance

strong enough to remove the dirty city smells from my hair. I remembered our family trips to the southern Adriatic and how the water there was so pure, so heavy with salt that it bit my skin for hours after swimming.

But that had been before. Those were childhood summers, at the end of which my brother and I were always browner, leaner, and swam as rapidly as fish. In those summers, there had been no television to interrupt the music of the crickets and no screaming traffic to spew out fumes on the blistering hot rock. I remembered stone houses and old men who congregated on a *riva* in the cooler evenings. The younger men, whose boats were moored to the stone blocks of a pier by thick salt-encrusted ropes, were busy mending nets and did not even look up—except when a pretty young woman walked by, and they gave low whistles to get each other's attention, returning a moment later to the steady rhythm of mending. The place I remembered had no name. It was an amalgam of places—a *malo misto*, a small town, with the noise of Zagreb hours to the north.

Lying in bed in my aunts' apartment during my 1993 visit, I felt *čežnja* for the sea as if I were its native daughter. The sounds from the street were an infringement upon the white rock and clear water I imagined each night before falling asleep.

BUT THAT TRIP TO THE SEA with my friend Tia had gone terribly awry, and we had spent hours underground during the mortar attack.

By early evening we finally climbed back onto the train and

found our compartment. A couple sitting across from us were going to Rijeka to visit friends. The man looked from his wife to the gaily wrapped bottle visible in her canvas bag, and then again at his wife.

"Don't!" she told him, reading his mind. "We don't have anything else to give them."

But he ignored her, taking the bottle and unwrapping it. "They'll understand," he told her, untwisting the cap and taking a deep swig.

She shrugged.

He looked across at us, offering the brandy. At first I refused, demurely, but then thought better of it. A Croatian adage says, *You should drink water after nobody, wine after some people, and hard liquor after everyone.* The fiery liquid made the back of my throat burn, and I coughed. He passed the bottle around the compartment until one by one we had all drunk from it. When we arrived in Rijeka, we stumbled onto the train platform drunkenly but without pain.

My *čežnja* returned with the first smell of the sea, and we revived ourselves sufficiently to push the day's events from our minds. The shelling of the train had been all we could speak of, but then silence descended, and we decided not to talk about it for the remainder of the weekend.

"We deserve to enjoy this weekend," Tia said, and I agreed.

On the island of Krk we met a young fisherman named Antonio. He had kind dark eyes and told us where to get the best *mušule*, and we took walks with him along the beach that weekend, laughing into a *bura*, a northerly wind that carried our laughter away. Carried it into the Lika hills, he said, so that when he went back to the front, he would hear it echoing from one mountainside to the next.

Everyone was in the war.

Then his face changed suddenly, and he began telling us how the fighting had started driving animals out of the Lika mountains. Wolves had been distracted from their ordinary hunting patterns. Brown bears had started wandering down into the foothills and all the way to the sea. Some of them had even swum the distance to Krk, black noses bobbing and legs paddling furiously. When they reached the island, they headed inland and were rumored to be attacking flocks of sheep.

"People are like the bears," he told us with a shy smile. "I spend each day in Lika wanting to swim home."

We grew sober when he mentioned the end of his leave, and he looked almost sorry to have said anything. "Look at you," he said more brightly, "coming back here when you could have stayed in America."

Perhaps because of the shelling, or perhaps because I felt sorry for Antonio, who would soon be returning to the front, I exchanged addresses with him. The letters I sent from Zagreb in the next few weeks were filled with chatter about my life and studies—the things I threw myself into in order to forget the shelling. I described my language teachers and the cafés where I met friends in the evenings. I ended each letter in the same awkward way. *I hope you are well. Take care.*

The letters Antonio wrote back were full of a sudden admiration that made me nervous. How smart I must be to have a place at an American university, and how beautiful I was. He wrote fragments of poems and songs, which he explained would sound better if he could sing them. His handwriting was the painful scrawl of the barely literate. When the letters arrived, my aunt Katja looked at me with raised eyebrows, but said nothing.

He wrote of the winds that blew out of all directions. And how he loved taking his boat from Krk to Senj in the summers, when no *bura* was blowing.

Tia shrugged whenever we discussed the weekend. "It was strange." A policeman whom she had met on the train had abruptly stopped calling.

As the autumn wore on, Antonio's letters grew more erratic, and he began speaking of things about which I knew nothing. It was as if he were leading a life with an alternate me. He wrote of places in Lika—gorges he walked through, the command center where they based their operations. He wrote of these places as if we had been there together.

He wrote of the trip we had taken to Senj, of how my hair had blown across his face, and of how we had pulled the nets into the boat, yelling in excitement at the catch. The fish had grinned up at us from the bottom of the boat, the moon turning their scales to silver pieces. I shivered, never having been to Senj. Never having been out in his boat.

I would like you to come visit me. It will be like old times. He told me that he had come home because his father was sick.

There is more wrong with me than my father, he admitted in his next letter, not mentioning my refusal to come to the island. *I am sure that I will die when they send me back. Please, don't stop writing.*

He told me that the wind pierced his head when it blew over their positions in the hills.

I told him that better times were sure to come, that the war could only last so long.

You understand nothing, he told me in the next letter. *You are a spoiled child living in a fantasy. They want to eliminate us all. I have looked into the eyes of the dead.*

I wrote more neutral things, hoping to calm him, but my hand as it held the pen was white.

He wrote back to me after a long silence. *If the possibility of you disappeared, there would be nothing left.*

I imagined that I bore a responsibility to aid in his survival. It's like a candle, I told myself knowledgeably. If you let it die, you extinguish him.

I would be leaving soon, going back to America. What was the harm?

I love you, I wrote. The lie looked up at me from the white sheet of paper. *Survive for me.*

A MONTH LATER I did return to America and to college. Once or twice I had nightmares about the train, about the sound the shells had made, streaking metal cutting the sky open like skin. Sometimes I dreamed about the little boy under the pear tree.

In the dreams, he is shattered by the explosion of the tree. The splinters go everywhere. They stab him through and through, and when he dies, he is listening to the weeping of his cows. On more than one occasion I wake up thinking that I am holding his wood-riddled body in my arms. I rock him like a baby, but he is already dead. The blood stains my belly, and there are splinters that have worked their way into my thighs that will not unwind themselves from my skin.

I took up swimming, spending long hours at the campus pool, gliding from one end to the other. I thought of my deceased aunt Ana's long-dead catfish, swimming from side to side in its tub in Sarajevo. My stamina increased, and I began to spend long periods of time in the water. Sound and color were muted there, and people moved gracefully. There were no sudden movements or sharp sounds.

I thought of Antonio very little, to tell the truth.

"I might die," he had threatened on the telephone before I left.

I had grown uneasy with his damaged voice, the crack when he admitted that he spent hours drinking. There was something about him that had withered in the weeks since we'd met.

I wrote a few more letters from America. I did so with a heavy heart, feeding the lie I had begun. In my mind, it was growing like a Frankenstein. There was a period of sudden silence, and then a letter explaining that he had been in Bosnia.

I kept your picture beside me, he wrote. *It watched over me through some black days. I wrote you letters while I was there, my hands so cold I could hardly write. I begged people to post them for me. But I believe that each letter was lost and that none ever found its way to you.*

Then came news that he had left the army, and I stopped writing. It's done, I thought to myself and, in a flash of ego, He's saved. I did not write again.

On the day I had left Zagreb for America, a few weeks after the shelling on my way to the sea, Aunt Iva waited on the platform beside my train. Small and dressed in black, she clutched a dusty handbag to her chest.

"Be good," she called up at me. "Study hard."

I nodded at her. "I'll see you, *tetka.* I'll see you later."

She smiled. The train began to move away. I hung my head out the window and watched her figure grow smaller, waving at me, at the retreating train.

"Don't forget us," she had called as the train started to roll forward, in a voice so small it was all but lost under the screeching wheels.

"I won't forget," I said to the curtains on the train, which were thick with dust and cigarette smoke. I repeated the words as I boarded the airplane in England, and upon my return to America, and all through my classes, when my professors' voices hung above my head, never fully penetrating my fog. I spent a year looking out of windows and imagining a different landscape, thinking even then about men who bore my brother's face, lost in the Lika mountains. In those mountains it was winter. Walking from crag to crag, their bare feet turned blue in the razor ice. They called into the still air, surrounded on all sides by walls of pine trees. Black eyes of startled brown bears regarded them from the darkness. Wolves circled the snow a mile or two downwind, stopping to sniff the cold air and whine low in their throats. But the words were taken from the lips of these men. They became frost and hung in clouds in front of their blind eyes.

WHEN I RETURNED to Croatia several years later to research women in the war-affected population, I saw Antonio again. But the tall, gentle boy who had walked with us on the pebble beach on Krk was gone.

We met at a bakery near the Korzo in Rijeka. He was drunk when he arrived, and he sat across from me with accusing eyes. His hands shook slightly, and he would not allow me to pay when the waitress presented our bill.

"You stopped writing," he said bluntly, "and I hated you."

I would not meet his eyes. Guilt made me cry, and tears fell on the tops of my hands. "I thought I owed it to you to write for as long as you were in danger," I explained to him. "That's all."

The belief that my letters were his salvation struck me suddenly as an extreme form of narcissism. But I had not promised him a life together, just words of comfort, I insisted to myself.

"I hate you," he said. There was a note of violence in his voice, and I was suddenly afraid. He rose and walked away.

I threw myself into my books, reading witness statements and human rights reports. I attended a conference in Zagreb and traveled to the former "Krajina" borderland region. It was a ghost land of destroyed houses and dead animals.

The last time I saw Antonio was in front of my apartment building. He had wild eyes and smelled again of alcohol. He had been calling me in the middle of the night, crying and screaming, until I stopped answering the telephone. He was a specter, stalking me over the wires.

Shock must have shown in my face, and I flinched as he moved closer to me. He was crying.

"All my fault . . ." he managed to get out. "The wrong coordinates. People in my unit died because I had the wrong coordinates . . ."

He backed me against the front door. He towered over me. I was not sure whether to believe him or if this was a misguided bid for sympathy.

"I'm sure it wasn't your fault," I told him in confusion.

"You." His eyes focused on me, as if he'd become suddenly aware of my presence. "After everything I went through . . . I deserve you."

"People don't deserve other people," I told him, looking nervously up the deserted street. "It doesn't work like that."

"I earned you," he went on. "And you won't see it."

"No." I felt color drain from my face and shook my head. "It doesn't work that way."

I turned to move away from him, but his hand wrapped around my neck. He squeezed, not hard enough to cause me any great pain, but with enough strength that I was immobilized and pinned against the wall, hard enough to let me know that if he wanted, he could snap my neck.

When he let me go and walked away, I slumped against the wall, running my hands along my collarbone.

WAR LEAVES NOTHING UNTOUCHED. In Bosnia I was a part of the forensic team because I rose as they did and donned the same blue suits; I excavated beside them and ate with them in the evenings at the mess hall. But I was not one of them, because I understood how the war had changed everything. I knew this because I knew how things had looked before.

When we finished excavating the site, we left the entire grave uncovered, a hole with a frieze of suffering at its bottom. Before the bodies were pulled out—thirty-three in both graves and fewer than expected—the press was allowed past the cordons to take photographs. Their faces were uncertain as they approached the depression. Journalists fell silent as they filed past. It was possible to pick out the seasoned reporters, like soldiers from the front. There was no shock on their faces, no disgust, only an expression that seemed to dwell somewhere between hardness and hopelessness.

I have since seen some of the pictures that were taken that

day. I recognized the graves and was able to trace in my mind where the arm of one dead person is flung over the man beside him whose body he partly covers. I was also able to recognize what the photographs do not show: myself. Sitting on top of a pile of dirt, filthy and sweaty, listening to the sound of the creek that ran just a few feet behind the grave.

It was a shallow creek. No more than a trickle, but it made a nice sound. From atop the dirt pile I could see the bleached stones of the dry parts of the creek bed, the tiny streams and estuaries that had survived the summer months. Behind me, photographers were snapping away. I heard the whir of their shutters. Children must have played in this creek, I thought. I could see them standing on the larger stones, dropping pebbles into the stream. Plop, plop, and squeals of laughter as they pushed each other into the water, the smell of soaked sandal leather following them as they scurried along the stream.

It was almost exactly a year to the day since the graves were filled with bodies. Had the people lain here underneath the sky for a while before dying? Could they hear the sound of the creek? Did it bring them back to some other place in those last seconds?

Don't. The voice was so loud the words seemed to have been spoken directly into my ear. No one else noticed. The photographers continued with their picture taking. The stream kept up its steady murmur. *Once you let them in, you are finished.* The pathologists and anthropologists had been telling me this since my arrival, and I think they gently pitied me for being unable to shut them out.

But there was another voice as well, as light as wind. It was a ghost voice, the voice that separated me from their ranks. It said, *You are finished if you keep them out.*

Later we pulled the bodies one by one. They made strange sighing sounds as they were removed from the ground. We placed the bones of their hands in plastic bags so that no piece of them should remain behind.

SOME MINES DETONATE on the ground. Others, like *PROMdžije*, jump into the air where they explode, ejecting thousands of shrapnel darts in all directions. The explosion occurs at chest level on a man of average height, but roughly at the level of a ten-year-old's eyes. There are antipersonnel mines and antitank mines. There are mines that explode under very little pressure and mines requiring a burden of several pounds to detonate. They can be mass-produced—in Bosnia they included examples of East German, Soviet, and Yugoslav manufacture—or homemade. They can remove a leg or a hand or turn vast portions of the human anatomy into ground meat. They can kill instantaneously or leave someone writhing in agony and the dissipating warmth of his own blood.

Children, curious and inclined to games, are particularly vulnerable. They stumble on mines accidentally, or they locate them but find the squat and cylindrical shapes ominous and fascinating. Although it seems implausible, they have a habit of playing with them. I know because my own mother, who was supposed to be a fairly sensible child, used to bang with a rock on an interesting piece of unexploded ordnance she found behind her aunt's house in Austria after the Second World War. She remembers suspecting that it might be dangerous, but she did it anyway.

In Croatia I had met a woman who counseled traumatized children. She was once asked if there was a special heaven where legs and arms might go. Her patient proceeded to draw a picture of dozens of limbs, all attached to helium balloons, floating gently in the sky.

Areas declared mine-free are often still contaminated. The immediate radius around houses is cleared, leaving orchards, fields, and woods untouched. When mined fields burn, on purpose or accidentally, there is a deafening pyrotechnics display.

Sometimes mines can be found on the sides of roads or on the roads themselves. When we got out of our truck one morning to start another day of excavation, an SFOR soldier from one of the Humvees happened to spot an unexploded mine on the side of the road. It was quite near where we had parked and exactly where we had been parking for the past several days. We had walked right past it. Not one of us had noticed.

The area was promptly rechecked for other mines and, when none were located, the vehicles moved. We were herded away from the area while people argued about what to do. After a short conversation they decided to detonate it.

Initially they suggested that we get into the WOLF, a South African monster of an armored vehicle. A group of us looked at it dubiously. Though it was barely eight in the morning, we were already drenched in sweat, and the WOLF's metal belly looked like the inside of an oven. We opted for one of the trucks, now parked a hundred feet away and on the other side of the road behind the blind of a Humvee.

We waited for the detonation in uneasy silence. When it came, it was louder than we expected.

"Do you think it was there before?" we asked each other as we got out of the truck again.

Although none of us had seen it before, we determined that the mine must have been there all along. Which was a more agreeable thought than the alternative.

THE NEXT LOCATION slated for excavation had not been cleared of mines, and the de-mining dogs had mistakenly been sent to Mozambique. But at dinner one night, Bill Haglund announced that he wanted to proceed to the site regardless.

Everyone around the table shifted uncomfortably. One of the American women with more presence of mind than the rest of us cleared her throat and said, "Forget it, Bill. I'm not going to a site that hasn't been de-mined."

He continued chewing his food. After a long pause he nodded. "Of course. Who else feels this way?"

My hand and several others went up.

He gave me a hard look, and I wondered if he had heard me telling cautionary tales to the others, warning them not to enter areas that had not been professionally de-mined. My voice sounded preachy and I felt like a schoolmarm, but I pressed on, connecting the dots that, in the flush of their Bosnian adventure, they could not seem to connect for themselves.

Even before that dinner with Haglund I had told the women I bunked with, "Nothing is worth losing a limb or dying. Not ever. They can't even keep track of the areas they know for a fact to be mined, far less the areas that they're unsure of." I related nightmare scenarios about returnees, booby-trapped areas, and mined thresholds. I remembered the story of a family that had returned home to start rebuilding their house in Slavonia. And of the leaf-covered present that had been biding its time for years, waiting for their son beside a well.

We finished our meal in silence.

A STANDARD DE-MINER in Bosnia must stab each square meter of ground roughly two thousand times. Most of the mines are antipersonnel mines, meaning that it would take less, rather than more, weight to detonate them.

A group of tall blond Swedes from the Norwegian People's Aid worked as our de-miners. They were, by far, the most even-keeled people I met working in Bosnia. They shared a quiet sense of humor and were perpetually good-natured. Each man worked with a dog, and the dogs were as agreeable as their masters.

A dog alerted its handler by sitting quietly when it found a mine. For the dogs it was a game, but they were also attuned to their handlers and to the gravity of the situation. One misstep, one missed mine, and the one they adored most could be blown into little pieces.

"The dogs, they can get upset," one of the de-miners told me. Too many days in the field, too much asked of them could compromise their performance. "We must take good care of them."

De-mining dogs undergo years of tough mental testing and training. They have to be healthy, well fed, and rested. When the de-miner learned that we had regularly drunk tap water in Tuzla prior to our water arrangement with SFOR, he was shocked. "We don't drink it. Our dogs don't drink it. You oughtn't drink it either."

Their organization had sent someone to test the water in

advance and found Tuzla's water supply a disturbing petri dish of bacteria and viruses. Theirs was not the only water test, he told me, and he knew people who had become quite ill.

I thought about all the children who drank it every day to wash down their rations of humanitarian aid, and I nodded.

"You must trust your dog an awful lot," I said.

They were like one body, he told me. They got into a groove that was something like meditation, crossing and re-crossing a field, moving slowly, never sure what lay underfoot.

One dog was stolen while I was in Bosnia. They were not trained as attack or guard dogs and were friendly to almost everybody. One day when the de-miners had left their field house, someone broke in and led one of the dogs away.

When the de-miners returned to find the dog gone, her handler was beside himself. Better they had taken his girlfriend, he told us later. His hand. He had been near tears, and enraged. But a neighbor had seen the culprit, recognized him, and given directions to his house, which was not far away. The de-miners set off as a group but made the dog's handler wait in the car. They found the dog tied up, tail thumping the ground at the familiar faces come to rescue her. The thief had meant to resell her for a few hundred marks. He needed the money, he told them nervously, and had not considered the consequences.

The dog's handler was overjoyed, but he grew more guarded after that. He began to look at the population around him with increased skepticism. He had felt less than whole without his dog, naked and unnatural, he told us later.

SOME TEAM MEMBERS did inspect the new site the day after our dinner meeting, reasoning that if the rest of us saw them return, we would shed some of our fear of mines and join them.

"A macho thing," one of the women said, shaking her head.

Nothing happened to them, but we were unconvinced.

The backhoe operator, who removed the top layer of dirt, was a friendly and affable man. He would have been the first to learn if the field was mined or not. He seemed to be under the impression that he would be fine, seated well above the ground behind his controls as a metal scoop scraped the ground.

Someone had pointed out what an explosion of metal on metal might do, and he promptly stopped smiling.

Since we weren't going to the site, I spent that day washing some of my clothes and my hair. I read a book, throwing it down on my cot a short while later to call my aunts. I had not spoken to them since arriving in Bosnia. They believed, like my father, that I was in western Slavonia, and I felt guilty for misleading them.

"*Je li sve u redu?*" my aunt Katja asked from Zagreb. "Is everything okay?"

"*Sve u redu,*" I confirmed.

"Are you eating?"

I smiled into the phone. "Naturally."

"Well, that's the important thing." And she shared a few choice bits of neighborhood gossip before hanging up.

As I walked back to my container, the wooden planks sighing under my feet, I imagined their apartment on Trpimirova Street. Usually I found it claustrophobic, but now I thought fondly of Katja's sewing machine, which stood like a guard at the balcony door, and I thought about the way she read the newspaper with a running commentary of "My God!" "Cretin!"

and "Devil take him!" Iva would be working away in the hot kitchen, stopping occasionally to watch children play in the courtyard below.

I got along with my great-aunts with varying degrees of success. When I had begged to accompany my father on his trip to Zagreb four years before, as much as anything it was out of a fear that I was forgetting them.

Fiery Katja was the last of the sisters to be widowed. She and Mile had lived with her twin, Iva, and older sister Ljubica. The fourth aunt, Draga, had died several years before, in 1990, in Posušje. My grandmother Anđelka, their oldest sister, had died in the late 1960s, a silhouette who existed in the sepia of family photographs and my father's stories.

Two dead and three living is the game's score, they seemed to say with quiet defiance. But my remaining aunts seldom spoke about their dead sisters.

"You're tall like she was," was all they ever said about my grandmother, and I knew to leave certain subjects alone.

Katja and Mile had been an anomaly among other couples of their generation, the majority of whom wore the black of mourning. They were like butterflies among moths, and while there was plenty of arguing, they seemed to take a certain amount of satisfaction from strife. Their married life had spanned five decades.

Together they had traveled all over the world—to India and Spain, Israel and Scandinavia. Ceramic plates from faraway places lined their walls. On Saturdays they went like teenagers to films.

Aunt Draga was one of the topics they avoided. She had been both a decorated Partisan and an alcoholic. On family visits to Herzegovina when we were little, my brother and I had been told that Draga was perpetually unwell. Her face had always been a strange color, but her eyes were green and lively. She had a ferocious laugh that drinking never altered. I could remember from childhood that unlike other grown-ups who were constantly shushing or sending me meaningful looks, Draga had been delighted by my hot-tempered personality. Timid Iva had been her caretaker in those days, and Iva was as tiny as Draga was large.

In 1969, when my father brought his intended to the hills of Herzegovina to show her where he had been born, Draga, Iva, and some other women who had been summoned for the event came out of the house in Posušje to examine my mother. In those days her hair was platinum, and she wore the shortest miniskirts that had ever been seen in the village.

The black-clad countrywomen with wrinkled faces had circled her and clucked their tongues in scandalized delight over the amount of leg visible beneath her skirt.

My father, fourteen years her elder, had already introduced her to family members and friends on the Dalmatian coast. There the women had looked at my mother and asked, "A ča češ ti sovom ditetom? What are you going to do with this child?"

"Crni Bero!" they had called him with smiles, wagging their fingers in his face.

"Black Bero" only grinned. He was as dark as a Gypsy, clearly taking after his father's family. He was mercurial and had a complex nature. Within the family his temper was legendary. But in the mountain village in Herzegovina, they asked about what kind of wife she would make him.

"Sluša li te?" Aunt Draga asked. "Is she obedient?"

He thought for a moment. "Not really. But I want a wife, not a donkey."

QUIET IVA had been disappointed in love and had never married. She was the idealist in the family. Even into old age she smiled proudly, remembering the time she was arrested at the age of twelve for singing "Rajsko Djevo, Kraljice Hrvata" in church. The hymn, "Virgin of Paradise, Queen of Croats," was banned.

She did not end up marrying either of her two suitors, she once confided to me, because the first had been unfaithful and the second would not marry her in a church, in front of God. The snide village gossips called her an old maid behind her back, clucking their tongues over her womb, withering further with every year. The second suitor had spent dark years in prison after the Second World War and was afraid that a church wedding would send him back to a Communist jail.

"I wanted a church wedding. A church wedding or nothing." And so she had remained alone, spending a lifetime taking care of others. Later, when I lived next door to them, she insisted on taking care of me as well, often to my irritation.

"*Nemoj švercati*. Don't get on a streetcar without a ticket. You may think you won't get caught, but you will." . . . "Don't walk through a red light. These drivers here are crazy, just crazy." . . . "Don't wear skirts that are too short, and if some strange man starts talking to you, just walk away."

And she spent hours in the kitchen, feeding me to the point of bursting.

Aunt Ljubica was the quietest of the sisters, and she sat on the couch with a drawn face from dawn until dark, speaking so little that when she did say something, it came out terse and angry, like an old hinge grown rusty that complained bitterly when someone tried to make use of it.

In her youth she had been married to a man from Livno who became a high-ranking officer in the fascist Independent State of Croatia. He was killed in the Partisan reprisals at the end of World War II on the *Križni put*, a death march. Ljubica became a recluse, seldom leaving the apartment after that.

I was curious about her, about a love that had left her waiting for so long, but I had learned to leave the topic alone, devoting all my energy to fending off unwanted advice about my appearance. When I lived in Zagreb those few months at the age of twenty-one, I had been sloppily collegiate, preferring the comfort of tennis shoes and jeans. I wore my hair in a ponytail, my only accessory the plastic band that kept it out of my face. But each of my visits in jeans and an old sweater was taken as a personal offense and was greeted by a clucking tongue. She culled pictures from magazines of well-groomed young ladies and presented them to me. She was not pleased with how I wore my hair, and she considered my clothes unflattering.

"And you, an American girl. What are people going to say?"

I started to laugh. "In America I wear nothing but jeans. Jeans to go to classes; jeans to go on dates."

She looked shocked. "People are going to think you are poor."

I shook my head. "We're not rich."

She was stung by this reminder, believing the stories of immigrants who arrived in America with nothing and built financial empires.

"Do you own any makeup?" she would ask.

And I would sigh. "I have makeup, *tetka*. I just don't wear it."

"You must take more care of your appearance, girl," she told me, reaching out a hand to lift my hair. "You should wear this up. You look better with it away from your face."

After Uncle Mile died, the sisters had all kept up their own appearances in spite of the widows' weeds. They wore the same formless black garments, black stockings, and black shoes, but they colored their hair and tweezed their eyebrows.

They wanted me to make more out of my long, dark brown hair.

I grinned at Aunt Ljubica, teasing her. "It's so hot during the summer. I may just cut it all off."

"No!" She bore a shocked expression, and I could see the wheels in her head turning. What man would want me then? She had been dismayed to find that a husband did not yet interest me, especially not the steady, dependable type she recommended. She looked at me suspiciously while I reassured her that I was only joking. I could see that she was imagining me shorn like a sheep, and husbandless.

One day during one of my childhood visits to Zagreb, my parents had gone into town to meet friends for coffee and left my brother and me in our aunts' care. Bored and sweaty from their edict that we take naps in the stifling heat of the dining room, we began to make trouble. We quickly tired of chasing each other around the room in bare feet, and I dared Andrew, who was then only six, to run naked through the living room, where a neighbor was drinking coffee with Aunt Ljubica.

Mile had lost his temper and cuffed my brother, who promptly burst into tears. Although he was used to our father's temper, he had never been spanked by another person, and the degradation was too much for me to bear. I burst from behind the doors of the dining room, eyes ablaze and dark braids flying, and seized my brother's arm with such ferocity that my uncle, aunts, and the neighbor froze. Stunned by my sudden and violent appearance, they looked at me in some amazement, and their reaction gave me a certain satisfaction.

"I hate you!" I screamed at them, and shepherded my brother into the bathroom, where I locked the door behind us and refused to be coaxed out by the cajoling and sweet tones coming from the hallway. Andrew, as I remember, had quieted down with surprising ease, thinking we were playing a game of fort, holding off marauders. When he got bored, he curled into a ball, rested his head on my lap as I sat cross-legged on the floor, and fell asleep.

Aunt Ljubica later claimed that my words had been directed at her. Years after, she was still able to mimic my eight-year-old voice screaming *I hate you!* in English with an accuracy that shamed me.

From the bathroom I heard them talking anxiously, wondering what my father would do when he came home. They did not have long to wait.

"Old man," he told Mile, a note of fury in his voice, "don't ever lay a hand on my children again."

When I finally unlocked the door, knowing that I had been responsible for the entire confrontation and afraid that my father would find out and punish me for it, I saw them standing as still as chess pieces. I stepped into a hallway so full of silent tension that no one noticed the addition to the strained tableau. My father's face had been taut with rage and his fists clenched. He and Mile faced each other like warring elephants. My aunts had closed ranks behind Mile, staring at my father with angry eyes. Even then I was aware that there was something more, that behind their expressions lay an undercurrent of something darker.

For years, when I asked him about it, my father would shake it off.

"You're just like him," Ljubica told me uneasily when I became an adult. "Same blood. Hot and unthinking, and filled with rage."

Later, after Aunt Ljubica had a stroke, she spent days disintegrating in her bed. When conscious, she would look at us as though we were visions she was none too pleased to see. One side of her body was paralyzed, and she could not chew properly or speak, save for one phrase that she repeated constantly. *Nosi njih.* Carry them.

When she needed to be turned or to have her bedsheets changed, bitter, hurt tears turned her eyes to glass. She would try to cover her nakedness from our eyes, with hands that twisted erratically like branches.

"It's all right, *tetka*," I would say, trying to soothe her. "I'm not looking."

But she became so agitated that Iva and Katja soon began to push me into the hallway, summoning me a few minutes later when the business was done and Ljubica was pale and staring sadly at the wall.

But even without speech she could communicate her displeasure. When my long hair fell over my face or when I came dressed in black, she would press her lips together so that they formed a thin line, and she would look away from me.

"You're dark," she had told me once, when she could still speak. "When you wear black, you disappear."

She thought I did it to spite her.

Sometimes I made a special effort for her, wearing dresses of pale colors, tying my hair back, and applying lipstick and rouge. Her eyes would brighten, and her lips stretched into what must be called a smile.

When I leaned over to kiss her white face on the whiteness of the hospital bed that we had dragged up to the apartment, she was like the shell of a cicada, like glass. But when I caught her unawares, I could see that some of her remained.

I believe that this war and the Second World War bled together for her at some point. That her life had become a collection of accumulated suffering, unclassified by years and without a strict chronology. I would see her on a Monday and then again on a Wednesday, but the way she greeted me, tears rolling down her cheeks onto the white pillow, made me think that she was unable to keep the threads of those days separate, that when I had been gone for two days, it may as well have been two years, and that all days were a punishment in which she was waiting to die.

Her sisters never gave up, though, helping her with often painful exercises that the physical therapist showed them, and tilting her so she could watch television. But she had lost interest in the mundane world, and her eyes would focus not on the screen, but on some intermediate point that very rarely brought the ghost of a smile to her face.

VARYING PATTERNS of vegetation can indicate ground that has been disturbed. This is particularly true if the disturbed ground has been filled with organic material. A trash pit, for example, or a compost heap. Sometimes there will be a perfect circle of flowers in an otherwise unremarkable field, a neon sign that can tell archaeologists where to start digging.

After a cataclysm, ground can settle and become even with surprising speed. It is more dynamic, more prone to flow than most people think, but vegetation markers can take some time to appear.

The graves around Srebrenica were a year old in 1996. Grass had started to grow back, but the outlines of the graves were still roughly visible. In the end, no difference in grass or bright flowers had ultimately been necessary to find many of them. Satellite photographs had revealed bald ground right away, and bone markers stuck out like brittle branches.

Once all the bodies had been removed and transported to the morgue, dirt was redeposited in the grave. The ground was packed down, but the edges were visible. In the months to come, the grass would blur the edges again, making them less distinct, but I was convinced that there was enough organic matter left behind in that pit to cause a chemical change in the soil that would one day subtly affect the things that grew from it. There had to be.

I imagined that one day, maybe years in the future, people in a plane flying over Bosnia would be able to see the differences from the air. Perceptible circles and rectangles, the sloppy edges of fields, continuing into the horizon.

WHILE THE CREW WAITED for the de-mining dogs to return from Mozambique, I made a request to move back to the morgue in Tuzla. I vastly preferred excavation to the morgue, but the field was chaotic. We felt constantly at the mercy of others—the SFOR soldiers who escorted us to the site, the mines that might or might not have been underfoot at any given moment. And I was disturbed by the fact that they were still using the Serbian laborers on the grave.

"It's not right," I had finally told Haglund, sounding more emotional than I wanted to. "There's a moral issue here."

"Moral?" he had asked.

Some time later a colleague handed me an article from a French newspaper. My French was halting, and he translated it for me. A reporter had cornered one of the diggers and interviewed him. The man admitted to being present when the grave was first filled.

"I only dug," he had insisted in the article interview. I felt ill.

My colleague looked at me, "What do you think?"

I laughed bitterly.

"You don't buy it?"

I shrugged. How could I tell him that I thought the massacred men had probably been forced to dig the trench themselves and then been deposited into it?

Colleagues told me later that Haglund was grumbling about elements on the team trying to cause problems, and he had decided the smartest course of action was to keep everyone in the dark and simply inform no one of future plans. "We have a schedule to keep," he kept insisting. Most days, though, he departed to debrief the press.

SEATED IN THE BACK of the truck on the drive back to Tuzla, I asked Haglund and the UN investigator when the de-mining dogs would return. A rumor was circulating that they were considering contracting a local de-mining team, and I confronted them about it.

"Why should it matter if it's a local team?" the UN investigator asked, glaring at me in the rearview mirror.

I was tempted to laugh. Equal opportunity seemed funny in Republika Srpska. "No one wants us here," I explained to them carefully. "What is one mine more or less if it stops our work because someone gets killed?" I was looking out the window, feeling as if I had entered a world where the ones with the least common sense were in charge.

A few of the SFOR soldiers had become frustrated with the way that some of our team did not seem to understand the seriousness of the situation in Republika Srpska. "There was a war here. Don't they get it?" One SFOR soldier had watched angrily while one of the cars in our daily procession back to Camp Lisa broke formation and drove back without armed escort. "This isn't a game," he pointed out.

UN personnel had temporarily been taken hostage that summer in eastern Bosnia, and people on the roads regularly shook their fists when we passed in our clearly marked trucks.

"What would a local de-mining team have to lose if it were to, say, plant a mine where we were to dig?" I continued on the drive back to Tuzla. "Their good reputation?" When they did not respond, I said, "They're happy with the status quo. No Muslims except dead Muslims."

Family members of the missing were not allowed near the graves, and this also upset me. In other parts of Bosnia they had been granted some access to the exhumations. But in Republika Srpska people worried that having Muslims present might further alienate local Serbs and possibly endanger future work. Several of the Latin Americans, acutely attuned to the fact that the missing had waiting family members, were also disturbed by this policy.

I thought of the families in their refugee rooms, following scant details of field developments through the newspapers each day. I thought of the people who should have access to the graves and who should have been present during the exhumations. "They don't belong here," one of the laborers had told me earlier, referring to the Muslim interpreter who had accompanied one of the journalists.

During the fall of Srebrenica, Ratko Mladić is alleged to have said, "It is going to be a feast. There will be blood up to your knees." We passed through Zvornik an hour into our journey. I watched the Drina River. It was murky and flowed quickly. What's one body more or less? The word Mladić is alleged to have used is *meze*. It is more than a feast. It is a slow, delightful process, grazing on delicacies when there is a little slice of something here, a little cut of something there, and each bite is savored.

The refugee cousins had looked at me with dull eyes. *The bodies came floating under the bridges. We looked to see who, but we couldn't recognize them.*

In the front seat, they were now talking about something else—a colleague, the weather. They existed in another place.

SARAJEVO

1933–1945

Give me your hand, my Dove.
I wish to climb up to you.
Cursed is she who sleeps alone.

—*from "La Tore," a Sephardic song*

ANĐELKA LIKED to watch the birds wheeling in the winter sky over Begova Mosque, like black leaves caught in a funnel of wind. She felt suddenly weightless when they fell in unison, as if they were teasing her, before resuming flight. Sometimes when she walked through Baščaršija, Sarajevo's market section, she would stop in the middle of the cobblestoned streets, a single immobile figure among the teeming shoppers, merchants, and pedestrians, and lift her eyes to the rapid darting of the birds in flight. Until someone jostled her or a sound from the street brought her out of her reverie, and she slid into motion again, holding the scarf that had come open at her neck and grasping her purchases more firmly under her arm, to resume her purposeful walk home.

Sarajevo was an exotic city so unlike Herzegovina that it had taken her weeks to get used to its noises and smells.

Baščaršija was a souk, with merchants hawking fabrics and leather, spices and jewelry from stands and small shops. Aščenice sold *pita* and *čevape* with creamy white *kajmak* cheese. And wandering vendors sold *salep*, a winter drink made from sassafras root. Bero had come to love the warm drink, begging for it on trips to town.

Five times a day muezzins called faithful Muslims to prayer from minarets in dozens of the city's mosques, and many women still wore *feredža*, the covering that hid their faces from the world. They seemed like ghosts to Anđelka at first, but in the oblique rays of morning sunshine their eyes became nearly visible behind the mesh of their veils. She had met them on more than one occasion—the quick black eyes of young women who were smiling into their veils, the tired eyes of older women who were struggling with their market baskets—and although she still found their extreme modesty strange, she learned to detect the personalities that lay behind the covering.

Though she had been at school in Mostar, a city with a mixed population, she had never before lived in a city as large as Sarajevo, where Muslims, Serbs, Croats, Jews, Czechs, Germans, and many other communities lived side by side. She learned to wish Muslim neighbors a happy Bajram and Serbian neighbors a happy Christmas in January. They ate at each other's tables on feast days and celebrations, and their children played soccer together in the streets.

She liked wandering the city's boulevards and narrow streets, and walking along the hesitant flow of the Miljacka River, crossing the river when the impulse caught her and recrossing at the next bridge, weaving into town in a circuitous route. If she sometimes longed for Herzegovina's clean, raw wind, or the uninterrupted blackness of its night sky, she enjoyed the fact that in Sarajevo she was nameless among all the other people hurrying to do their errands. Here no one thought of her as Marijan's widow or the eldest Jukić girl, and she did not mind one bit.

She walked the streets with her children, balancing Zoran on her hip and holding Bero's hand as he toddled, head bent forward, watching the street pass beneath his shoes in such wondrous concentration that she had to give his hand a little shake every so often in order to make sure he did not stumble. Few people did more than smile at them. No one gave unwanted advice.

When they first arrived, they had lived with Marijan's brother and sister on Ćebina Street. Ivan and Ana had meant well, helping her to get settled and to make Marijan's tiny pension stretch as far as possible. But during the oppressive days, when Ivan was working on the railroads as an inspector and Ana missed no opportunity to assert herself as mistress of the home, Anđelka would look out the windows and long for air.

Within a year she had found an apartment for herself and the children on Điđikovac Street. There was a large park at the bottom of the steep street, with plenty of trees for shade in summer, and hills for sledding when it snowed. Sveti Vinko Catholic School was just beyond the park, and Anđelka was already planning for her sons' education.

For the first time in her life she had a key that opened a space belonging only to her. For the first time, she could breathe. Waking up in the mornings, giving the children their breakfast, throwing the windows open to let the sunlight in— she began to enjoy the intimacy of these tasks and the fact that no one else observed them.

Her sister Ljubica threw up her hands in consternation on

one visit. Wasn't she lonely in the big city? Anything could happen to a woman on her own in such a place.

Zoran shifted in his sleep on her lap, and Bero was playing with toys underneath the table, talking to them as if they were an entire army of playmates. Anđelka did not respond. Theirs had always been a tense relationship, fraught with arguments and recriminations. Anđelka had married at sixteen, as soon as she was able, leaving her orphaned sisters behind. Ljubica had married Ante some years later. The two sisters shared blood but not much common ground. Anđelka was resolute, while Ljubica was moody and more susceptible to being hurt. Ljubica had still not become a mother, which created an ever wider gulf between them.

But Anđelka felt sympathy for Ljubica. She imagined her sister living in exile with Ante and struggling month after month to give him a child. She had sensed a propensity for anger in her brother-in-law, and she did not know if her sister's face was pinched because she endured his beatings or because of his bitterness over the fact that they were still childless. Or perhaps her own disappointment was the cause. Ljubica felt cheated, she could see that.

These were subjects about which they seldom, if ever, spoke.

"I'm not lonely," Anđelka said finally, to her sister's prodding. "I'm not alone."

A world began outside the Điđikovac apartment building, spread through the sloping park at the bottom of the street, and went on to embrace a landscape of limitless possibilities, of which Sarajevo was only the first outpost. Marijan's death had been difficult, and it meant she would have to raise the boys alone. It had also set her free, and she wondered why her sister could not see that.

• • •

IN THOSE FIRST YEARS, the children were often sick. It seemed that no sooner did they recover from one fever than they burned with another, conscious only when they begged her for water. She spent many nights sitting by the bed, worried that if she fell asleep, they would be stolen from her by dawn. She had premonitions that she would go to bed at night only to awake with the two cold bodies of her children on either side, like lifeless sentries. She believed fervently in the protective powers of her vigilance.

It was the only time she talked to her dead husband, pleading with him. "Djinko," she would tell the room, her voice sounding hollow. "They mustn't go."

When Bero came down with pneumonia that first winter in Đidikovac, she sat on a wooden chair beside the bed. A day went by and then a second. Bells began to ring outside, and the sound confused her until she realized it was Christmas Eve.

In the evening a neighbor sent her daughter by with a plate of cakes. The girl had been an angel in a church procession and was still dressed in her white costume.

Bero's fever broke while the girl was speaking to his mother. His eyes flickered and opened. He parted his lips, but he was so thirsty that no sound came out. He closed and opened them again, caught sight of the angel, and smiled.

"Angel," he called out in delight, and fell immediately back to sleep.

IVAN CHECKED IN on them from time to time. He was Marijan's eldest brother, as rooted as Marijan had been wild. Of all her husband's five siblings, Anđelka liked this gentle, polite man best. He did not ask prying questions or wonder what his brother's widow got up to in the city.

"When you need me, I am here," he had told her on more than one occasion. Anđelka felt a little sorry for him. Ana kept house for her brother and watched over him like a lioness. The poor man could hardly move without feeling his sister's watchful gaze.

After she had moved to Điđikovac, Anđelka had accompanied him for a walk down Aleksandrova Street. Ivan noticed the appreciative glances his sister-in-law received from other men, and when he attended a mass with her, he saw that some even waited for her arrival outside the church, though she seemed unaware of the attention.

"You are young," Ivan had told her awkwardly on their walk. "Your life does not end at twenty-two."

Anđelka looked at him curiously. She felt that she had been given his blessing, although for what, she was not sure.

That night, passing the mirror, she stopped to look at herself. She went to open the curtains to let some light in, then returned to study the woman in the glass. She made an inventory: Tall woman. Average build. Square jaw. She was able to make out a pulsing branch of veins in her forehead, just beneath her hairline, and she pressed a finger to that drumbeat. She looked again, imagining the body of a tiny black bird resting beneath her hair. When she opened her mouth, she half expected the moonlight to catch the gloss of its wings.

She began to feel the glow of the sun on her dark brown hair when she walked through the city. Bringing vegetables up through the park in her basket, she became aware for the first time that when her heart beat faster from the climb, the air she inhaled was sweet with the smell of the trees. And when she entered the apartment, if she caught sight of her reflection, her skin was rosy from the outside air.

A FEW YEARS LATER, as she walked past the Jonekla storefront on Aleksandrova Street, she glanced matter-of-factly at her reflection in the glass, not stopping to adjust her hat or fix her lipstick. She seemed in a hurry, but something about the way she looked in the window made Josef Finci think that she had seen him, that she had caught sight of him staring at her from the other side of the glass. He knew that couldn't be so. The sun was shining outside, and the interior of the hardware store was dark. But there was a knowing quality to her eyes, and a smile played at the corners of her mouth.

He jumped to his feet. "I'm going out, Father." A gray-haired man looked up absentmindedly from his office, but returned a moment later to his newspaper.

Josef had watched this woman pass the storefront several times on her way to shop at Lukić's grocery next door. The first thing he had noticed about her was the way she walked, with a quiet dignity that accentuated her height. He did not believe she was from Sarajevo. She lacked a city person's artifice, and he spent hours wondering where she might be from and what had brought her to Sarajevo.

From the sea? he guessed, observing her nut-brown hair. She was a Catholic, certainly. He had seen sun glance off the tiny gold crucifix on her neck. From the mountains, he decided finally, observing her clothing, excruciatingly plain and immaculate. He liked the almost stony line of her jaw.

But there was something different about her gait today. She might never choose to walk down this street again, he thought, or she might be traveling somewhere far away from Sarajevo and its mountains. He put on his hat and stepped out onto the street, and when he passed his own store window, intent on catching up with her, he did not glance at his reflection.

Something about his voice made her think the "Excuse me" was directed at her, although later she could not be sure what had given her that impression.

He removed his hat, revealing light brown, curly hair. "Yes?" she asked him expectantly.

He seemed at a loss for words. "Please. Would you accompany me for . . . a coffee . . ." His voice trailed off, and he looked suddenly shy, as if his first burst of bravado were evaporating.

She stood a moment in quiet shock. *I'm a widow*, she almost told him. *I'm a widow with two small sons and hands that are red from scrubbing, washing, and cooking. What do you want with me?*

But as he drew closer to her and offered his arm, she was thankful for the gloves she wore, and she placed a graceful hand on it, as if her skin were as smooth and uncracked as the belly of a dove.

THAT WAS HOW IT HAPPENED. They began to see one another secretly. Anđelka did not tell her sisters. They were far away, and besides, it was none of their business. Josef's sisters and mother knew he had a sweetheart, and they teased him, but they did not know who it was. His younger sister, Klara, was sure it was the girl whose father owned the jewelry store not far from their hardware store. She was a nice girl, small and plump with blue-black hair. His other sister, Nela, had gone to school with her, and Klara began to joke with him about it. *"Ken es esto en la ventana, que me amostra tanto amor?"* She danced around him, singing, "Who is it in the window who is showing me so much love?"

He laughed at her nervously. "Don't be silly," he said. "I have no sweetheart."

Their mother admitted to her daughters that she would be satisfied with such a match. They would make a big wedding, his mother thought happily. Josef was her gem, her only son. She and the girl's mother would make the plans, and Sarajevo would be talking about it for years to come. She smiled at the woman on the street whenever they ran into each other in the town or at the synagogue. The woman smiled back at her. Josef's mother was content. It seemed the families shared a secret so fragile that it could not be brought into the light. They would not talk about it yet; rather they would wait for the two young people to reveal their true feelings.

Josef was blissfully unaware of all of this.

"THE CHILDREN WILL HEAR," he whispered, holding her on the first night in her bed. He touched her hair and the gentle pulse. It kept a steady tempo, and he thought of water drops falling from an icicle in the winter sun.

"The children are asleep." She smiled and took his hand between both of hers.

• • •

A YEAR WENT BY, then two, and his parents grew impatient.

"But why do you go sneaking off?" his mother asked him, wringing her hands.

He grew annoyed. "I do not sneak off. I see my friends. We go drinking, and one thing leads to another . . . and I don't come home until morning. Is that so strange?"

But she was suspicious. He had been acting strangely for a long time. Her husband had told her to leave the boy in peace, but she had to know. She could not sit idly by without knowing.

JOSEF COULD NOT VISIT during the weeks when Anđelka's sister Draga was visiting, which made them both unhappy. They met in Veliki Park, sitting side by side on a bench that was far from the street, holding hands beneath their coats.

"I'm going to tell my parents," he insisted one night after Draga's departure. "I'm a grown man, and this has gone on too long."

Anđelka shrugged. Although he was the older one, she felt somehow that the reverse could be true. He was from a privileged family and had never known hunger. His family belonged to Sarajevo's tightly knit Sephardic community, and she knew a Catholic wife would be unacceptable, much less a widowed mother of two small sons. For her part, she was from Herzegovina, where Jews were not only so few that she could never remember having spoken with one in her youth, but were also reproached for everything from the death of Jesus to the current state of the world.

"I love you," he pleaded. "We have nothing to be ashamed of."

She smiled into his eyes and placed a hand on either side of his head. His eyes were like blue ice, and when she was with him, the hard years melted from her.

Draga returned to Posušje with her own suspicions. Her sister had acted strangely during her visit, answering questions angrily and shortly.

Bero and Zoran had been too young to remember Marijan, and they were too young to question Josef's appearance in their lives. One morning, the children had talked about Uncle Josef, asking when he would come again. Draga's intelligent green eyes had been fixed on her sister's back.

Anđelka stood at the stove making *palačinke*—thin, flat pancakes that she would fill with sweet preserves, a treat for the children. She could feel Draga's curious eyes even while the children ate happily, smacking their lips at the jam. When her sons said his name, she felt her shoulders tense, as if a jolt of electricity had shot from one blade to the other. But when she turned around, Draga was no longer looking at her.

When she and Josef were alone and the children with a neighbor or at the cinema, they lay side by side on the bed or embraced in a flurry of limbs, unafraid to make sounds. Her skin was white, his a shade deeper, and together they resembled milk and honey, a comparison that drew a smile from him.

"COME ON, *Seka*," Draga told her when she returned to Sarajevo several months later, this time with Katja in tow. "We know you've got a sweetheart."

Anđelka glanced at her dryly. "Look to yourself, sister."

Draga had started to gain a reputation in Posušje that had reached Sarajevo. The middle Jukić girl was reputed to like drinking and the company of men to a degree unacceptable in country girls.

But Anđelka's sisters would not let the matter go. "So what if you've got a boyfriend?" Katja said. "You don't need to hide him from us."

And Anđelka finally told them the truth, so tersely that it left no room for debate.

"He's Jewish?" Draga asked. Katja only shrugged. Later, when Anđelka went to the marketplace and left Bero and Zoran in their care, Draga taught them a rhyme. Zoran was still a toddler and Bero four years old, and they were delighted to learn.

"Repeat after me," she told them with a sly grin. "*Ćifuti, repati, skoro ćete krepati.*"

"What does it mean?" Bero asked, ever curious.

"Never mind, just say it after me." She repeated the words, and he said them, slowly at first and then building up speed to match her cadence while she nodded encouragingly.

Katja, who had been watching the exchange nervously, warned him, "Don't repeat that to your mother . . ."

Bero began to run around the apartment, giggling and singing out the rhyme. Zoran trailed behind him, calling out random words.

"*Ćifuti, repati, skoro ćete krepati!*"

When Anđelka returned home, Bero ran to her with a shout and sang the verse gleefully. "Yid, with a tail, soon you'll die!"

Anđelka stared at her oldest son for a moment before dropping the market basket and twisting his arm. "Do you know what you're saying?" she shouted at him.

He looked up at her, surprised, and burst into tears.

She slapped him once across the face, hard, and he ran away from her, sobbing. "Never!" she shouted after him. "Never repeat that."

Draga and Katja, who had fled to the kitchen, emerged shamefaced.

"You!" Anđelka told them accusingly. "You taught them that?"

"It was only a joke," Draga protested.

"He didn't even know what it meant, but you let him run around singing that trash?" She was shouting so loudly that a neighbor began to pound the ceiling from below.

"Out!" she hissed at her sisters. "Get out."

Katja began to cry, but Draga was defiant. "You'd throw your own flesh and blood into the street?" she shouted back. "Over something so stupid?"

Anđelka walked out of the room, slamming the door behind her.

FOR JOSEF, discovery came in the form of a suitcase. He had arranged to go to the seaside for a couple of weeks.

"With whom?" his mother asked, her brow furrowing. He listed some names of people she barely knew, this one and that. She was not pleased with his answer.

He shrugged. "I promised Father I would help him do inventory tonight," he told her, delivering a kiss to her cheek. "I'll be home later."

She did some last-minute ironing of pants and cotton shirts. He and his friends were going to Gradac the next morning. They would catch a train to Metković, where they would go by ferry down the Neretva River and then out into the sea, following the coastline until they reached the little town.

His mother turned on the light in his room. His bed was neatly made, the suitcase standing ready in the corner of the room. "Silly boy," she said aloud. She was holding the ironed clothes in her hands, and she tilted the suitcase onto its side to open it and place the folded clothes on top. A lump in one corner of the suitcase caught her eye, and she pulled back the carefully folded clothes. It was a red ball. She looked at it dumbfounded and began pulling other items out of the suitcase. In the end, she was sitting on the floor, staring at an assortment of children's toys.

"AH!" They watched the red ball sail over the blue water. Bero was quicker than Zoran and reached it with a kick of his legs. He could hear splashing behind him as his brother closed the gap between them. He hoisted it above his head triumphantly and threw it to Josef, who grinned and threw it closer to Zoran, smiling when the fairer head reached the ball with a happy shout. Anđelka was sitting on the beach, shading her eyes with one hand. Even from the water Josef could tell from the way she tilted her head to one side that she was smiling.

She had almost wept when he told her of the argument with his parents.

"It makes no difference to me," he had told her. "They know now. We don't have to sneak around, and we can live as we want."

Now both families knew, and neither approved. But An-delka and Josef did not care. Objections had been lodged, dire warnings issued, but that was the beauty of adulthood in a city—they were answerable only to themselves.

"I'm glad it's over," he had told her. "There's no reason to hide things anymore."

Josef turned and dived beneath the surface, swimming underwater until he saw the two pairs of thin legs drawing nearer to each other expectantly. He almost laughed as he swam, a line of thin bubbles rising vertically above his head. They had figured out this game, and he imagined them trying to predict where he would surface.

He popped up between them, water pouring from the crown of his head, and the sounds of their squeals filled his ears. He had a boy securely under each arm, and he told them each to take a deep breath.

They did so with exaggerated volume, anticipating their dive, and Josef sank with them several feet to the sea bottom, where he stood on a large mossy rock. He looked from one to another of the two boys, who were clamping their noses shut with their fingers, and he squeezed them once before letting them go. They sped quickly away, their legs kicking them into vertical darts, and he watched them break through the ceiling of the sea into the hot air. He stood a moment longer underwater before swimming to the surface and retrieving the ball.

PRELIMINARY GERMAN AIR ATTACKS during the early spring of 1941 strafed Sarajevo, leaving many dead. The war had begun, and the city's residents learned to hate the sounds of the planes, especially the screams of the Stukas, which would dive at a target and drop bombs before rising once more.

Just before one attack Anđelka and her children had been seated in the kitchen eating breakfast. There was the sudden, faint ping of glass breaking, so quiet she thought she had imagined it. A quick search of the kitchen revealed a glass on the counter that had cracked mysteriously in half, its base broken from its rim. It had not fallen or shifted, but stood eerily intact.

It was an omen, she thought, and she bundled the boys out of the apartment, leaving everything where it was. The street outside was nearly deserted, but she took each boy by the hand and hurried them in the direction of Bjelave. They had climbed less than a few hundred yards when bombing began. There was an explosion a short distance behind them.

They took shelter under a bakery's metal awning. It seemed that no one else had shared Anđelka's premonition of impending disaster, and the majority of people on the street had been doing their morning shopping. They jostled each other for position under the awning, some crying and others standing tensely silent. Smoke and dust rose in plumes from the city center, which lay just beneath them. And each time a bomb made an impact in the city below, debris clattered onto the metal awning. Then the pieces of brick, wood, and shrapnel rolled onto the pavement, littering the street before their frightened eyes.

THERE WAS SOME FOREWARNING before the next large raid that year. Ivan came to collect them, having arranged for them to go to a farm outside of Sarajevo that was owned by the farmer who sold them milk. They would spend a few nights in her barn until the bombing abated.

They made their way to the train station, but just as they reached it, the attack began. The station was a prime target for the German planes, and everyone nearby fled, screaming, trying to escape. A Stuka roared and swooped behind them as they scrambled up a hill behind the station. The plane's gunner strafed the panicked crowd, and Ivan screamed at Anđelka and the children to get down. They fell onto the hillside, covering their heads with their hands as the gunner punctured the ground around them. When it was over, Anđelka rose, righted her sons, and brushed the dust from their traveling clothes with a shaky hand.

In the countryside, they slept on hay amid the sounds of animals and the creaking of the barn. Bero and Zoran bore troubled expressions even while they slept. They had been forced to leave their German shepherd, Lux, in the yard behind their building. He was a stray they had adopted, and even though they left him unchained, with some food, the boys were worried.

By the time they returned to Sarajevo the next week, the Germans had taken the city. There was tightness in Anđelka's chest when they turned onto Điđikovac Street and saw that their apartment building had been damaged. Their home was still standing, but Lux lay in the yard, dead, with blood-matted fur.

TEN DAYS after German tanks first entered Sarajevo in April 1941, Josef returned from the south, where he had been serving in the Yugoslav Royal Army. Ill-equipped, disorganized, and overpowered, their defenses had been easily smashed by the Germans.

Josef came first to the Điđikovac apartment, where he shed his military uniform, took a bath, shaved, and changed into civilian clothes.

"It's no good," he told Anđelka flatly before leaving for his parents', deeply troubled that Sarajevo's fate—that all their fates—lay in German hands. He had been following what was happening to Jews elsewhere in Europe and had struggled to explain to his father that the same thing could happen in Sarajevo and that they should leave for neutral Switzerland, where they had family.

But his father demurred. "I've been doing business with Germans for years. This is our home, Josef."

The panzers rolled through the city for days on their way south and east. Residents of Sarajevo spent nights listening to the steady roar from the city's main thoroughfares.

On April 10, 1941, the Independent State of Croatia, a fascist dictatorship under Ante Pavelić, was declared. The kingdom was dissolved. Pavelić, or *poglavnik*, as he was to be known, wasted no time instituting racist policies. He and his Ustašas, a formerly fringe fascist group, had spent years of exile in Italy. He immediately ceded vast portions of Dalmatia to Italy, preferring to maintain control over "historically" Croatian territories, which included Bosnia-Herzegovina.

"Gangster," Anđelka had muttered to Josef, fear just beginning to enter her assessment of the current situation.

She despised politics, the memory of those years in exile with Marijan still fresh in her mind. She listened as Pavelić made his proclamations about purging the Croatian race of "alien elements." In the spring and summer of 1941 the first racial laws against Jews and Gypsies were introduced.

All she and Josef wanted was to be left alone. It was not, she would point out to God, as she knelt in Sarajevo's cathedral, too much to ask.

On the day the Ustašas burned the city's large new synagogue, a cold hand reached through her rib cage and clawed at her heart. After hearing the news and before she could properly think, she took her sons to see it. By the time they reached the building, it was a smoldering ruin.

The hands with which she held her children's hands were white at the knuckles. Bero and Zoran were so young, she thought, too young to understand what was happening. They had been frightened by the bombing. The day they had returned to find Lux dead, she had heard them cry themselves to sleep, but they did not understand the proclamations, the troop movements, the executions that had already begun. They did understand the need for quiet, however: the need to avoid any and all notice, to shy away from drawing attention to their family's situation, in which their mother loved a Jew. That was how the world would look at it now, she thought glumly, how it had perhaps always looked at it, and she had been fooling herself all along to think the world capable of more than what its shriveled, black heart could manage. Anđelka Brkić, mother of two surviving sons, loved not a man with a name and a history and a tender heart that returned her love, but a Jew.

Anđelka studied the expressionless faces outside the synagogue. After that day, she would not remember the physical details of any one of them, but she thought she read satisfaction in some of their eyes, quiet grief in others.

Zoran was tugging her hand. "I want to go home, Mama," he whispered to her.

She pulled them both to her. She could withstand anything, she thought at that moment, as long as she had her sons. And Josef. "We will, darling," she told him. "But first I want you to look." She watched smoke rising over the building. She did not lower her voice. "First I want you to look and see what human hate can do. And I want you to remember."

And they looked, and they remembered.

POLICE BEGAN ROUNDING UP JEWS all over Sarajevo. The prominent Finci family was among the first on the list. Several days after returning to Sarajevo, Josef heard them banging on the door of his parents' house. He heard the splintering of wood and the breaking of glass, and he froze for a moment. His mother was screaming, but his father grabbed him roughly by the collar. "Get out," he told him. "Get out, get out, get out!"

Josef ran up the flight of stairs to the top floor and climbed through a window to the roof. Behind him, he could hear his mother sobbing. He jumped to a neighboring roof. It was as if he were made of paper, tossed by the breeze. The city was underfoot, and he passed raggedly above it.

ANÐELKA WAS DRINKING COFFEE in her kitchen with her upstairs neighbor, Sida Montiljo.

"Things are getting bad." The pupils of Sida's eyes were large. They both knew about the raid, and Sida knew that she and her husband, Rafael, could be picked up at any moment.

Where were the people being taken? The question hung, silent and heavy, between them.

Anđelka's hand shook while she tried to grasp the coffee cup. She wished she could lock her children and Josef in a special room where no one could enter. She would stand guard like a lioness, she thought. She would be capable of killing for them. But what kind of world locked men and boys in airless spaces? And so she let Bero and Zoran play in the park and in front of their building. She swallowed her fear and checked on them frequently, calling them in to rest or to eat or to sleep when she thought she could not stand another moment of their being suspended and vulnerable in the world.

And she waited for Josef. She looked at the murky bottom of her cup and the residue of tarlike grounds. She waited for him, hoping fervently that he was managing to avoid detection and that he would again fill the rooms of her apartment in his familiar, smiling way.

Today's roundups had taken her by surprise. When she and Sida heard gunshots in the distance, her neighbor's smile was forced. "You're good at reading those." She nodded at the cup.

Anđelka lowered her head, hiding her own smile. She had stopped such nonsense because the readings had given her a certain power over superstitious people that she did not want. Her sister Iva had been especially enamored of fortune-telling. A famous seer had come to Sarajevo the year before, and Iva had insisted on sending her cup to him to have it read. Anđelka had given the white porcelain cup with its grounds dried into patterns to Ignac, one of her sons' friends. He was instructed to pretend he'd visited the seer and to appear with the cup when her sister had returned from the market. When her sister came home, laden with vegetables, and Ignac entered on cue a moment later, Anđelka pulled three chairs to the table.

"Now, listen carefully to your future, sister," she had said, nodding to the boy that he should also sit. "This is the message he sent . . ."

She had made up wonderful things in her sister's absence, the coffee grains looking like black gold: a rich future, a handsome husband, and many children. She had rehearsed with the boy, telling him what to say, and she smiled as he repeated the predictions with a credulous face.

Now, seated at the kitchen table with Sida, she looked deep into the cup. The coffee grounds were black, trapped together in a dark sludge—nothing out of the ordinary.

"What do you see now, Anđo?" Sida could not help but ask. They were all a little superstitious at heart.

Anđelka shook her head. There was a strange lump in her throat, and the territory behind her eyes ached. "Nothing, just nothing."

SHE WAS BARELY SLEEPING when she sensed him approach. All night she had heard shouts. All night she had listened to her children's shallow breathing. She had been trapped somewhere between her waking self and the self that walked in nightmares. The sweat on her forehead and between her shoulder blades made her cold.

She heard the apartment building's front door open and then footfalls on the stairs. She sat up in the bed, her eyes wide and scared as a rabbit's. A man cleared his throat in the hallway and stopped outside their door. She shot out of bed and ran to the door, not stopping to put on a housecoat.

Her son stirred from the other room, but she did not hear him. She put her hands on the wooden door. On the other side of this door is a man, she told God. Let that man be Josef.

He entered the apartment like a ghost. He sat at the kitchen table and put his head in his hands. "They took my parents," he told her. His sister Klara, her husband, and their baby girl had been arrested separately, at their own home.

It felt as if their lives were being lived by other people, as if the world, straining for so long, had finally split its seams. "Where will they be taken?" he wondered out loud. "What is going to happen now?"

JOSEF MOVED into Anđelka's apartment, which was barely habitable after the air raid. A few weeks later they moved, all together, to Brankova Street. When Josef went out, always at twilight and just before the curfew took effect, he did not wear the identifying yellow star and Ž on his sleeve. On the streets he learned who had been taken and who remained, as well as rumors of upcoming raids.

Anđelka lived in fear while Josef was out of the apartment. Summary arrests were common, and she sat paralyzed until he returned.

Once, he found an elderly Viennese man wandering the center of town. The man had worn the yellow Star of David, and Josef had drawn him quickly into an alley. He learned that the man had barely escaped Vienna, fleeing to Sarajevo by train and leaving everything behind. He had managed to avoid being stopped but had nowhere to go.

Josef tore the patch from the man's sleeve and brought him home. Anđelka placed sheets on the bed in the small room.

He was a kindly gentleman who communicated with them through a series of hand signals and their own halting German. After a few days he also began going out onto the streets in the evenings without his yellow band. Weeks later, when he did not return, they knew he had been picked up. He had given Anđelka his only remaining possession of value—a gold pocket watch—to sell for food. She avoided selling it, keeping it hidden in a drawer. When he did not come back, she took it out and opened its cover. She caught sight of her reflection in the glass, hovering over the delicate Roman numerals of the hours. She thought about how his reflection would never again shine from its face.

The man had been kind to her sons. They had wondered aloud at his absence, and she let them think up all sorts of scenarios that ended with his safe escape. But when she looked into their faces, she knew they did not believe their own stories.

ONE NIGHT, when they knew another raid was imminent, the remaining members of Josef's family fled to Anđelka's apartment. Josef's sister Nela had so far avoided arrest, but she lived in constant fear for her husband and two children.

They came singly or in pairs, filtering onto Brankova Street in a slow trickle before the curfew so as not to draw attention. Bero and Zoran acted as lookouts, letting them into the building and leading them up to the apartment, excited and scared by their prominent role.

Anđelka had never been invited into their homes, and they had never been to hers. She could see that they did not know what to say to her, and she did not know what to say to them, so they said nothing and turned off the lights. They remained frozen for hours, listening for the sound of a truck in the street and the voices of angry soldiers.

When the policemen came, they beat on the Montiljos' door upstairs. "Open the goddamned door, Jews!" There was no answer from the Montiljos, and the next sound was of fracturing wood. There was a young voice. "They're not here." And then the sound of cursing. The policemen were furious. The Montiljos had left the night before, taking only what they could carry, and had fled into the forest outside Sarajevo.

No one in Anđelka's apartment breathed; no one moved. In the trickle of lamplight from the window, Josef could just make out Bero's and Zoran's ashen faces. All the children in the room had ashen faces. Children should be playing, Josef was thinking to himself. Children should be playing.

Later they heard footsteps recede. Trucks started on the street and drove away, but everyone remained still until they were sure that the policemen had departed. Early the next morning, after the curfew had ended, the people in hiding began leaving the apartment in twos and threes. Bero and Zoran fell fast asleep, but Josef lay in bed shaking.

"What is it?" Anđelka asked him quietly, so as not to wake up the children. "We got them out."

"That was too close. It's too much of a risk," he whispered. "I'm going to end up killing all of us." He took a deep breath. "Soon it will be time for me to go as well."

She cringed. They had planned this. It was the safest for all of them. He would escape the city and join the resistance. Someday this would all be over, he would come back, and it would be like before. Or if not like before, they would at least be together.

He felt the shuddering of her body as she cried in the dark. He held her hand to his chest, cupped in his. "Ando, we deserve for this to end. This *will* end."

They began to hold each other in a new way. There was something anxious in their routines, even when they embraced, trying to burn the weight of each other's arms into their memories. Trying to preserve in imagination the exact shade of each other's eyes.

His are so blue, she thought, like underwater.

Her eyes are brown, he thought, closing his own, making sure he could conjure hers. Brown like wood, brown like earth.

BEFORE JOSEF LEFT, he had to smuggle Nela, his only surviving sister, and her family from the city. With Anđelka and her children, they planned a trip to the Adriatic Coast, which was under Italian occupation. Word had spread in Sarajevo's remaining Jewish community that those who made it to the coast were relatively safe.

Josef paid an exorbitant amount to secure forged traveling papers. A well-dressed man in a fez came to their apartment, and he and Josef struck a deal over a pot of Turkish coffee. Josef decided not to buy documents for himself and to remain in Sarajevo. Two men out of uniform would draw twice the attention. On a train, there would be numerous soldiers conducting identification checks, guns slung over their shoulders, fierce-looking dogs at their sides. He decided that his brother-in-law, Ovadija, should escape the city and that he would stay behind.

When Anđelka and the boys returned, he would make preparations for his own escape.

IT WAS A LONG TRIP. The train went from Sarajevo all the way to Dubrovnik. A narrow-gauge railway, it was a relic of the Austro-Hungarian Empire, and the train chugged with maddening slowness up hills, over bridges, and through tunnels. The children played, but with a frightened look in their eyes. Bero was twelve and Zoran ten. Perla was six, and she clung to Anđelka. Mordekaj was almost two years younger. Anđelka started a game to distract them and pass the time, but her gaze kept returning to the train windows.

She was posing as Ovadija's wife, and she and Nela had swapped children. They were afraid of being stopped and asked to recite the Hail Mary or some other prayer. Officials often ascertained one's ethnicity through faith. Nela's children were young, and Anđelka could say the words to the prayer for them. Bero and Zoran had been altar boys, and there was no prayer that they did not know. Ovadija would try to avoid attention as best he could.

"Just a little longer, children," she told them softly, stroking Perla's hair. "How nice it'll be to reach Dubrovnik."

Her sons were sitting across from her. Zoran was fast asleep, his thin chest rising and falling. Bero was looking out the window, his mouth white around the corners. She caught his eye, and he smiled. It was a quick smile designed for his mother.

"Just a little longer," he told her.

• • •

CHECKPOINTS HAD BEEN SET UP between the Independent State of Croatia and Italian-held Dalmatia. They were not stopped, and their papers were stamped without question. When they reached Gruž, just outside the city center, Anđelka felt her knees weaken.

She and the boys would stay a few days to help Nela and her family settle into a stone house at the foot of Lovrijenac Fort. Anđelka was consumed by the fear that Josef would grow restless and leave the Sarajevo apartment. She knew, at least, that he was not starving. At the beginning of the war he had brought sack upon sack of beans and flour, and cans of cooking oil, to her apartment. They had been living off of those supplies for months, supplemented by what little money he had and by the meager pension she received.

It hurt her to think how quietly he would be moving around the rooms of the apartment now, how studiously he would be avoiding the windows. She thought of nosy neighbors listening through their walls and ceilings. Josef had told her that he was beginning to feel like hunted prey. He was practically climbing the walls when she went to the market or to run an errand, so afflicted was he by his virtual imprisonment and loneliness. Anđelka could not sleep, thinking of him in the apartment alone, waiting for her. But the children were happy by the sea. They were always happy there, and Anđelka watched them racing around the alleys of Dubrovnik.

In order to receive food here, one had to register with the police for food stamps, a lengthy process. Nela's family had begun the registration, but in the meantime, the children were resourceful. Lovrijenac Fort had been commandeered as a barracks by Italian soldiers, and each night the Italians filtered down to the Old City to their mess hall. The children stood on the steps leading up to the fort and smiled winningly, begging for *"Panjoka!"* when the soldiers returned to the barracks, their pockets filled with bread. Each evening the children scrambled to meet them. The men could not resist Perla's shiny dark curls or sweet smile, and they bent to pat her head. Most nights she walked away with her pockets filled with bread, which the children shared once they got back to the house.

The boys learned how to scrape *ćuke*, tiny sucking clams, from the stone piers of the city. Anđelka smiled when her sons returned with their "catch," so happy to contribute. She smiled at Nela as they drank coffee in the house's small kitchen, Perla playing in the sunshine just beyond the stone doorway. But it was a tight-lipped smile, because there was a howling animal hidden behind her teeth, and she could not let that animal be seen. Not by Nela, and especially not by her children.

ANĐELKA AND HER SONS returned to Sarajevo, to the Brankova Street apartment where Josef was waiting for them. When he saw her, he held her for a very long time.

"We're fine," she insisted. "We weren't stopped once."

His face had grown gray in their absence.

The atmosphere on the streets had changed. The roundups had netted almost every member of Sarajevo's Jewish population. Josef felt like the sole survivor on a ship that was sinking fast. He no longer went out at dusk. He did not know whether to escape or to wait out the war, which had every indication of lasting for years. If he was arrested on the street, he would be the only casualty, but if he was arrested in Anđelka's apartment, they would all suffer, and this knowledge ate away at him as the months passed.

He stayed away from windows and doors. He spoke softly for fear that the neighbors would hear him. He grew thinner and paler, felt himself shrinking, and could do nothing to prevent it. In the hours while the boys were outside playing, Anđelka held him. She comforted him, but in his heart was the fear that his presence would end up killing them all.

Marijan's brother and sister, Ivan and Ana, were resistance sympathizers and knew of Josef's presence in the apartment. Ivan brought him newspapers and told him how the war was going. Sometimes they listened to rogue broadcasts of the BBC, outlawed in Sarajevo but listened to nonetheless. Most of the news was not good. Anđelka's own sisters, who lived in Posušje, had no idea Josef was staying with her.

Bero and Zoran learned to act themselves when outside the apartment, but to make no reference to Josef. They lived in constant fear of discovery. The world was a divided place in which people either knew or did not know their secret. And even to those who knew, they said little.

After a few weeks the boys made an escape plan for Josef in case of an emergency. They placed a coiled rope on the balcony that overlooked the yard. Josef would slip down to the balcony beneath them, and their Serb neighbors, who also knew of his presence in Anđelka's apartment, were sure to hide him. The boys would run and untie the rope while their mother stalled for time with the police. It would be like in the films, they insisted—a clean getaway.

Josef and Anđelka smiled at one another. "Yes," they agreed, "it would be exactly like that."

At night, while the boys lay in bed, the plan gave them comfort, and they slept.

ONE DAY while Anđelka was at the market and Bero was playing soccer on the street, Zoran appeared at his brother's side in tears. Bero heard a commotion behind him and turned around. The edges of the world blurred, and at its center was a building that no longer looked like his own.

A police van was standing outside, and a few men were milling about, smoking. Zoran had held them off for as long as he could, he told Bero. He had protested shrilly that his mother was not home and he was not allowed to open the door to strangers. This was precisely what he was supposed to say, but Josef froze. Ana, who had been drinking coffee with him, keeping him company in Anđelka's absence, had pushed him into the storeroom, then fled into one of the rooms where she pretended to be sleeping.

Josef's expression panicked Zoran most of all. He and Bero had spent months devising the plan, as heroic as any they could think of. But after months of near incarceration, Josef was weak and in shock. He lacked the strength to shinny safely to the balcony below.

The police found Josef immediately, striking him viciously across the face. Ana shrieked, and Zoran slipped away in the ensuing melee. Now the brothers ran to the corner of Aleksandrova Street to intercept their mother on the way home.

She saw them from a distance and waved. But when she saw their frantic expressions, something grabbed at her throat. She sped up, and by the time she reached them, she knew.

They did not know what to do, and they stood there in the street for several painful moments. Anđelka's sons were nearly hysterical, fighting hard to maintain control. She felt like weeping, brushing angrily at the burning in her eyes. They could run. She could take them to Ivan's. She could flee with them to Herzegovina or to Dalmatia.

Instead, she clutched the market basket to her chest. "Stay here," she told them.

She could see them already forming objections.

"Stay here!" she ordered, leaving no room for argument.

They began to shake, watching her walk away. They watched her approach the apartment building and weave her way through the policemen on the front steps.

The boys moved closer to the building. They did not know what to do and could not bear to look at one another.

Josef and Anđelka were led from the building after what seemed like hours. Bero and Zoran drew nearer and watched as their mother was placed in the van first. They surged forward, and Josef saw them in the crowd. He managed to place a hand on both boys' heads, quickly. "I'm sorry," he told them quietly.

Josef and Anđelka were both taken to Sarajevo's Beledija Prison. Bero and Zoran were left in the street. Josef and Anđelka might never return, and this knowledge created motionless statues of the two little boys. A Serbian neighbor, a widow with many children, had watched the arrest. Something about the way the boys were standing told her that they would stay like that until they were moved. The policemen had started looking at them, shifting from foot to foot. Without thinking, she grabbed their cold hands and hurried them into the building.

The woman checked on Bero and Zoran for several weeks

while they waited for news of their mother and Josef. The punishment for helping a Jew, knowingly or unknowingly, was execution. Posters on every third building in the city proclaimed this. At night in the empty apartment, the brothers lay wordlessly side by side.

It occurred to Bero that if he could find his aunt Ljubica's husband, Ante, he could get help for his mother. Ante had last been garrisoned at Žuta Tabija, just outside the city, and one morning Bero instructed Zoran to stay in the apartment until he returned.

"But I want to go with you!" Zoran said, near tears.

Bero considered this for a moment, then shook his head. He put an end to Zoran's objections, telling him, "What if she comes back to find us gone? One of us has to wait for her."

At the age of twelve, Bero's universe consisted of just a few Sarajevo neighborhoods. He had never roamed the more distant reaches of the city alone, his mother too afraid of what could happen to him during wartime. But he knew how to get to Žuta Tabija by foot, secure in the knowledge that when he found Ante, his uncle would know what to do.

Ante was a towering man with a stern voice who had always scared Bero, but Bero now imagined him marching through the gates of Beledija. He would find Anđelka, bribe whoever needed to be bribed, make up whatever fictions were necessary, and bring her home. He might even be able to help Josef. But even as this thought occurred to him, Bero recognized it as a delusion.

When Bero reached the gates of Žuta Tabija, the sentry shook his head. "They're pulled out already. They're halfway to the front by now."

Trucks and soldiers seemed to be moving around him at

dizzying speeds. The small hope he had nursed proceeded to drown. He felt alone in the world, alone in his grief. He imagined climbing the stairs to their apartment and having to tell Zoran.

IN BELEDIJA PRISON, Anđelka stared at the walls. She stared at a chipped cup full of brackish water. The food smelled of rot, but she could not bear to eat in any case. She closed her eyes and inhaled the smell of the water. She tried to imagine the blue. But she could only see his eyes as he was being dragged away from her. Blue of electric sorrow, so sure that he had killed them all.

THERE WAS AN INVESTIGATION, but it did not start immediately. First Anđelka spent weeks in a cell in the women's section of the prison. She wondered what crimes her cellmates in the small half-lit room had committed. Some were younger than her own thirty-one years, some much older. They were uniformly quiet, with dirty, unkempt hair and sad faces. She wondered if they had been guilty of anything at all.

Rats and other vermin invaded the cell at night. The first night, she did not sleep at all, but sat stiffly upright against a cold, perspiring wall. She could hear the squeaking and scurrying on the floor. When she felt something climb over her ankle, she drew her knees to her chest and tried to make herself smaller. Josef had explained circumference to one of the boys only the week before, helping him with a mathematics assignment. She had been listening with one ear from the next room and now tried to decrease her circumference.

On the second night, she fell asleep but awoke with angry red bites on her legs. Too small for rats, she thought, only somewhat relieved. On the third night, an insane woman was added to their cell, and the woman shrieked with laughter until morning.

At first Andelka thought there was a design to her waiting, that perhaps they were trying to bring her that much closer to a confession. But as one day bled into the next, it occurred to her that they had simply forgotten her, or could not be bothered to do anything about her—that ultimately, her confession or her silence made no difference to them. It occurred to her that she might not feel real sunlight for years, or ever again. She might never see her sons, or Josef.

She knew Josef was in the men's prison. At night she imagined that she could hear shouts carrying through the tiny window in her cell or down the dirty prison hallways. She imagined him being abused, denying everything for her sake. He would deny it in order to save her.

When she entered the apartment on Brankova Street on the day of the arrest, the police had shoved her into a separate room to question her. Through the door, which was slightly ajar, she could hear them interrogating Josef. *They hit him right away*, her youngest child had blurted out on the street—a slow trickle of blood had stained the cotton shirt he wore. She had ironed that shirt the day before, she remembered, as the children were finishing their breakfast.

They had found his toothbrush beside hers in the bathroom, they told her, and his shaving things. His possessions were scattered about the apartment in a way a boarder's would not be. *That indicates familiarity*, one of her interrogators said with an irate expression. *With a Jew.*

Those banal objects would be part of their undoing, she realized then. She imagined the toothbrushes in the bathroom, slender handles, bristles flayed like arms held open to one another. She noticed that she was still grasping the wicker market basket, and she placed it gently on the floor beside her.

She answered their questions for what seemed a very long time:

—*He is a Jew. What is a Jew doing in your home?*

—*He is a boarder*, she repeated. *I am a poor widow. I needed the money.*

—*Boarders need to be registered. Why haven't you registered him?*

Then they were led downstairs and onto the street. Some neighbors came to see what the commotion was about, and she could feel others looking at them through the peepholes of closed doors.

Her children had been waiting in the street. She wanted to fold them into her arms, to tell them everything would be all right again, but the policemen pushed her into the van before she could say anything. She should have told them to run away, she thought later, but where could they have gone?

Ljubica's husband, Ante, was a high-ranking Ustaša officer. He was very frequently in Sarajevo, and Anđelka thought for a moment of turning to him for help. Perhaps he could help salvage the situation. Her sisters did not even know she was in jail. They certainly did not know Josef had been hiding out in the apartment for months. They never spoke of such matters and, if anything, assumed he had fled to Dalmatia or joined the Partisans. They rarely mentioned him before the war, and she could imagine their relief thinking she and Josef were separated. In her sisters' eyes, she was safe now.

Ante had become a powerful man, she knew. He had even moved Ljubica to Sarajevo, to a beautiful apartment on Koševo Street. Anđelka and the boys had gone to visit them, admiring the large rooms and the high ceilings. She had neatly avoided most visits from her younger sister. When Ljubica did come over, Josef stood uncomfortably and quietly in the tiny storeroom while the sisters drank coffee at the kitchen table.

Ante had connections, but Anđelka despised those connections. And she knew even he could not help her now.

At night, when she thought she heard men screaming, she pushed her shoulders against the wall. She pushed until she thought she would pulverize the bone or bring down the wall. Then all the walls of the prison would fall. When she fell asleep pressed against that barrier, she dreamed that the walls would dissolve and that Josef would find her in the huddle of crying women.

WEEKS INTO HER INCARCERATION, she was finally led from her cell. She was steered through dimly lit hallways, her arms hugging her chest. In the interrogation room, she noticed that her dress was filthy, her hands covered with grime, but she smoothed the skirt over her knees and took some deep, shuddering breaths. The man seated across from her, the police investigator, frowned.

"My name is Ćuk," he told her, adding that he was from her

village. "My *Posušjanka*," he told her sternly, not waiting for her to respond, "what have you gotten yourself into?"

Anđelka would not look at him directly. He was from her *rodno mjesto*, the tough piece of earth where she was born, and even as hope was smothered, it gasped for breath.

"I am a poor widow," she told him quietly, "with two young sons." She looked at the palms of her hands and remembered her village. She might think that she had escaped it, but she had not. A woman inside her began to laugh until the tears rolled down her face. But the woman outside, the *Posušjanka* with bones made of stone, was calm. "Please," she asked him. "Let me go back to my sons."

She and Josef had practiced their story.

I rented him a room, I did not know he was a Jew.

I rented a room from her. She did not know I was a Jew.

They said the sentences again and again, through hours of questioning and incarceration. They were questioned separately, each imagining that they sat together.

It became clear that someone had informed on them. The police knew too many details of their lives, such as how they had helped smuggle Josef's family members from Sarajevo.

Anđelka thought it was the man who forged the documents, but she did not know his name, and she was not told the name of her accuser. She kept a running list of other possibilities: neighbors, parents of her sons' friends, distant cousins. Each time, she came back to the man with the fez.

On one occasion, as she was being led back from questioning, Josef was being led to the room. Her eyes grew wide, and she felt them fill with tears. He pretended to trip, and as he rose, he was able to slip something into her hands. In the cell, she saw that it was a note, written on a scrap, a flimsy gray page that looked like it had been torn from a notebook or a ledger. He had filled it with his steady, neat script and words of love.

Your sacrifice is painful and weighs upon me heavily. In the turbulent storm and mighty blows which my destiny has delivered, I am still unable to consciously gauge the true pain caused by the loss of You, my eternal love. I know only that it is something of immense significance to my life, and for my peace. The only companion able to comfort me was torn savagely and calculatingly from my arms, maybe not forever, but who can know! I again saw your genuine love, and the warm breath of your feelings toward me, which will always revive me in my most difficult moments, and ease the heavy burden of violent fate. Justice must smile one day on we who sorrow, providing happier moments and the deserved comfort of joy. I live in that hope and with that expectation I go to accept the fate meted out to me and to the other innocents of my race. I am happy because you also love me in this way and that calms me greatly. Be the watchful guardian of your dear sons. I will be happiest when I meet you all again, and find you healthy and happy. I remain forever yours. J.

BERO AND ZORAN spent their days sitting anxiously in the main room of the apartment, as if waiting for guests. They opened the door to the hallway countless times, listening for footsteps on the stairs.

They ate meals with the neighbor and her children, for

which they were grateful, but they could hardly bear sitting at her table, listening to the carefree slurps of the other, unburdened children. Bero and Zoran gave each other sidelong glances and wished they were eating at the table upstairs, with their mother serving them soup from a pot on the stove. They pictured the way she cut bread, holding the loaf upright to her chest, working her knife around it.

They had heard stories about Beledija. Uncle Ivan had been imprisoned there during the Kingdom of Yugoslavia. They imagined their mother in its stinking darkness, with murderers and lunatics, and the images would not let them sleep.

"YOU TELL ME what really happened," Ćuk said, trying to draw her out. "Or do you want to be in trouble so deep that I can't help you?"

She willed every line in her face to fall into a blank expression of emptiness.

"For the sake of our Posušje," he told her softly, "tell me."

He told Josef, "If it comes out, what do you think will happen to them?"

And still they clung to their story.

Josef thought of her sons. They had never been without their mother. He imagined them going through the motions of their days like orphans. Worse, he imagined their detention. There were rumors of camps for children, from where none returned. He thought of his sister Klara, the baby of the family, and her own baby girl. He knew that they were dead.

For days they stubbornly maintained the story of the rented room. Ćuk told them finally that while there was nothing he could do for Josef, he could try to save Andelka. But he demanded the truth, and finally, they told him.

ĆUK MADE THE STORY of the rented room sound more plausible and entered it into the register. He secured Andelka's release shortly thereafter, citing a lack of evidence. But Josef would be sent to Jasenovac, a concentration camp in the north, on the next transport.

She had thanked Ćuk stiffly when she was set free. *For the sake of our Posušje,* he had told her. Herzegovina had saved her.

When she returned home, her face was gaunt and her eyes had a disturbing emptiness that her sons did not recognize. Her body crawled with lice.

She spent hours in the bathroom, scrubbing the filth of the prison from her body and her hair. She instructed her sons to burn her prison clothing in the kitchen stove. They watched the cloth turn orange and yellow in its slow conversion to ash, and it emitted a sad smell.

All my mother's tears, Zoran thought.

His brother was staring at the flames as well. If only things could go back to what they were before.

And each time they passed the bathroom door, they slowed to hear her weeping.

SHE HAD MANAGED to hide the note through all the days of her incarceration. At home she held it to her face, to her belly, to her breasts. She breathed in the smell of it and hid it between the leaves of a book for safekeeping.

God began His slow death in those days, for all of them. In Posušje she had been a religious girl. She had learned to say the rosary from her mother, reciting the prayers aloud while her mother looked after her younger siblings. She had believed in a God that was merciful and just, and she had prayed often to His Holy Mother for intercession. Thus had she weathered the deaths of her brother, her parents, her own children, and Marijan. And still she had believed in His mercy.

When the archbishop of Sarajevo, Ivan Šarić, began his rants about the Jews, she decided never again to enter the cathedral when he held Mass. In her eyes, he was a degenerate who worshipped a God different from hers. In addition to his sermonizing, he inflicted his own miserable, uninspired verses—dedicated to that murderer Ante Pavelić—on the general populace. "O, great and noble leader," she and Josef would joke through the days that he hid out in the apartment. "O, flower of the Croatian nation." They would say the words in a falsetto, mimicking his high, effeminate voice.

"There are limits even to love," he had told his congregation. "It is stupid and unworthy of Christ's disciples to think that the struggle against evil can be waged in a noble way and with gloves on." The Ustaša were known for never asking for mercy and never showing it, and Šarić was their mascot, with the entire weight of the Roman Catholic Church falling squarely behind him.

IN JASENOVAC, Josef was able to avoid immediate liquidation because of his metalworking skills and the fact that he was young and able-bodied. His experience in his family's hardware store saved him. He worked in the *lančara*, the metal workshop in Camp III.

In the *lančara*, the prisoners were forced to make special sickle-shaped knives that could be fastened to the hand with leather covers. The knives were regularly used to kill prisoners in the camp.

Anđelka sent packages as often as she was allowed. She packed them carefully, holding each item until it grew warm in her hands. She doubted that everything reached him, but she held each one nonetheless.

She knew that some of them did reach him. He was allowed to send her occasional notes on standard-issue camp forms. Each note could be no longer than thirteen words and was read by censors. He did not write anything personal in them other than *How are you? I am fine.* He thanked her. *Coffee. Cigarettes. Razors.* She imagined him writing each word slowly, instilling them with love.

Each time she saw the familiar handwriting, her heart expanded and died, then grew again.

She sold everything she could to send him what he requested, including what was left of the family gold he had salvaged. He had left it with instructions to sell only if they were starving. She imagined that he was starving.

She took only a part of that money to feed her own children. There was no meat, no eggs, no fruit, but her sons did not complain. They knew that whatever their situation, Josef's was worse.

When she was alone with his notes, she closed her eyes and touched the paper. She placed her lips against them, this paper that his hands had touched.

• • •

JASENOVAC WAS A STRING of five camps located on the Sava River. The ground inside was swampy, making it hard to walk, especially when it rained. When prisoners fell in the mud, they were beaten. When they rose, they were beaten.

On the other side of the river was the deserted wasteland of the Gradina.

There were only birds. Sometimes their black, free bodies darted against snow-filled clouds. Some flew south. Some flew as far as Sarajevo.

In 1942 the prisoners built an earthen dike. The water-saturated ground kept collapsing beneath them. They died from exhaustion, starvation, beatings. Their bodies were immediately buried in the dike.

At morning musters in the main camp, the Ustaša guards picked out the weak or old. Their hands were bound with wire, and they were executed.

The authorities were not above taking children, and there were places designated for their execution. Gone were their playthings and the lace of their bibs. Gone were the sugary treats packed in white bakery paper with which their birthdays and holidays were celebrated. They died from famine and cold. They were drowned in the Sava.

In 1943 there was an attempted escape. The prisoners were promptly caught and taken to the *lančara*, where chains—made by the prisoners—were welded around their legs. The guards beat them.

The food was rotten. Its stench poisoned the stomach. But

the inmates were starving. Some who went outside the camp on work detail brought grass back for the others.

They buried the dead and brought back grass.

EACH OF ANÐELKA'S SONS had a pact with God, but they had stopped attending Mass during her incarceration, and she did not have the energy to make them go back.

Across the street from them on Brankova lived a beautiful young Slovenian woman whose husband was a prisoner of war in Germany. She was the object of much admiration, and every boy on that street loved her secretly and fervently. They waited for her to emerge from her apartment, playing beneath her windows, hoping she would walk onto the balcony and smile at them.

Sometimes she would place a few coins in an envelope and throw it down to them, asking them to buy her bread or milk. They shoved each other out of the way to catch the prize, each determined to do her bidding.

Anđelka had seen them jostling for position. Bero, she saw, was especially smitten, spending long hours kicking a soccer ball beneath her building, looking up at her balcony every so often to see if she had appeared.

He was heartbroken when one day Božidar Brale, a priest and secretary to Šarić, had walked out bare-chested onto her balcony, stretching proudly so that the entire neighborhood could see that he was bedding the beautiful *Slovenka*.

Anđelka had already heard the rumors by the time Bero sat at the table that night, glum and without appetite.

"He's a priest," her elder child said, stabbing viciously at the plate in front of him with a fork. "A representative of God."

She had sighed and stroked his cheek. Božidar Brale, rumor had it, was guilty of far more than the sin of lust. When she saw the good priest walking in her direction, she often turned the other way.

"How could she let him?" Bero asked her, sounding betrayed. "He's disgusting."

Anđelka looked away. "Maybe she had no choice," she offered a moment later, squeezing his arm and beginning to clear dishes from the table. "Maybe he promised that he would help her husband."

In the coming weeks she watched the *Slovenka* walk down the street. There were women in the neighborhood who would not speak to her. But every time Anđelka passed her on the street, she nodded slightly. She could recognize a woman who was waiting. The war could not last forever. They were waiting.

THEY LISTENED TO THE BBC on a shortwave radio. Starting in 1943, they were able to chart the beginning of the end. The tide of refugees into the city increased, and the Allies began making gains all over Europe. The Independent State of Croatia was increasingly undermined by Partisan attacks.

Just a little longer, she told Josef at night when sleep would not come, imagining that he could hear her. *Just a little longer, and then we'll be together again.* He had managed to survive until now; his notes were evidence. Please God, she begged the ceiling of her room, help him survive just a little longer.

The Germans were the first to pull out of Sarajevo. They left quickly, without ceremony. They had entered the city triumphantly, on shiny motorcycles, in trucks, in cars. They withdrew in horse-drawn carts.

Fearing reprisals, the Domobran, the regular Croatian troops, were pulling out as well. In their columns were her cousins, some neighbors, her friends' husbands. Some had borne deep convictions and loyalties to Pavelić. Most were caught up in the time in which they lived, with little in the way of ideology to guide them. They were peasants or laborers. They were conscripts.

One of her cousins was little more than a boy. He was frightened, she could see that when he came to say good-bye to her. He had been responsible for running errands with a motorcycle, and he brought the contraption to her, asking her to hide it in the basement of her apartment building. "When things are over," he told her, "I'll come get it." At the end of the war, if nothing else, at least he would have a motorcycle.

Ustaša units were also retreating, to Zagreb. Ante planned to go first; then Ljubica. Katja, who was unmarried and had been living with them in Sarajevo, would travel with her. The sisters would be separated again, and Anđelka was saddened by this. But her desire for Josef to return was more fervent than her desire that her sisters should stay.

Ante came to say good-bye the night before he left. Even seated at the kitchen table and drinking coffee, he filled their apartment with an angry energy.

"Your Partisans are coming," he told Bero, unable to hide his bitterness. "You must be happy now."

Bero turned white and looked away. Anđelka remained silent.

Ante rose to leave, and they all embraced awkwardly. He placed a hand on Bero's shoulder. "Take care of your mother," he told him. He lifted Zoran and embraced him. He had wanted a son so badly, Anđelka knew. Ante set the boy down and then, as an afterthought, turned to Bero. "They won't be what you think they are," he told the boy quietly. "You don't know what they're capable of."

His nephew shivered.

Anđelka shut the door behind him and gathered her sons in a quick hug. She let them go and turned to clear the table. How long until the camp was liberated and the prisoners set free? How long would it take Josef to make his way back to them? Mother of God, she thought. I ask for mercy now and not another thing for as long as I shall live.

TUZLA

1996

Blood is my light and my darkness.

—*Ivan Goran Kovačić, from* The Pit, *Stanza I*

But how will you go, so tiny, into the world
How defenseless you are
Because of that we will never part
We will never part
Never body of my body
Soul of my soul
Never

—*Mak Dizdar, from* Lullaby

I RETURNED TO TUZLA, relieved to be in free, Federation territory again. The town's now familiar summer greenness, the pockmarked buildings, the market and surrounding hills, all these things elated me. There were cafés, restaurants, and newspapers, and in the hours after returning from the morgue, I could wander the streets as I pleased. I could disappear into crowds, swept along in the direction they walked, propelled by no other force, it seemed, than the joy of being anonymous again. I was not confined to an SFOR base, an insular albeit comforting bubble of prefabricated America in the middle of Bosnia. I did not travel daily to places of execution where I was, some would say ridiculously, afraid.

How many times during those days back in the Bosnian Federation did I pass the families of the missing on Tuzla's streets? How many times did I stand in line at a kiosk, waiting to buy a newspaper, behind a woman whose son was at that very moment decomposing in some unmarked grave, or whose husband lay in the freezer outside the rundown factory building that was our morgue? How many knitters of socks, patchers of trousers, and sewers of shirts did I nod at unwittingly?

I spent the first day of my return eagerly contemplating how I would disappear from the base house that night after dinner and walk alone into town. I would buy some chocolate, I thought, or drink a coffee and read a newspaper.

That evening, I did walk alone, past the shops and markets, past the hotel where humanitarian-aid workers, reporters, and some members of our own crew drank themselves into stupors. I wandered inadvertently into Kapija, the social center of the town, where people congregated at outdoor cafés.

I had avoided the square until then, knowing about one late spring evening just over a year before, when young people had converged upon it to enjoy pleasant weather. The war had been in full swing then, and I had been told that there was the sound of shelling in the distance, which was not out of the ordinary. The week had been relatively tranquil, and the square was filled with voices and music. The young people of Tuzla had been spending days and nights inside their apartments and houses. They were bored and tired, Nedim—Jadranka's husband—had told me. They wanted to listen to music and drink. They wanted to see their friends who had endured similar days of cramped stagnation. That is why the single shell that landed there at around 8:30 in the evening, killing seventy-one people who were mostly between the ages of eighteen and twenty-five, had so devastated the town.

Tuzla had already survived several years of war and shelling, but nothing in its recent history matched the horror of that night. The town was not so populous, he pointed out. And there was nobody who did not lose someone.

After the shell landed, limbs littered the square in pools of blood, and headless bodies remained seated in café chairs. Parents converged upon Tuzla Hospital in a panicked search for their children.

On my walk back from Kapija I met some colleagues for a drink in a café nearer our base house. I realized that I had not bought my newspaper or eaten my chocolate. I had stood there looking dumbly at a plaque surrounded by candles and flowers. I read every name and age.

Over a beer, I mentioned the plaque and the names, effectively ending all conversation.

"Why do you always do that?" one of the women I worked with asked me later that night in some frustration.

At the café, young people passed our table. They seemed not to notice or care that we had grown silent and were watching them. Some had surely lost siblings and friends that night. Around the table, we were unable to meet one another's eyes.

I knew from Nedim that some young people had happened upon the square running late to meet friends they would not see again. Some had sped frantically over the bloody ground and tracked the blood of that night into their homes, into their bedrooms and their beds.

Walking past our table, the young people of Tuzla embraced and sang drunkenly, seemingly committed to enjoying youth until it slipped away or was seized from them.

AT THE MORGUE we hired three local Muslim men to wash the clothes from the corpses. Unlike the field-workers, they had much in common with the bodies from which the clothing came—aside from the obvious. In the weeks to come, they held the articles with a care that bordered on reverence.

I explained the terms of the work and saw that two of them were not really men at all, but in their late teens. They needed the money, they told me, and I did not have the heart to point out their youth to the pathologists.

"It's hard work," I explained to them. "It is unpleasant." They looked at me without expression, then at one another.

Yes, they had expected that.

"You're not to touch the bodies, just the clothes," I instructed, and I sensed a sudden shift in the air. They seemed relieved.

Omer, the eldest of the three, had bright eyes, like polar ice, set in a suntanned face. He grinned at me rather awkwardly. "We will be fine," he told me. His two companions were stone-faced.

I brought out the first set of gum-colored clothing and set it in front of them on the tables. I showed them where the detergent was kept and where to get water. I showed them how to soak the cloth and how to scrub. It was a dirty business, and they stood in a cluster, smoking and watching the filled buckets as I demonstrated.

Omer threw his cigarette away, a sign that they should begin. I walked away to leave them to their task, knowing that my presence in those first few moments was unwelcome. An hour later I went to check on them.

Amer—a tall, handsome young man who had greeted me that morning with the easy swagger of a village boy—had turned his back on the clothes and was retching into the grass. Each time he tried to speak to me, dry heaves caused him to turn around and bend over. Though he was nearly crouching, I could see that he was red-faced with shame.

Seeing me, Omer held up his hand. "He'll be fine. He just needs to get used to it."

Dževad, the third one, was silent, barely looking up from his bucket.

Later, during a cigarette break, I fell into conversation with Omer. "It doesn't bother you?"

He responded with a half smile. "I was in the war and saw men die. A dying man bothers me, but not this." He nodded in the direction of the buckets.

I learned that he was married and had a daughter, and we spoke a little about the war. I referred to it carefully, skirting around it, but once started, he did not mince words. His mother had been killed by a shell in front of their house.

"I'm sorry," I told him. "When?"

He knew the date and what day of the week it was. He knew the exact hour and minute.

OF THE POPULATION we saw each day on the roads of Kalesija, some were local residents, but many were refugees expelled from other, occupied, areas of Bosnia. They were living with extended family in the small town, near the border with Republika Srpska, until they could return home. They were so near the border, so close to their occupied towns, that some were just a few kilometers away. They might as well have been on the other side of the world. Return, it seemed, was not imminent, and the lives they led in Kalesija were ones of excruciating suspension.

While working in Zagreb, I had visited the refugee camp in the Špansko district several times. It was populated by Slavonians who were already five years into exile. Some men worked odd jobs, earning money under the table in order to bring their wives and mothers a rare gift. The cramped rooms housed as many as four or five people, and the only luxury in the camp seemed to be an occasional television. The sets provided visions of a world outside the barracks.

There were certain favorite shows, and when they came on, a hush fell across the camp. The children stopped playing, and the women halted their chores, turning on their televisions or going to visit neighbors if they didn't own one themselves. People jostled each other for a good spot, occupying chairs, beds, and cushions on the floor. For a few minutes, the years of refugee life, the dead, the lost houses and fields faded into the background.

And then the show would end, followed by news bulletins. The children clamored out again into the sunshine or drizzle or frost. The women returned to their ironing or sewing or shelling of peas, looking around them at their reduced lives, and they sighed.

Sometimes I intruded on them, sitting at their tables and drinking coffee or brandy. The children giggled at my accent, and their parents shooed them outside so that we could talk in peace. We discussed politics and, sometimes, the war. But I was always a visitor there, a foreigner for whom opportunity had not shriveled into a dry husk.

They would ask me questions that I answered as honestly as I could.

"Where are your parents?"

"In America."

"Does your father work?"

"He's retired now, but he still works some on the side."

"Do you have a big house in America?"

"Fairly big. Comfortable enough for my parents, cramped when they have visitors."

They always wanted to know the details of our house, its dimensions and furnishings. The women asked about gardens and kitchens. They described the houses they had left behind, at times punctuating their sentences matter-of-factly with a grim prognosis.

"I don't expect to see that again."

"We heard it was destroyed."

"Our neighbor is living there now. Imagine, he was our neighbor for forty years and couldn't wait for us to be evicted."

Talk invariably turned to plans for the future, and with it came an entirely new set of questions. "You need a husband," the wives would tease me. "Wouldn't you like to get married and start a family?"

This was a favorite topic of conversation with my aunts as well, and I would answer them with the same sly smile. "Why marry," I asked, "and spoil all my fun?" I entertained them with stories of my aunts and their matchmaking that sent them into fits of laughter.

Later I always asked them the same question: "What will the future hold?"

They would sit at the tables looking at each other and at me as if it should have been obvious and the question slightly infantile. "We're waiting," they would say. And then, as if to make me feel better, "*Bit će bolje.* Things will be better."

• • •

THE THREE WORKERS outside the morgue were caught in
the same glue, a sticky substance in which one is stuck while
years are lost.

They had taken the job at the morgue to make some money
for their families, Omer said. They had a similar philosophy. *Bit
će bolje*. It will be better.

There was some discussion initially about whether they
would be allowed to use our shower facility after work. They
were the first ones done in the evenings, and hot water was at a
premium.

I had put my foot down, insisting that they be allowed to
wash the smell of the morgue away, just as we did. I cited reasons of hygiene and decency. But the truth was that I could not
bear the idea of sending them to their families smelling of death.

In the next couple of weeks I took my breaks outside by the
station where they washed the clothes. It was easier somehow.
The morgue doors yawned like a haunted cave in a children's
fairy tale, and I was grateful for every opportunity to emerge
into the sunshine.

I had been put in charge of them. They teased me respect-
fully, teaching me Bosnian words, filling out my vocabulary.
According to them, I needed to learn these things because my
father had grown up in Sarajevo, a revelation that had won
smiles from them despite strained relations between the capital
and other towns in Bosnia, and despite tensions between Bosnian Muslims and Croats.

But each time I brought out buckets of the soiled clothing,
they became silent and watched me.

Sometimes, in the course of the day, I did not feel like talking to anyone. I would walk to the very back of the building, where there was a deserted loading dock. To get there, I bypassed a dark room with ankle-high debris and hanging cables. I ate my lunch sitting on the loading dock and looking past the factory fence, over the yellow summer fields, and toward the hills a few miles away.

"They are in those hills," the workers had said.

I sat back on my heels, looking at the broken glass and scattered bullet casings that covered the cement floor. I looked up into the hills.

"Can they see us from here?" I had asked, feeling foolish for the tremor in my voice.

Omer chewed the inside of his cheek. "Not with the naked eye. With binoculars, perhaps."

I stopped sitting back there. It was not only paranoia about a sniper that made me uneasy. It was the odd beauty of those mined fields, of the fertile greenness of the hills and the fear of losing myself in them.

I WAS SURPRISED that the autopsies did not affect my appetite. Before work, I helped Jadranka make sandwiches in the kitchen for our lunch break, wrapping each one in waxed paper. The square parcels we turned out reminded me of sandwiches my mother had made for me and packed in my metal school lunchbox.

At noon we filed into the bathroom to wash our talc-stained hands. We ate in the same large hall where the autopsies were performed, but at the far end. It was less than pleasant, but we turned our backs on the tables, open body bags, and flies and, somehow, ate the food untroubled.

Sometimes we drove into the town. Most residents knew what we were doing at the factory, and the children regarded us with trepidation, as if the vehicles were filled with bogeymen intent on kidnapping them. One day we asked a group of boys playing football for directions to a market.

"*Dečki!*" I called from the car window. They stood stock-still, the soccer ball gliding unnoticed into a cluster of weeds. Waiting for me to continue, they did not even seem to breathe, but watched me with wide, serious eyes. When I asked them for the market, they looked relieved. They indicated the direction, and my colleague gunned the engine before driving off. In the side mirror I could see that the boys did not resume their game, but stood frozen in the middle of the road watching us go.

WHAT I REMEMBERED from my previous trip to Bosnia with my friends Judita and Belkisa a few months after the war were the old faces of small children. In Gradačac we had walked up and down the hills and through the rubble of a destroyed school.

The tired woman who had been the schoolteacher told us that the children wanted to come back to school, but were now years behind. She had turned and looked out of a school window. The glass, long shattered, lay in shards in the schoolyard, where children had not played since the shelling began. A discomforting melancholy set in at the sight of abandoned children's toys, and we left the school solemnly.

We had hoped to revive ourselves at a stand outside the destroyed hospital. While we sipped our coffee, a woman came to buy bread, a little boy holding her hand. When she let his hand slip to fish into her tattered purse for money, the boy howled, burying his face in her hip and grasping her leg through the material of her skirt. The schoolteacher turned around and crooned to him, "What is it, little one?"

His cheeks were wet with tears, but he had wise eyes set in a wiry child's face. She told us later that his stricken expression did not unnerve her. It filled her with grief.

I WAS, naturally, not alone in my quirks. The people at the morgue were a motley crew of varying ages, nationalities, and experience, and everyone dealt with the work differently.

Laura, a young woman from Scotland, sang to the bones when she washed them, readying them for inspection by the anthropologists. She's crazy, I had decided when we first met. She and Amer, one of the clothes washers, had been flirting across the morgue. She told me that he reminded her of a puppy with big brown eyes.

"Why do you sing to the craniums?" I once asked her impatiently.

She was at a loss at first. "They had mothers and sisters. Girlfriends. It's a terrible thing to be without a name."

There was another young woman from California who worked on the computer database. She spent her days adding details from each corpse to the list: estimated age, degree of decomposition, cause of death. I had once helped decipher some of the pathologists' notations. "Multiple GSW." Multiple gunshot wounds.

She was pretty and blond, and she did yoga on the porch before work.

One day when Jadranka and I were washing up the dishes after dinner, she asked about the girl with the short blond hair.

I shrugged. "She seems nice enough."

"Yes, but there is something wrong."

"Wrong? How wrong?"

She hesitated, rinsing a dish in a bucket of water that had been collected two days before, when water was running.

"I was cleaning upstairs. I heard someone crying."

I waited.

"She was sitting on the upstairs porch just sobbing."

I patted Jadranka's hand awkwardly. Her eyes were large and concerned, this girl who had survived the war. I did not tell her about our work in the morgue, even when she asked. At night when I dried the dishes she washed, I brushed past questions about the day. I did not tell her that it might be a relief to cry.

José Pablo, the Peruvian, was a confident and capable anthropologist. He had spent years working in the field, but when decomposition touched his bare flesh—an occasional unpleasantness others took for granted—he jumped as if burned. Snapping off his gloves, he would flee the autopsy room in a panic, hurrying to wash off.

Some of the men drank, and some of the women did too.

Barbara, an Austrian student, had come to Bosnia as an intern and was responsible for organizing the interviewing of family members. She put together a team of people who would handle survivors from Srebrenica and ask questions about the missing. She was about twenty.

One night we went together to a hotel bar in Tuzla. José Pablo had a crush on her and invited us both for drinks. She was the object of interest and I the grudging chaperone. She lent me a dress, and I brushed out my hair.

When we got there, a group of reporters were already seated at the table. José Pablo knew many of them and introduced us.

"Where did you find these two?" one of them asked him in Spanish.

José Pablo shrugged the question off. "What can I say?"

"Not bad," said the other one, eyeing Barbara. "But I have no fucking energy for chasing anything."

I pretended not to understand.

"Maybe we should switch to Catalan," one of them said idly, glancing at me.

"No, no, man, it's okay." José Pablo had become engrossed in conversation with Barbara.

There was a drunken Englishman sitting across from me. He was telling story after story of his travels through Bosnia. When he called the waitress over, he attempted to order his fifth glass of liquor in Bosnian, but he gave up, finally, under her frosty stare.

"How old are you?" he asked Barbara suddenly, when he had waved the waitress away. "You look about sixteen."

"Twenty."

He rolled his eyes. "Jesus. They're sending children now."

Then he turned to me. "Tell me, how can you bear it?"

I stared at him. "What, exactly?"

"What you do." He waited a moment, and the table became quiet. "You people are ghouls." He spat the words at me. "I am sitting at a table with ghouls."

I was quiet for the rest of the evening, which, mercifully, did not last much longer. When I rose to leave, one of the Spaniards handed me my bag. He was a photographer for Reuters. "We're not very good company tonight," he said.

I shrugged. Barbara and José Pablo had gone ahead.

"I'm sorry"—he sighed—"but the repetition of certain events can make you hard."

Hard as nails, I thought.

THE NEXT DAY a Srebrenica refugee told Barbara of a detention camp operating at a farm in Republika Srpska, mere miles away. She told me that night, and I sat helplessly across from her as she started to cry.

Rumors like that were common after the war in Croatia as well, with people insisting that their loved ones were being held at secret camps in Serbia, or in prisons. There was no way to substantiate the rumors, short of going forcibly to the identified site, and no one was ever willing or able to do that. In Croatia some of the reports had turned out to be true.

In May a group of Bosnian survivors from Srebrenica who had been wandering Republika Srpska since the massacre flagged down SFOR. They had managed to survive nine months in the wilderness, but SFOR, instead of taking them to free territory, turned them over to local Serb authorities. They were in custody and awaiting trials on trumped-up charges. Observers noted that they appeared to have been beaten.

There was nothing we could do aside from registering the matter with the Red Cross, but we needed to have eyewitnesses. Barbara would go to the Red Cross the next day, she said through her tears. She would make them write it down.

MY FATHER still did not know where I was, and I got a sinking feeling when I thought about it, which was often, because I saw his face everywhere: in the soccer-playing children on the roads of Kalesija, in the teenage boys who helped their mothers down from Tuzla's buses, in the older men who stared expressionlessly at the white, hurtling UN vehicles, looking away a moment later with barely concealed contempt.

There are irrefutable truths I know about my father's past, and I carried them into Bosnia. In my childhood they were like the remaining tiles in a mosaic that had been stripped by flood and fire: charred ground with a cryptic inlay of cobalt and rust.

The rare stories of his childhood, of Herzegovina and Sarajevo, were vivid parables for my brother and for me. There was the one about nearly getting drafted by the Partisans; the one about the girl who painted hearts on her eyelids and winked at him across the classroom; the description of church picnics in Posušje, during which someone was inevitably stabbed. There was the love story of Anđelka Brkić and Josef Finci, and the day he had approached her on a Sarajevo street.

Between the narratives were gaps, but we learned to ask for the stories we knew by name and overlook the rest. His telling of them marked his good moods, which could last for months before the darker ones set in. He told them with such animation that we were transported to that distant terrain where we met him as Bero, the little boy. Our grandmother, who had died before we were born, stood out in technicolor, so that she was with us in spite of death. In my sleep I could taste the bread she baked, and when I woke, I could describe the dusting of flour on the crust and the way the scent made the sharp corners of the kitchen blur ever so slightly. We did not see him as the editor of tragedies then.

After arguments that struck with the randomness of light-

ning, he would retreat like a wounded bear into his den, sometimes failing to emerge for days. Like other new Americans
who seek to reinvent themselves, he let weeds and dirt overtake the past. But he was never entirely allowed his reinven-
tion, the obliteration of his mosaic past, for his daughter was a
stubborn demander of stories.

As a child, I tried digging at the silence. I scooped away
layer upon layer of burned earth, sensing that it was covering
something. I was eager to discover the nature of what lay underneath. Too abrupt an excavation could cause irreparable
damage, but I dug carefully. With my ear to the ground, I could
hear something raging. It raged through the stories he told and
raged still more in the stories he could not bring himself to tell
until much later.

"There are things one does not tell to children," he says
now by way of explanation. But as we grew older, we were
led intuitively to those holes in our father's otherwise intact
history.

I WAS CONCEIVED on a trip to Africa in 1971, two years after my parents married. A more precise point of origin, my
mother explained with a shy grin, was Mombasa, where the
sandy beaches ached in their whiteness and the sea was a constant motion.

"Do you remember?" she teased.

Science has proved that a fetus in the womb is sensitive to
light and sound, and that it learns to identify its mother's voice.
A fetus is soothed when its mother is happy, but its heart rate
rises sharply when she is upset. Psychologists who toy with re-

gressions into past lives and the moments before birth claim that you can remember conversations that occurred while you were in utero, heard through the thin layer of your mother's swollen belly. As if you were leaning your ear against her navel to determine what awaited you, or putting your eye to that keyhole in order to discover the shape of territory to come.

I was told that the elements present in those moments were a mix of forms and sounds: There was the meal that they had eaten a few hours before, the bottle of wine that they had shared, and the inhaled pollens of plants that they could not identify. There were circumstances that stretched back in time, long before that evening when my mother stood barefoot at the window listening to the sounds of nighttime Kenya and my father turned down the bed.

My mother brought wanderings to their union like post-cards: the sun on Lebanese cedars, sweet lychee fruit from Thailand, and the smell of glacial lakes whose floors are edged with leeches. My father brought fierce energy and darkness: the whisperings of martyred poets and recollections of war and hunger.

It was not until they reached a coastal Moroccan village several weeks later that my mother sensed her pregnancy. In the harbor, her stomach rolled and she became dizzy.

"You look pale," my father told her one day. They had been wandering through a souk and had stopped at a fabric stall.

She smiled, insisting that she was fine, and continued examining the skeins of fabric—cobalt, black, and gold.

I was born nine months later, dark and with a thirst for wandering. At the age of twenty-three I wandered into Bosnia and turned twenty-four.

Why did you come? I was asked repeatedly by the people I met there. One of the workers at the morgue had shaken his head, not unkindly, but in utter bewilderment. *Your father got out, didn't he, and made a new life for you in America? What on earth possessed you to return?*

I neatly sidestepped the question. I had no answer, just a recurring vision: My father at twelve stands on the street as his mother and Josef Finci are removed from the Brankova Street building. Josef has carried him on his shoulders. He has brought him blood oranges from a Sarajevo marketplace, the flesh so red and sweet that it makes the back of his throat ache in expectation. Josef has wrapped loving arms around his mother, making her shake with laughter, making her eyes warm.

The man is dragged away into darkness, into nothingness, and somewhere the twelve-year-old senses his fate. Like the gentleman from Vienna who simply failed to materialize one evening, Josef will not return. The boy's mother is arrested, and although she will return, she will not truly return.

The years spiral out from him. He looks down their grim length and weeps.

———

ON THE EARLY SUMMER MORNING of a rare day off, I drove into the center of town with one of the UN investigators. He dropped me off on the main road, and I walked the last several hundred meters to the Tuzla bus station.

The girl at the counter smiled as she pushed the ticket to Sarajevo in my direction. "Are you Arab?"

Because of my dark hair and olive complexion I had frequently been asked this question since coming to Bosnia. There
were a large number of relief agencies from the Middle East
who had come to assist Bosnia's Muslims. Some were operating
strictly as relief agencies. Others had more political or religious
aims.

America had grown concerned about the proliferation of
these groups. When the West refused to lift the arms embargo
and Bosnian Muslims became desperate for weapons with
which to defend themselves, sectors of the population became
aligned with Arab countries who were more willing to contribute weapons and supplies. The West worried, a little belatedly, about reports of Muslim freedom fighters who had come to
Bosnia during the war, including a number of mujahideen.
These men were reported to have stayed in various strongholds
throughout Bosnia long after the war had ended.

"No," I told the girl, "I'm not Arab; I'm American."

"Oh." She nodded, looking disappointed. But she was
bored, and she asked, curiously, "Why are you going to Sarajevo?"

I tucked the ticket into my wallet. "My father grew up
there," I told her. "I'm going to visit friends."

She looked thoughtful. "Well, don't expect it to be like you
remember it . . ."

"I hardly remember it. It's been so long."

"That's good," she told me, shutting the partition window as
I turned to leave. A moment later she opened it again, calling
after me. "It's also a shame. It was a beautiful city before they
killed it."

A man waiting on the station platform had overheard our

conversation and nodded at me. "A lot of things were beautiful before they killed them."

IN SARAJEVO I took a streetcar from the bus station to Ilidža, a suburb that had been under Serbian occupation during the war. My father's childhood friend, Ignac Cezner, lived there with his wife. I had become friendly with their son, Lado, who had escaped Sarajevo in 1993 and was studying at the university in Zagreb.

The streetcar ride from the bus station was a tour of pancaked architecture. There were entire buildings whose walls had collapsed and whose floors lay neatly stacked, one on top of another. Other buildings were skeletons that had remained intact but whose flesh was completely gone. The *Oslobođenje* newspaper building was a wreck, having been the target of repeated and sustained attack during the war.

I felt linked to Sarajevo even though I had been so far away. I was drawn to it because of my father's stories and memories of his childhood. And then there were my own memories, so faint as to be almost invisible. Aunt Ana of the Turkish slippers had died, mercifully, several years before the war began.

Many people were drawn to Sarajevo's suffering—not sufficiently to do anything about it, but it made good copy. Sniper Alley and the Marketplace Massacre became well-known far from Sarajevo. For most people the city had been a vision, glimpsed briefly through the footage of the 1984 Olympic Games, which my father covered for the Voice of America.

I remember how proud he was when he prepared for his trip there. Our mother had bought him long underwear and woolen socks, and he told me stories about his childhood as he packed, remembering the winters in Sarajevo when ice covered trees like a second skin. We followed the Olympics on television, looking beyond the skiers and skaters for my father's familiar tan parka.

That same footage was later unearthed in order to show poignant then-and-now shots of fractured architecture and an annihilated infrastructure. The whole world became a voyeur, watching the slow ebb of the Miljacka River underneath a bridge where the "Romeo and Juliet" of Sarajevo were shot and bled to death. Sarajevo was a sound bite in which snipers neatly took out cemetery mourners who rolled efficiently into open graves and where children at play were killed in the middle of the street, picked off like cardboard cutouts in a shooting gallery. In Sarajevo, people ran like tiny, frightened mice. The West, in its utter fascination, had ceased thinking of them in human terms. *See how they run. See how they run.*

IGNAC AND HIS FAMILY lived in a sprawling house surrounded by a garden. We sat in the *bašča*, at a table under the trees.

His wife, Nevenka, had prepared savory stuffed peppers and mashed potatoes. After weeks of MREs and cafeteria fare, I attacked the meal hungrily. It was food that smelled of home, and they even brought a bottle of wine up from their cellar to toast our meeting.

"We had an entire collection of wine," Ignac told me ruefully. "Lado and I spent years putting it together, and then . . ." While Ilidža was under occupation, Serbian Army volunteers had come and ransacked the cellar, taking some bottles and breaking others. Very few had been spared.

He poured me a glass and shrugged. "Well, it is only glass and liquid." And we toasted each other's health and the end of the war.

In 1992, after the war had started and Ilidža had been severed from the rest of Sarajevo, Ignac's children, Lado and Regina, escaped into the city center, which was not under occupation. Their mother marched down to the self-appointed authorities who were expelling non-Serbs from the district.

"I was born here," she explained to them. "My children were born here. The only way I am leaving here is dead."

Their corner of Ilidža went largely unscathed during much of war, though there was one Serb neighbor across the garden who had borne a grudge. There had been a dispute about the border between their gardens and a fruit tree. He shot at them several times when they were in their garden. Nevenka was terrified each time her husband stepped out the kitchen door that she would hear the whizzing sound of a bullet. And then one day it happened. A bullet lodged in Ignac's leg. The neighbor then came and knocked Nevenka down, breaking her arm.

When the Serbs left Ilidža, they went on a rampage of burning and terrorizing the people who stayed behind.

Nevenka looked over at the neighbor's dark house and waved her arm. There was a knot on her forearm where the bone had been set improperly and healed poorly. "We heard that he was killed on the front line," she said with a slight smile. "A sniper got him."

Mostly they had been afraid for their children. Lado had

been in the Croatian Defense Council, the HVO, which was regarded suspiciously in Sarajevo. He and other men had been sent, unarmed, to the front to dig trenches. When off the front lines, he had lived in the center of town caring for his ill uncle Slavko. In 1993 he went on a "field trip" with a group of other Croats to Međugorje. He did not return to Sarajevo again until the end of the war.

Regina, their daughter, was now living in Zadar, in Croatia, where she studied archaeology. The siblings were able only rarely to get word to their parents. And so the family lived for several years, spread out and cut off from one another.

In Zagreb, Lado studied electrical engineering. We had met occasionally for coffee, and he helped me with my Croatian vocabulary. I was having tremendous difficulty with the technical terms I came across in my research and work. *Zolja*. *PAP*. *Ručna bomba*. Rocket. Semiautomatic rifle. Hand grenade. They were terms of war. There was one I could not make sense of, and I asked him about it.

"*Fenjer*." He grinned and pulled out a piece of paper, drawing for me. "Like a lantern. It comes down out of the air and lights up the entire terrain so they can see you to shoot at you."

"Like a flare?"

"It lights up everything, makes the night day."

While the war had been going on in Sarajevo, this young man—who was then only in his early twenties and had not grown up so differently from my brother and me in America—had express wishes for his burial. He knew the piece of ground he wished to occupy, and he had even written down the post-mortem instructions. I wondered if he carried the note on him or left it with someone else for safekeeping.

Before returning to Tuzla that afternoon, I walked through the garden with Lado and Regina, picking up fruit to take back to the base house. We filled a bag with tart apples and hard green pears.

The garden was larger than I'd thought. It sprawled behind the house, down to the property of the sniping neighbor, and was filled with flowering bushes and fruit trees.

"Come here," Lado said, gesturing down the hill. "There's something I want to show you."

We walked around one tree to a piece of circular heavy metal that was embedded in the ground.

I jumped back when I realized that it was an unexploded shell whose tip was buried in the brown dirt. The exposed part of it came up to my waist. Lado chuckled. I reached out a hand to touch it, but then reconsidered.

"It landed a couple of years ago and didn't go off. The army was supposed to send some people out to make sure it's defused, but they haven't gotten around to it."

"How can they live with this thing in their backyard?" I asked. "It could go off at any moment."

"It could, but it probably won't. Besides, you'd be amazed what you get used to living with."

Lado's father, Ignac, and my uncle Zoran had been in the same class in Sarajevo. My father was a couple of years older, and Ignac's brother Slavko, older still. But they had all attended Sveti Vinko Catholic School and grown up together in the same neighborhood.

My father remembers how proud Ignac's mother had been of her little son's curls, and how she would dip a comb in sugar water before running it through his hair, so that the spirals would keep their shape. I told them this, and Ignac nodded his head, smiling.

Lado hooted at his father. "Sugar water?"

"And I remember your grandmother," Ignac said, grinning at me. "She used to feed her sons egg yolks and sugar, so thick you could stand a spoon in it. She said it gave them strength."

It was my turn to laugh. I could see my father standing in the kitchen, beating raw egg yolks and sugar with intensity. They start out golden yellow and become paler and sweeter. Finally they make thick ribbons that stand on their own. I remember my brother sitting on my mother's lap, reaching out for the spoonfuls with longing arms. The first taste of the *batulin* is a shock of sweetness, the sugar grains brushing roughly against the back of the throat and making one cough. The second is the opening of the universe, the cracking open of its thin sides, the warm yolk pierced and running out of it.

SOMEWHERE BETWEEN THE GRAVES and my return to Tuzla, the tip of my index finger had begun to burn. It felt as if a splinter had become embedded under the whorl of my print and expanded just a little each day. I rarely thought about it while working, but at night, lying in my cot, I would worry it with my thumb. In the morning I tried to dig it out, but it was the tiniest sliver, and I couldn't find it.

Igor, one of the men hired for logistics, was a medical student from Zagreb, and he examined it under a lamp in the field house.

"There's something there," he said. "But I can't see what it is."

He recommended antiseptic.

But I had the terrible feeling that a splinter of bone from one of the bodies had made its way into me and lay buried under my skin.

By the time my Tuzla bus left Sarajevo's outskirts, dusk was falling, and I watched the fields turn gray beyond the windows. My finger throbbed, and I pressed it against the cold glass, trying to tamp the ache. I was exhausted. We had worked a long time without a break, and I thought of returning to the morgue the next morning with a heavy heart. Personal effects from the bodies were kept there under lock and key in a special cabinet. By that point we had amassed quite a collection, from bullet-pierced photographs to scraps of paper. There were amulets and rolled-up prayers, and heels of bread in plastic bags. One letter, largely destroyed, had asked the recipient (name illegible) to provide the bearer (name illegible) with food and shelter.

THE THIRD WORKER at the morgue, Dževad, was so young that it was hard to watch him cleaning the clothes of the dead. His blue eyes were set in a mature face, but his voice gave him away. There was something unnerving about the way he washed the clothing, the way he concentrated on it. He was completely absorbed by his work, but he watched everything around him.

"He's a *kibicer*," Omer told me with a wink. One who watches.

In the beginning, Dževad had asked me where the bodies were from. Because we were under orders not to disclose the details, I waved my hand nonchalantly. "They're from a long way away." The graves were at least two hours by car from the morgue. I could see that my answer did not satisfy him, but he returned to hanging out clothes on the drying racks.

During a cigarette break some hours later Omer told me that Dževad's father was missing. I didn't understand at first.

"Three years ago. They never found his body."

Comprehension dawned on me slowly.

Omer inhaled, the lit tip of his cigarette almost sparking. "He's looking for his father's clothes."

I felt the color drain from my face. I thought of the buckets filled with putrid water and how he stood over them day after day, never uttering a word of complaint.

"That is why he asked you where the bodies are from." Omer stubbed out the cigarette and squinted into the sun.

I finally found my voice. I stumbled over it, and the words came out tersely. "The bodies are from Srebrenica. These men were killed last year. You should tell him."

Omer nodded. I turned and walked back into the fly-spun darkness of the morgue.

I BEGAN HELPING FRANS, the Dutch policeman, catalog the washed clothes. He was a crime-scene photographer, and he shot reel after reel of the objects recovered from the bodies. The photographs would later be shown to surviving family members for purposes of identification.

I had seen photographs like that in Croatia—entire stacks of forlorn objects waiting to be recognized. I had seen women study them carefully, inspecting stitching that might have been their own handiwork. They would turn the photographs this way and that, struggling to remember the details of shirts and belts.

Frans and I worked out a system where I would bring the clothes from the drying racks in the sun outside and lay them out on two tabletops that had been placed side by side in the morgue. While I did this, he changed his film, adjusted the lighting, or moved the stepladder from which he took the pictures.

I laid out the clothes in the shape of a man. Shoes at the bottom, then socks. Trousers, then shirt and jacket. I tucked the shirt into the trousers and left underclothes to one side. When I saw something distinctive—a pair of handmade socks, which were in abundance, a special patch or label, a tear that had been mended—I pointed it out, and he knelt next to the object to take a close-up.

I could sometimes tell from the size of the clothes that they had come from a boy. In such cases, I pored over the articles, looking for a crack in the sole of a sneaker, a button sewn on and not matching the rest, an undershirt that had been hastily fashioned from a larger one. From the boy's father's? I wondered. Was he also here?

BACK AT THE BASE HOUSE one evening, Jadranka cooked us a pot of Turkish coffee after dinner. I savored the bitterness, looking at the black bottom of the cup. I'd never liked American coffee, the weak wash from percolators and coffeepots. Turkish coffee has a strength that penetrates the bone.

The anthropologist sitting next to me had drunk her portion and was examining her cup pensively. I told her to flip it over.

"When the grounds dry," I told her brightly, "I'll tell your fortune."

WHY DID YOU COME TO BOSNIA? Dr. Peerwani had asked me. *Are you looking for something?*

I was, in fact, looking for many things. I was a veritable mine of questions.

I asked the silent twisted bodies in the morgue.

I asked the UN workers I met, wondering, How could you let it all happen?

But they ignored me and went on drinking their cold beers in any of several restaurants that catered to them on the scorched earth of Bosnia.

I wanted to ask my fellow team members, *How can you stand day after day and keep standing?*

But I shielded my alien nature from them as best I could, and even joked and talked as they did.

Our group was constantly revolving. People had been hired from all over the world, and when they returned to their countries at the end of their stints, they were quickly replaced by well-rested reinforcements who came from Sri Lanka, Scotland, Denmark, America. A good-humored woman from Texas named J.R. joined the team. Her name won grins even from the local workers, who had seen subtitled episodes of *Dallas* before the war.

Like many of the other excavators, my sojourn in Bosnia was open-ended. I could cut and run at any point, I assured myself. And not a day went by in which I did not think of leaving.

Dr. Peerwani left Bosnia to return to Texas. I missed him. There was no one left who could help me fathom, to however small degree, what it all meant.

Do you think it will make you understand? he had asked.

IN 1988 my father covered a fifty-year commemoration of *Kristallnacht* at a Maryland synagogue. There he met Flory Jagoda, a Ladino musician from Sarajevo. Slightly older than he, she had left the city as a girl and had spent the war years on the island of Korčula. Her entire family had been exterminated in the camps, including her grandmother, from whom she learned a repertoire of Sephardic songs.

This is how I keep our dead alive, she seemed to say through her haunting songs.

Although my father did not know this woman, she seemed immediately familiar. He sat in the synagogue while people around him said Kaddish over the dead. He bowed his head and listened to the voices around him, and he prayed as well, saying his own Kaddish for Josef Finci.

That night, the dam that had been holding back all my father's memories of those years burst. Fully formed stories emerged. We had known about Josef Finci and even about the arrest, but our knowledge had been partial and incomplete.

When my father filled in the details, his eyes grew wet and his hands shook. We were astounded by his tears. He was a man given to intense emotion, but always in the form of booming laughter or bitter anger. We had even come to recognize the latter as a proxy for sorrow, and we accepted that his darker moods were often not a product of his immediate environment, but a residue of something else. But the sudden tears shook us, for all that they gave us relief.

At night the moon hung low over the porch in Tuzla, and I crawled out to watch it cross the sky. I thought about the waste of Josef Finci's death and of the lean, lonely years that followed. I have mined the stores of my father's memory, trying to make sense of the years that contaminated every year that followed, right up to the present.

I thought about the men we had dug out, about the women who were waiting for them. Those men had been husbands and fathers. They had teased their wives and played catch with their children. They had hoisted their sons onto their shoulders, so that now there are thousands of boys who dream nightly of those moments when they grasped their father's ears with one hand and touched branches, ceilings, and the tops of cornstalks with the other. Those children were growing up without fathers or father figures, just as my father had done. Fifty years later, the utter absurdity of this waste had not lessened.

Dr. Peerwani was right. I still did not understand.

AMER'S FLIRTATION with Laura, the Scottish girl, had progressed, and she had gone home with him one day for lunch. Home to his mother, to whom she gave some Vichy hand cream. Home to a cramped room where she could not understand what was being said to her, but where she was moved deeply by their hospitality.

But our supervisors had seen her walking with him down the road outside the morgue, and they deemed her behavior inappropriate. She had gotten a stern talking-to and had cried. She was young, an archaeologist like myself, and had only just finished school.

Amer wrote her a note in Bosnian. Would I translate it for her? she asked. And not tell the others what it said?

Just that day, I had tried to decipher a soggy letter, overlooked in a jacket pocket from one of the bodies and accidentally taken outside for washing. One of the workers had brought it to me, cradled in the palm of his hand like an injured bird. He was upset because, as he pointed out, people inside the morgue were supposed to check pockets first. Had he known that it was there, he would have been able to save it.

Little paper survived anyway, I said, trying to comfort him. What did was already wet and ruined from the grave. I said I would try to open this one and see what was written on it, but he hunched his shoulders and walked away. I laid it on the table, but the longer we waited, the more the ink ran, expanding from neat letters to fill the pulp of the paper with indistinct bruising. Ronald, an English policeman, helped me try to open it with tweezers, but some of the ink had already run, and it was largely useless, the paper tearing like tissue. An occasional word could be made out, but nothing that made sense. I was near tears for the first time in days.

Ronald put a hand on my shoulder. "We'll photograph it," he told me gently. "Maybe someone will recognize the handwriting."

When Laura came to me with her love note, my impulse was to shove it back at her. "I'm tired," I had said in irritation.

But there was something so earnest about her face, a gust of fresh air from the outside world, and so I took the letter with its words of boyish admiration and translated them.

EARLY IN AUGUST a wave of excitement swept across the entire crew. The Swedish UN battalion was organizing a big party, and we were all invited. We had worked hard, and here, finally, was a chance to relax. There were rumors of a barbecue, music, and booze.

We got lost on the way, driving down one long dirt track after another. We passed groups of refugees who appeared to be living in the woods. We passed an old mining camp with refugee children who scattered into the darkness of the shacks at the sight of our truck. The adults looked at us over barbed wire with tired faces and angry eyes.

A slow drizzle started. The roads of Bosnia unwound outside the windows of our car like faded ribbon. We finally found the correct road, only to be told by another truck coming from the opposite direction that the party had been rained out and moved. We backtracked and found some familiar faces sitting on the terrace of a small, unremarkable restaurant.

We were late. A lamb that had been turning on a spit all afternoon was cold. It had been chopped into pieces and was heaped onto serving plates together with salad and bread. The food now disgusted me, and I left it on the plate. I found myself drinking glass after glass of wine, though my tolerance for alcohol has always been low. Voices rose and fell with shrieks of laughter. It was like listening to music constantly expanding and shrinking, and the sound sat on my skin and made it crawl.

Laura sat across from me, beaming. I knew that she took out the letter and looked at it several times a day, despite the fact that she could not read the Bosnian words. Clea, the American girl who had been in Rwanda, sat next to me. The Chilean and the Guatemalan were deep in conversation. The former had recently learned that his wife was expecting a baby. The latter was slated to return to Guatemala in order to testify against powerful men responsible for the killing of civilians. There were concerns about whether it was safe for him to walk into court. He had the gentlest face I had ever seen on a man. When he was asked if he did not fear for his own life, he spoke softly and smiled. "I must go. That is all."

I saw all this, and still I felt removed from them. I drank another glass of wine, its acid working its way through my empty stomach.

Everyone was still talking excitedly, but suddenly I realized I could not hear them. They were opening their mouths wide, and their teeth were huge and bearlike in the half-light of the restaurant lamps. But they were making no sound, their faces fading in and out of focus. I was not aware of rising from the table, but later I would remember the wooden slats of the restaurant terrace moving beneath me as I made my way to the street, back to the car. I ran around it, to the dark side, like an animal running for shadow. Time and space fell away, and my name and history ran off me like water. I leaned against the car, looking up at the sky, and wept.

A few moments later the stars were blocked out, and arms were cast around me. They tore me from the side of the car and held me upright. I was shaking violently, but I became aware of a voice, of someone singing to me, and I looked up at José Pablo. But somewhere through all the thick cotton of drunkenness I realized that he was not singing to me; he was not even murmuring. His words were insistent.

"You are alive." He was shaking me. I tried to sink down onto the ground, but he would not let me. He got me into the car, and I lay across his lap, trembling. *The eleven-year-old boy*, I wanted to tell him. The words came out garbled, and I realized I was not speaking English. I could not find the English words, but I was telling him anyway. At some point on the drive back to Tuzla, I got sick out the window. For months to come I would be embarrassed thinking about it, but at that moment it was just one more piece of the darkness I wished to be rid of. Letting it out of my belly was a relief. José Pablo helped me to sit up, and he held my shoulder as I vomited, to prevent me from falling out of the jeep. I lay down across the seat, my head in his lap, babbling hysterically.

I was aware of getting back to the house and being half carried up the stairs. José Pablo laid me on my bed and unfastened my shoes as I continued to cry quietly. My finger was on fire, the bone splinter stabbing at me. I rubbed a hand across my thighs, feeling other splinters in my legs. Tree splinters, splinters of that eleven-year-old's bones.

He shut the door. I heard the sound of crying, but could no longer distinguish it. It had grown out of me. I thought it might have been José Pablo or the girl from California, or the Dutch policeman who had driven us home, his face a controlled mask in the harsh light of oncoming traffic. He had small children at home, he had told me as we photographed the clothing. When he telephoned his wife, he could hear the sound of their laughter in the background.

I couldn't tell who was weeping. In the end, I decided it was the eleven-year-old, crying as he died.

LIBERATION

1945–1959

All the silver and gold of this world, all the lives in it, cannot buy thy pure beauty!

—*Ivan Gundulić, from "Hymn to Freedom"*

O N THE MORNING of April 6, 1945, stillness descended on Sarajevo's streets like a thick blanket. No children shouted from city alleys, and there was no sound of soccer balls being kicked from one pair of scuffed wartime shoes to another. There was no hum from shoppers on their way to the center of town, and no pitch of streetcar wheels against metal tracks. The city usually only achieved such silence in the thickest heat of summer, when the sun greased pavements with mirages and the air stood still. But the breeze that slid hesitantly through half-cracked windows that morning was cool.

Anđelka and her sons listened to the quiet from the Koševo Street apartment, which had been abandoned by Ljubica and Katja when they escaped to Zagreb a few weeks before.

"The Partisans are coming," people had whispered to one another in the preceding weeks, going about their daily business in a state of excruciating suspension. "The devil is at the gate," some people had determined, with dire predictions about the weeks to come. Still others could not hide their relief. "Liberation is close at hand."

"Take our apartment, *seka*," Ljubica's voice had echoed through the empty Koševo rooms. "We'll be happy in Zagreb, and I'll feel better about you being here. It's larger than your apartment, and cooler in summer." The practicality in her voice had fooled no one. "We'll send word as soon as we can."

When they embraced, Anđelka felt a stab of sorrow. She realized that she might not see her sisters for years, or ever again. The war was an unrepentant gobbler of people—no sooner did it gorge on one than it moved onto the next. But survivors did occasionally return from its black belly, and this was the hope that buoyed her in those last days of the war. Liberation also meant that Josef might be restored to her, so she waited with barely concealed exhilaration.

While Bero and Zoran embraced their distraught aunts, bidding them farewell, Anđelka thought of the tiny Posušje house they had all shared as children—five lean sisters and a dying boy—and it seemed another lifetime.

She and the boys left Brankova Street as the last Ustaša units were pulling out of Sarajevo. She hurried them from the apartment. Josef's absence taunted her from every empty corner, and it was as if they were escaping a plague-contaminated town. Điđikovac, their first Sarajevo apartment, was the scene of her sons' childhood. Each remembered it warmly despite the Stuka raid that had left long, horizontal gashes in its walls and killed their beloved Lux. When she passed Veliki Park on her way to the market, she remembered her sons sledding there in the years before the war. She remembered sitting on its benches with Josef before they were discovered, holding hands furtively under their coats, and she remembered the clatter of dishes and laughter in the apartment above the trees.

But the day of the arrest would forever stain the Brankova Street apartment, as would the tense years of waiting that followed. Shadow seemed to cling to its corners, and she could not bear the gray light of its rooms.

She had recently realized that a consequence of the war had been her sons' silence. They had learned to move mutely through the world and to reveal nothing in their dealings with strangers. They were cautious, like old men who had lived entire lifetimes of persecution. In the years since her return from prison, they had hovered uncertainly around her, aware of her waiting, quiet and distressed, unable to reach her.

But after they moved into the Koševo Street apartment, she had the impression that her sons felt suddenly more at ease. Perhaps it was the bright lamps that hung from the ceilings, or the relative size and airiness of the rooms, but the boys' complexions grew immediately less sallow. They stood taller and smiled more easily now.

Initially she had been afraid that Josef would grow alarmed when he returned and did not find them at their old address. She imagined him turning onto Brankova and climbing the stairs with his last shred of energy, only to find the apartment deserted. But her neighbors knew where they had gone, she told herself, less than ten minutes away on foot.

Once the Partisans took Sarajevo, the camp's liberation could surely not be far behind, she had told one of her neighbors. She saw pity flash across the woman's face and realized that the neighbor believed her delusional.

"He's coming back, you know," Anđelka told her, aware that

stubborn fury had climbed into her voice. She put her gloves on with such angry speed that they jerked the ends of her fingers. "It's just a matter of time."

"Of course he is," the neighbor told her, a beat too quickly for either's comfort. "They all are."

THE KOŠEVO STREET APARTMENT faced the *vojna pekarna*—the military bakery—and on the morning of April 6 they realized that the bakery was deserted. Nothing moved in the entire building, which ordinarily teemed with laborers, soldiers, and delivery trucks. Bero and Zoran sat on the windowsill watching for any sign of movement on the street. The air seemed taut to the point of snapping, and made the trees and buildings outside appear strangely misshapen.

There had been several days of bombing and artillery fire as the Partisans drew closer to the city and the Ustašas pulled out of it. In order to prevent her sons from leaving the apartment in those days, she thought up a dozen time-consuming tasks for them at home. Despite the fact that they were nearly grown, or perhaps because of it, she could not bear to let them out of the apartment. Bero was fifteen, the slight shadow on his upper lip already threatening to become a mustache. Zoran, at fourteen, was slighter, paler, but catching up. There were stories of even younger children being drafted and taken to the front.

"Do not dare," she told them repeatedly through those days, "set foot out of this apartment." She was perpetually terrified that if they left, a bomb would kill them.

And except for brief forays to the building's main doors, during lulls in shelling and while their mother was contentedly humming in the kitchen and dreaming of Josef's return, they had largely contented themselves with watching for signs of life from their window.

AT TIMES the shelling was so strong that the windows shook. The shelling was nothing compared to the Stuka raids at the beginning of the war, or the Allied bombardments that followed. But one of the bombs that fell in the final days of the war had exploded in front of the tobacco factory on Brankova Street, a stone's throw from their old apartment. With uncanny precision it had landed directly on Valter Perić, one of the leaders of Sarajevo's underground resistance, a man whom Anđelka knew quite well.

When word made it around the city that he was dead, Anđelka shuddered. "See!" she told her sons in the next breath. "He made it through the whole war, and now, one moment of stupid chance ended it."

No one knew if it was a Partisan shell or an Ustaša shell that had killed him, and she had nearly snorted aloud when the visitor who brought the news speculated as to its origin. It made no difference whose shell had killed him, she thought. He was dead just the same.

Some days later Bero visited the site beside the tobacco factory. He imagined Perić's figure lying proudly in the street, hands folded across his chest. Perhaps someone had draped it with a snow-white sheet out of respect. He expected to find some type of marker indicating where the man had died, but there was nothing. Pieces of his intestines, however, had been left hanging from the top of the factory's iron gate, and Bero

watched their trailing ends for a few horrified moments before
returning home.

WHILE BERO AND ZORAN were watching the *vojna pekarna*
on the morning of Sarajevo's liberation, their friend Rici burst
into the apartment.

"They're coming!" he told them excitedly. Rici's brother
had been fighting with the Partisans since the middle of the
war, and his family had been starving through most of the rest
of it. "They're here!"

Bero and Rici decided to go out to explore, but Zoran could
not be coaxed from his position at the window.

When Anđelka saw Zoran alone at the window, she stopped
in her tracks.

"Where's your brother?" she asked her younger son a little
sharply.

Zoran shrugged and turned to her with a guilty smile. "He'll
be back soon, Mama."

Anđelka joined him at the window, leaning out in order to
look up the block in either direction. The street was deserted,
and she felt panic settle like cold steel on the back of her neck.

"He'll be back soon," her son repeated, still staring at the
street.

She sat down on the couch and took out her mending, but
put it down a moment later, sighing. Almost an hour went by
before she heard him speeding down the hall outside. She
crossed her arms, ready to unleash a tirade. *All I need to worry
about is something happening to you too*, she would tell him.

It was not Bero but Rici who burst through the door a moment later. "They've taken him!" he told her, barely able to contain himself. "They've made him a Partisan! They're taking him to fight."

She felt the blood drain from her face.

Bero and Rici were the same age, but Rici was deemed too scrawny for them, he told her with some disappointment. They had immediately drafted Bero, however, adding him to a group of young men being shepherded to a mobilization station.

"He's fifteen!" she had shouted. Rici grew suddenly quiet, shifting from foot to foot a little sheepishly. "Where?" she demanded in some panic. "Where did they take him?"

But Rici did not know.

"Go home!" she ordered him a little wildly. "Go home so that your mother doesn't have to worry about losing two sons!"

Hours passed, and she paced the apartment in a rage. "Waiting," she muttered under her breath. "Always waiting." Three years of waiting for Josef was nearly more than she could bear already. And now her fifteen-year-old son was being sent to the front as a Partisan. A sob rose in her throat at the thought of it. Partisan soldiers had little food and shoddy equipment. They don't even have helmets, she thought hysterically. Then, I'll beat the hell out of him when I get my hands on him again.

She turned to Zoran, shouting through her tears. "I told you, both of you, to stay in the apartment!"

The Partisans had nothing but stupid cloth *pitovke* to protect their heads. Head wounds among them were commonplace, and she thought of their bleeding, seeping injuries. She had even heard Ustaša soldiers joking about it. Why waste ammunition aiming for their bodies when one clean shot to the head was all it took?

• • •

A FEW HOURS LATER Bero returned home, frightened and
out of breath. He knew that Rici would have told his mother
what had happened, and that she would be hysterical. At the
convent where troops were billeted, he had given a false name
and address and inched to the back of the room. When the unit
received orders to move out, he slipped away in the ensuing
commotion and found a cellar door. He barricaded himself in a
toilet he found there, and he waited until the sound of footsteps ceased overhead. He emerged too early from his hiding
space, however, and an armed guard stopped him from leaving
the building.

The man glared, closing the space between them, rifle in
hand. "I've come to see my cousin," Bero had said, surprised at
how the lie flew from his mouth as if on wings. "He's the com-
missar." He delivered his words casually. "But it looks like I've
gotten here too late and they've all gone."

He offered the sentry a cigarette, withdrawing it from his
pocket with a hand that barely shook. He could see that he had
surprised the man, and in lighting the proffered cigarette, he
was calm enough to discern the soldier's interest in his silver
lighter.

"I've another one at home just like it," Bero said airily, pre-
senting it on the palm of his hand. "Why don't you take this
one, comrade?" He backed away as the man focused his grudging attention on the bribe, and he broke into a run the moment
he was out of sight.

"I told you not to go onto the street!" Anđelka shouted
through sobs when he entered the apartment, slapping him

with her open hands. But her eyes were frightened, and in them he read another message: *You're not to disappear as well.*

AFTER SARAJEVO'S LIBERATION, shops reopened and streetcars ran again. Children went back to their games in the street. Life regained some semblance of normalcy.

On Saturdays, Bero and Zoran went to the cinema. In the dusty darkness of Sarajevo's theaters—the Imperial, the Apolo, the Drina, or the Volga—they sat mesmerized beneath the flickering black-and-white films. They had always loved this world, where the hero was clearly marked by his attire and the villain received his righteous due.

Films during the war generally came from Italy or Germany, but for a short period afterward there were American films about gangsters, gunrunners, and pirates. Bero and Zoran, fed on a childhood diet of Karl May's tales about the American West, loved Westerns particularly, the hero's face angular under the brim of his cowboy hat.

Later there was a series of cinema verité films about the war. In one, a small blond girl runs with her parents as German planes carpet bomb the road. The refugees are slaughtered, and, her parents dead, the girl climbs from beneath them to wander the road with skinned knees and a tearstained face. Bero and Zoran watched her unsteady path quietly, as if breathing could dissolve her trembling outline, a portrait that seemed drawn entirely out of dust.

Many years later, when they were adults, the brothers realized that those Saturday afternoons at the cinema had started as a chance for their mother and Josef to be alone, a weekly respite from the family routine and the demands of noisy children. By the time Josef was arrested, the cinema trips were already tradition. *On-screen the couple embraces. There has been conflict, misunderstanding, and danger. But by the film's end, they have found each other, and the woman's face lifts up to her lover's like a flower to the sun.* Bero and Zoran watched the screen spellbound. Here, finally, was justice.

THE END OF THE WAR brought both relief and disappointment. Although not Communists, Anđelka and her sons had celebrated the Partisans' arrival in Sarajevo, believing they were a liberating army. The war was over. Now Josef would return.

But Bero's near conscription had made them wary, abruptly tempering their euphoria. The boys drafted on that day were sent to the front in northern Bosnia, to Odžaci, a hill town where the Ustašas made their last stand. Even after the fall of Berlin the Ustašas continued to fight, and many of those boys—schoolmates and neighborhood friends—did not return.

Less than a week after Sarajevo's liberation, two men had shown up at the Koševo Street apartment asking for Ante Mamić. Anđelka looked at them in studied bewilderment. "No," she told them, "there's no Ante Mamić here."

Then Branko Stikić, an old neighbor from Brankova Street, came to their apartment with three Partisan soldiers in tow. "*Drugarice,*" he had told Anđelka, "these men are here for the motorcycle. Give it to them, comrade, and there won't be any problem."

Anđelka had never liked or trusted her old neighbor. "Motorcycle?" she repeated, trying again to sound bewildered.

"I believe you keep it in the basement," Stikić told her with a smirk.

It was not the fact that they took her cousin's motorcycle that bothered her. It had only been a matter of time before they discovered it and commandeered it anyway. It was the fact that a neighbor had informed on them that needled her.

"Be careful what you say to whom," she counseled her sons. It seemed that there was no end to the silence.

THEY WERE EVICTED from the Koševo Street apartment a few weeks later, but allotted an apartment on Vrazova Street, back in the Marin Dvor section of the city. Anđelka's pension was cut off.

Jasenovac, the concentration camp, was liberated, but Josef had still not managed to return. At night she lay awake listening for him. She imagined him coming to her under cover of night, although there was no reason to be afraid anymore. She remembered his arrival the night he had evaded the roundup that snared his family. He had been lucky then, she thought. He could surely be lucky a second time. O Mother of God, her mouth moved in the darkness. It is such a small thing to ask.

Ultimately she did not mind their eviction and the fact that they had returned to Marin Dvor. It would be easier for Josef to find them.

Harsh reprisals began. Tens of thousands died in Austria, at Bleiburg—Ustaša and Domobran troops as well as civilians—as they surrendered to British troops but were pushed instead into waiting Partisan lines. Still others died on the *Križni put*, a death march from Bleiburg to Belgrade.

Božidar Brale, the cleric who had conducted the loud affair

with Brankova Street's blond *Slovenka*, had fled with her to Slovenia. When the Partisans came, however, she immediately turned him in. He had been sent back to Sarajevo, where he was executed, but the Slovenian woman never returned.

"I wonder if her husband ever came back," Bero mused aloud when they heard the news.

Anđelka wondered as well.

When the first shipments of mail resumed, there was a letter from Zagreb, from Ljubica, addressed in her sister's pretty hand. But the penmanship inside was unsteady, and Anđelka had the feeling that if she shook the paper, the letters would become dislodged from the white sheet like tiny wisps of hair. Ante had also disappeared. Somewhere past the Slovenian border he had been separated from his brothers and not seen again.

RADNE BRIGADE, manned by Sarajevo's teenagers, removed rubble from neighborhoods filled with war debris and wreckage. Bero and Zoran worked that summer from dawn until evening on the Marin Dvor brigade. They returned home in the evenings exhausted but strangely happy. With the war's end had come freedom to roam the city's streets.

Bero was voted leader of the Marin Dvor work brigade, something his mother teased him about. He turned red, pretending that such a distinction meant nothing at all, but she could see that he was pleased to have been chosen. Two days later, however, he was approached by members of Communist Youth. He could not be a brigade leader without also being a member of SKOJ, they told him. He declined, more out of stubbornness than ideology. They also asked him to surrender the pistol he had found with his friends while prowling through the city's abandoned bunkers at the end of the war. He kept the trophy hidden at home.

Worse, they wanted him to denounce another boy from the neighborhood. He was to testify at a SKOJ meeting that he had seen him in an Ustaša uniform.

Bero turned pale, incredulous. "But I didn't. How can I say that I did when I didn't?" They waved their hands at this technicality.

"No," he told them tightly. "No, thank you. I don't want to be a member of SKOJ."

They were somewhat surprised, and relieved him of his position as brigade leader.

"I told you," his mother reminded him. "Stay away from politics."

In the end, they made him surrender the pistol anyway, and the boy was denounced by someone else.

ĆUK, THE POLICE INVESTIGATOR who had saved Anđelka's life, was put on trial. His wife tracked her down, appearing at their front door in tears one day, and begged her to testify on his behalf. Anđelka went before a tribunal, swearing that while he had been unable to help Josef, she was alive because of Ćuk. Others came forward as well, but to no avail, and in the end he was executed.

Communism spread like slow poison. School began in the fall of 1945, but students studied a whole new array of subjects. Bero and Zoran liked some of them. Darwinism, for example, had never previously been taught because of Church objections, and they found the theory fascinating. Other subjects involving political indoctrination were as boring as they were one-dimensional. Russian-language instruction neatly replaced German.

Bero's school friend Vlado tried to convince him to join SKOJ. It would mean more opportunities for him: he would be eligible to join other clubs at school, and his teachers would look upon him favorably. Communist Youth meant advancement, his friend insisted. So what if he did not believe?

But Bero was adamant. "Do what you like," he told Vlado, "but it's not for me."

Later his teachers recommended him to the School of Foreign Service in Belgrade. He was a member of the Forensics Club. "You're a good debater, Brkić," they told him. "You could have a promising career in diplomacy."

But membership in SKOJ was a prerequisite, and to their consternation, he declined again. He did not mention their offer to his mother.

HOPE WAS FADING. Every time her sons looked at Anđelka, they could see it, even as she went through the motions of her days.

It had been months since the camp's liberation, months since the Partisans had found a handful of emaciated prisoners and set them free. Stories about the camp, both accurate and inaccurate, were told and retold. Men were returning to Sarajevo all the time, Anđelka told herself in spurts of forced optimism. Partisans, Domobrani, former prisoners of war. They had been trickling back since the end of the fighting. One of these days, she told herself firmly, Josef will be among them.

She attempted unsuccessfully to find other returning prisoners from Jasenovac. She asked people who had been fighting in
that area of northwestern Bosnia, and she even tracked down
some who claimed to have liberated the camp. But each time,
they looked at her blankly, apologetically. They had not come
across a Josef Finci.

OUTSIDE THE CITY, burned earth looked blackly at the sky.
Roads were churned and rutted, and bridges started across
rivers only to end in thin air. "This is what they have done to
us," said the government in radio addresses to the constituent
peoples of Yugoslavia. "The Germans, the Fascists."

Youth brigades rebuilt the country while indoctrinating
teenagers into *bratstvo i jedinstvo*, brotherhood and unity. In forays made to look like high-spirited camping trips by grinning
authorities, students who manned the brigades were sent to
build dams and bridges.

In the summer of 1946 Bero's high school class went to
build the Banovići-Brčko Railroad.

"No!" Anđelka had told him. "Not yet!"

Working in the neighborhood was one thing, but leaving
her for months at a time quite another. Besides, her son had
undergone two hernia operations and was, she reasoned, still
too weak for the heavy labor the trip would demand.

But acquaintances from the neighborhood chided her. "We
don't like it any more than you," they told her, "but now they
might make it difficult for him to go back to school in the fall.
You should have let him go."

Even her brother-in-law Ivan, who had been appointed to a
position in the city's administration, thought it a grave mistake.

In the end, he arranged for Bero to fight forest fires around Sarajevo that summer. Civic duty could quickly become a matter of State involvement.

Bero was the youngest on the crew and city-bred, but the older men kept an eye on him, steering him around the dangerous spots. They fought fires that broke out in the dry, creaking pines around Pale, on the Romanija Mountains, and nearer to Sarajevo. Sometimes they came across burned areas where the ground was covered with carbon. Bero would have walked through them had the other men not held him back. Such areas were deceptive with their uneven, burned floors. Where huge trees once stood, holes left by burned roots extended far beneath the surface of the ground. He had seen men walk along only to disappear in a sudden flailing of limbs, the rest of the crew scrambling to bring them, screaming, back to the surface.

Bero's face became blackened with smoke, but with time, the hand that brought the cigarette to his soot-stained lips steadied. He imagined himself a hero in one of his favorite films, and the idea appealed to him. The justice of such films was that the hero rarely died. Such men were surely not sucked into ash-filled pits.

He returned to Sarajevo at the end of that summer.

"You look older," his mother said when she opened the door. She could see that her words pleased him and that all vestiges of childhood had fallen from him like leaves from a tree. She burst into tears, and his face fell. He moved quickly to embrace her.

Josef was dead. He and Zoran had known this for months, although for her sake, they had not been able to say the words aloud. But as her tears wet his neck, he realized that hope had died permanently in his absence.

AT NIGHT HER DREAMS were of imprisonment—her own weeks in Beledija Prison combined with images of Josef trapped behind a wire fence. Sometimes she dreamed that her sons had been placed in dark jail cells where the walls climbed with vermin. Occasionally she dreamed that they had simply disappeared.

When she woke in the middle of the night, she would enter their room as if to assure herself that they continued to sleep, that they continued to breathe. In the daytime she attempted to control her panic, her wild premonitions of their vanishing. Her sons were nearly grown. Bero would start university next year, and Zoran the year after. She knew that they needed a measure of distance from her now, and that she should not reveal the full extent of her terrors to them.

The idea that Bero was in some type of trouble had obsessed her lately. She believed that the authorities might one day connect the scared fifteen-year-old who had escaped conscription at the end of the war with the high school student who adamantly and repeatedly refused to become a member of SKOJ. She was aware of the tightrope he walked in his quest to be left alone. They lived in times when even shunning politics had political overtones.

She decided to send him to Zagreb, where he could make a fresh start and finish his last year of high school. He could live with her sisters Katja and Ljubica and be free from whatever in-

formation people had compiled on him in Sarajevo. She feared
those people, whoever they were, writing down his every move,
even while she knew that their counterparts existed in Zagreb.
Rumor had it that everyone had a dossier, a tabulation of per-
ceived slights against the State, compiled by anonymous members of the population. People could be summarily arrested,
imprisoned, and not heard of again. It happened every day.

Bero had acquiesced for his mother, and he hated it. He
missed his friends, his family, his girlfriend. In Zagreb he was a
stranger, and he felt both foreign and awkward. Standing on
the main square, he was aware how different his accent and
mannerisms were from Zagreb's population. He had been polite
to his aunts, but he longed for the mountains that surrounded
Sarajevo and the familiar haunts he frequented in the city. Zagreb was a snobbish place, with habits he found strange. He
missed Sarajevo's market, its *sevdalinke* songs. His grades began
to slip, and in letters home he spoke repeatedly of wanting to
return.

The decline in his grades concerned Anđelka. She was not
educated, but she understood the power of a university degree.
If he finished the year with such poor marks, his chances would
be limited.

When he came back to Sarajevo for Christmas, she gave in,
telling him that he could stay and return to his old high school.
He hugged her with such exuberance that her feet lifted from
the floor.

FOR HIS FIRST SEMESTER of university Bero was assigned to
the School of Engineering in Ljubljana. Anđelka remained
with Zoran in Sarajevo while he finished high school.

Bero had Marijan's black hair and coloring. He had a mental agility that alternately took her breath away and worried her. Things came easily to him, and he was adept at earning high grades with only a minimum of effort. But while he had some of Marijan's charisma, she was thankful that he had inherited none of his father's penchant for carousing. Her son was no *bećar*. With the exception of once, after his high school graduation, he had never been drunk, and the blinding hangover earned from that event was enough to ensure future moderation. He had been the man of the family since the age of twelve, a responsibility he took very seriously.

Her older son had a certain toughness, like the Herzegovina stone she had carried to Sarajevo in her skirt pocket and kept in her drawer. Although she worried about him in the distant Slovenian city, she knew that ultimately he could take care of himself.

Lately it was Zoran who worried her. None of them had been the same since the day of the arrest, but Zoran, who had been in the apartment with Josef at the time, bore the deepest scars.

Although he had always been of a slighter, frailer constitution than Bero, he possessed a stubbornness that could be maddening. He seemed to reside in a world independent of them all. It was not that he did not have friends. He had many, but there was a part of him that was remote and unknowable. His grades were good, though never as good as his brother's, and he did not earn them with the same facility. He would stay with a mathematics problem for hours, turning it this way and that until divining the answer.

And Zoran was easily wounded. After an argument he could spend hours in troubled and angry silence. Anđelka was fiercely proud of the fact that both her sons were individuals. But Zoran troubled her.

THE LAWS GOVERNING EDUCATION in Yugoslavia changed, and after one semester in Ljubljana's engineering school, Bero was able to choose a different course of study.

He liked languages and literature, and he switched to Slavistics in Zagreb. His friend Vlado, who had also been studying engineering in Ljubljana, switched to Zagreb as well. The two boys lived together with another friend from high school, Iksan Takhmidžija.

Although they all hailed from Sarajevo, they were a strange combination. Vlado was the son of an ardent ethnic Czech Communist and a Serb mother. A leading SKOJ member, he had been deeply involved with Communist Youth since the end of the war. Iksan was a mathematical genius whose theories had already appeared in international academic journals. A Bosnian Muslim, he was also an epileptic, deeply ashamed of a disease that most people did not understand and regarded suspiciously. Bero was a Croatian, but because he was bred in Sarajevo, Zagreb was as strange to him as it was to his friends, despite his high school semester there.

Iksan and Bero were studiedly apolitical. And whatever Vlado believed or did not believe, politics was never a part of their discussions. Anđelka liked both boys and knew that Bero was happy living with them. In the spring of 1949, however, she learned in a carefully worded letter from her son that Vlado had been arrested, and fear resumed its slow march. One night, after the boys had gone to sleep in the room they rented together, they were awakened by a pounding on their door. A bright light shone in the windows, and a voice boomed out, "Which one of you is Vlado Šatni?"

Vlado rose unsteadily in his pajamas, Bero and Iksan looking confusedly at one another.

"You're to come with us," the voice behind the flashlight said. And then, like an afterthought, and not without irony, "And bring your toothbrush."

ARRESTS WERE TAKING PLACE all over Yugoslavia that year. In the beginning, Anđelka was relieved that Bero had left Sarajevo, because the majority of his high school class had already been detained.

In 1948 Tito had broken with Stalin and the Comintern. When Soviet invasion seemed a credible threat, Tito put his decision to a vote of confidence by all cells of the Communist Party of Yugoslavia. He asked them, simply, whether they thought he was correct in his Marxist interpretation, or whether Comrade Stalin was. The SKOJ cell in the Sarajevo high school, and many others besides, sided with Stalin. In the months that followed, mass arrests neatly rounded up the injudicious voters.

Because they were not SKOJ members, Bero and Iksan had not been detained. Despite their friendship and cohabitation with Vlado, they did not know anything about the affair. On the night that he was ushered out of the room by the police, they had sat in stunned silence. They did not know what had precipitated the arrest. They could not sleep the rest of the night, worried and afraid, looking at the emptiness where their friend had slept. Bero remembered the burned forest, and in his eyes the bed became a thing of ash and cinders: a loosely packed and burning well that had swallowed Vlado whole, leaving the air empty where his friend had been.

ANĐELKA MOVED TO ZAGREB with Zoran, and he enrolled the following year in the agricultural department of Zagreb University. Bero came to live with them, and she was relieved that they were together again. At first they lived with Ljubica and Katja. Katja soon married Mile, who was studying to become a lawyer. Iva and Draga remained in Posušje.

Anđelka knew that Bero was worried about Vlado, although he rarely discussed it. There had been no trial, and they knew nothing about his whereabouts. But rumors abounded about Goli Otok, an island gulag for political dissidents. Barren Island was alleged to be a moonscape of rocks and blinding sun, cleared, like other Adriatic islands, of its pine trees centuries earlier by the Venetians.

Although Anđelka's pension had been reinstituted, it was a meager amount, and her elder son was uncomfortable living with his aunts while contributing so little. Katja worked as a seamstress, and the money she and Mile made fed them all.

"Never you mind," his mother told him. "Finish your studies, and then you'll get a good job, and we won't have to worry about it." She was concerned that he would interrupt his education to find a job.

In 1949, barely a semester into his study of Slavistics, Bero answered a Radio Zagreb advertisement for announcers. Out of hundreds of applicants he and a handful of others were selected for the job. The station's Party cell had also voted erroneously against Comrade Tito, and arrests had caused drastic under-staffing.

Bero consoled his mother. The university would allow him to continue his studies part-time. He would attend special night classes and earn money at the same time.

Unhappy as she was, Anđelka understood the practicality of the arrangement. Barely twenty, Bero would be making ten times the amount of her pension. And she too had worried that they were becoming a drain on her sisters.

They managed to move into a separate apartment in the same building, but the State would only allow it if they lived with another family. A woman from the island of Brač with three daughters soon moved into the other bedroom.

ANĐELKA MISSED SARAJEVO TERRIBLY. She had spent half her life there, and she felt as much a stranger in Zagreb as her son had during his unhappy semester of high school. But with Josef's death, Sarajevo had also lost its purpose for her. She felt rootless, and moving away had been an easy decision. Her sons were her entire life now.

They had a stiff, polite relationship with the family from Brač. And it was both a comfort and a hardship to be so close to her sisters. When she and Ljubica sat together drinking coffee, they would occasionally become lost in their own thoughts. Then they would look abruptly at each other and continue their conversation or their baking of coffee beans or their shelling of peas. They never spoke of their lost men, but the figures hovered on the outskirts of each conversation.

It had taken Ljubica years to give up on the possibility of Ante's return. In the beginning she had believed with a certainty that he would come back for her. Men did come back, all the time. Or women would receive news somehow from abroad, and that news would sustain them through all the gray days that followed. She might hear from him years later, she knew. There were all sorts of crevices and caves that could swallow a man. One had only to believe, fervently, that he would dig himself out again.

Anđelka was excruciatingly aware that Ante had belonged to the regime that murdered Josef. There were times, however, when she wept for her younger sister. Ljubica had grown whip-thin and angry. Her face had the sharpness of broken glass, and her voice a barely contained edge. One harsh word, and she would break into angry tears, and Anđelka would squeeze her sister's shoulder, knowing that the tears had nothing to do with their squabble. And Anđelka would remind herself that she had two children, but Ljubica had been left alone.

Dressed in black, Ljubica withdrew slowly from her life. She rarely saw friends and stopped going out. Katja's husband, Mile, was dead set against the Communist regime, but whenever he spoke of the Independent State of Croatia, Ljubica would wave him angrily away. She cared not one whit for politics or nostalgia. What had they ever brought her but grief? What use were aspirations when Ante was gone?

She and Anđelka had an uneasy silence together, but she frequently preferred it to the comforting words of others.

BERO SWITCHED from Slavistics to the Academy of Dramatic Arts. He continued to work at Radio Zagreb and had branched out into acting, directing, and writing. In 1951 his radio play *Jutarnja Tišina* won the Ljubljana Competition and was performed all over Yugoslavia in the year that followed.

Anđelka was proud of Bero, but he had interrupted his studies to take care of her and Zoran, and part of her feared he would never finish.

"Mama," he would tell her with benign exasperation, "things are going well."

And for the most part, they were. He had money to support them, and money to take summer vacations. He had even been able to spend his first honorarium at the Theatre Café, where he bought one drink after another for the Bohemian poets Tin Ujević and Frane Alfierević, until they were in an advanced state of inebriation and his honorarium wholly depleted.

Later that same year, a stranger approached him at the Hotel Dubrovnik café, addressing him by name. When Bero did not immediately recognize him, the man smiled strangely. "I *have* changed." They had been high school classmates in Sarajevo, but the man, now wholly unrecognizable, had been a prisoner on Goli Otok for several years. Vlado Šatni, he told Bero, was still there.

Bero had heard accounts before. The stories crept off the island and kept an already apprehensive population in check. He registered what the man told him and added it to the pantheon of the island's horrors, where every story took on Vlado's face.

"In the first year," the man with the stranger's face told him, "the stones were heavy on my back." Their sharp edges bit into his neck as he walked on a path through a wilderness of dry and barren ground. When they reached the other side of the island, they were allowed to throw down their burdens and return for another load.

"Are we building something?" he had asked in the beginning.

The others looked at him with tired, hungry eyes.

"What are we building?" he asked again. "Some kind of structure or wall?"

The days passed, and the pile of stones grew. His arms became as thin as cords, and his face was blistered and raw from the sun. A seawall? he had mused to himself. Clearing fields for planting? But there was no dirt beneath the stones, just more stone that seemed to fracture and chip away from the earth layer after layer. The island was a place of death. Men fell underneath their loads, collapsing from heatstroke. Dead fish washed up on the shores.

Months passed, and the pile of stones made a tower. You could stand upright in its shade in the morning before the sun crept too high.

"Enough!" the guards called one day, stepping around the pile, admiring its height and breadth.

Now? his face asked. The guard caught sight of him and walked over with a round grin. He patted him on the back.

"Congratulations, comrade. You have completed the task. Now you can carry them back to where you found them."

VLADO'S FAMILY had not gone hungry in the years following the war. They were staunch Communists, and his father was a government minister in the late 1940s. None of that, however, had saved his elder son.

Bero remembered that he had gone home once with Vlado, and his friend had scrambled fifteen eggs in one skillet for just the two of them to eat. At the end of the war there had been no milk, no eggs, no fruit, and Bero watched the steaming pile of eggs in amazement. His own family had been surviving on humanitarian aid, and he could barely remember the taste of an egg. As they were finishing their meal, Vlado's father returned home and began lecturing them on the benefits of Marxism to the workingman. After the squarest meal Bero had eaten in days, the older man's political words floated like so much dust in his comprehension.

Bero had loathed the Ustašas. They had taken Josef, arrested his mother, and shown him that the ground beneath his feet was flimsy at best, but he despised the insidious nature of the Communists as well. Partisan wartime promises had degenerated into a system of police and police informers, and he had grown restless and angry in the years since Vlado's arrest.

Most of all, he despised the fact that he had to temper the language of his writing to their politics. And although he believed that he had managed to avoid their attention thus far, the tightrope he walked grew increasingly taut beneath his feet.

Then, in 1954, he helped organize a trip to Italy for his class at the Academy of Dramatic Arts. They planned to see the frescoes of Assisi, the canals of Venice, and they even received funding from the Ministry of Education for the trip. But when the approved list of names came back from the Ministry of the Interior, his was not among them.

It was the first sign that something was wrong, and it unnerved him.

He had survived the war and the forest. Later he even survived the army, which in those years bore every similarity to a gulag. He was discharged earlier than usual, with a pneumonia that left him weak and coughing blood.

HE WAS PICKED UP for questioning a few months after his release from the army. It had been years since Vlado's arrest, but he assumed it must have something to do with their friendship.

They referred to it euphemistically as an *informativni razgovor*, an informative conversation, and they began by asking if he had ever spoken against the government. He looked at them in dismay. They continued, quoting his own words of outrage from the Hotel Dubrovnik. His old schoolmate turned out to have been an informer for the secret police.

"Did you say these things?" they asked him.

The questioning continued for some time.

In the end, they took out a copy of *Jutarnja Tišina*. They asked him questions about the play. What had he meant by this? What was his point in writing that line?

Finally, "Why did you make the American a sympathetic character?"

And still he was not prepared to leave. What would become of the life they had built? Of his mother? What could he write in a foreign country, where his language would not be understood?

He clung to the idea that he could maintain his silence and evade them. He made peace with the fact that there would be no advancement without Party membership. But he did not want to join them. His life was not so bad. He could support his family; he could buy as many cigarettes and books as he wanted and take yearly vacations on the Adriatic Sea.

Zoran had also started working for the radio, and he wrote children's plays as well. He was more vocally negative about the regime than his brother, and Anđelka frequently worried that he would get into trouble for his political opinions.

Like Bero, he had used his student status to postpone military service until the age of twenty-seven. But in the months before his birthday he had grown increasingly bitter.

"I'm not doing it," he told his mother and his brother. "One way or another, I'm not serving in their stinking army."

Anđelka was perturbed. Bero had nearly died in the Yugoslav Army. When they sent him home to recuperate from pneumonia, she had already started to worry about her younger son. If Bero had not been able to withstand those years, how would Zoran?

She and Bero spoke about it frequently in those months.

"He's got to leave," she told Bero finally. But what would he do when he left? She was desperately afraid that he would be unable to fend for himself.

Sometimes in the evenings, when Zoran worked on his writing, she would hover outside the door of his room. The shoulders that hunched over the paper in front of him were thin, his head bowed. Zoran created fantastical children's plays, populating them with characters that made her smile as she listened to them being performed on the radio while she was dusting or mending. Where had these characters come from? she wondered. For that matter, where had either of her sons found any of their stories?

She had endured her own life. There had been no room for fancy, no time for stories. Even childhood had been something to be withstood. To escape, she had married early and had babies early. She had attempted to create happy, carefree childhoods for her sons, but the war had undermined her. This im-possible country had undermined her.

She had tolerated their writing, but she wanted them to put down their pens and finish sensible degrees, and she ached that they had not done so. Now she had to send them away.

At night she cried herself to sleep, but in the mornings she forced a smile onto her face for their sake. She stood up very tall, did chores around the house with blinding efficiency—folding sheets so that they formed perfectly square corners, vigorously scrubbing the bottoms of pots.

Whenever they would look at her uncertainly in the midst of planning their escape, she nodded at them with encouragement. Once they reached Germany, they would find a way to send for her. It was the only way.

"Get out while you still can," she told them. "And don't come back."

ZAGREB

1996–1997

The roar of the storm grows above our heads.

—A. B. *Šimić, from* Despair

THE MORNING after the rained-out party, I woke up early with a piercing hangover. I knew that the illusion of controlled emotion that I had carefully cultivated over the past month had faded along with the bad weather. The sky that morning was preternaturally clear and seemed to leave the still sleeping town oddly exposed. But I forced myself through the robotic motions of getting dressed, aware only of the pain in my head.

In the morgue I could not meet other people's eyes, remembering how I had gotten sick on the drive back to Tuzla and fallen asleep in the base house weeping. I remembered that I had made other people cry as well.

Halfway through the morning, I approached José Pablo at one of the examination tables. "I'm sorry," I told him miserably, shame flushing my suntanned face.

He was unusually pale. "You're too close to it," he told

me, almost groaning. "And it's hard on everyone because you are."

I LEFT TWO DAYS LATER. It was like walking out from a shadow, and in my first few weeks back in Zagreb I thought I had made a clean escape.

Then one day I saw an abandoned sock lying discarded and forlorn on Branimirova Street. Though obviously unattached to a body, it seemed remarkably full, and I watched it for several frozen seconds to make sure that it was uninhabited. A week later, while cleaning chicken from a breastbone, I began to retch uncontrollably at the sight of blood-soaked cartilage. *Perimortem* trauma, I thought, and placed the whole thing in the refrigerator, where it stood for days until I wrapped it in a plastic bag and threw it away.

Weeks went by, and I thought, Finally, victory. I have extricated myself completely. Until I awoke one morning, having escaped a tight, cold space where bodies were stacked into a tower in a cubicle remarkably like the refrigerator in my kitchen, the one with the coils that whirred incessantly at night. Except that in my dream it had been completely silent and was the size of my bedroom.

The dreams could not be classified as nightmares, because they did not, in fact, frighten me. I was an anesthetized observer, and I spent many waking hours trying to make sense of my cold removal.

There followed a dream of a swimming pool with an assortment of severed male torsos at its bottom, all perfectly bloodless and still beneath the water. Then there was a dream of an evening in my aunt Ana's apartment in Sarajevo, where a group of us hunched against a wall as a sniper shot through the kitchen windows. But I dreamed feeling nothing.

On the streets of Zagreb I wandered halfheartedly to job interviews and meetings with friends. I refused to enter enclosed places and spent hours wandering down Ilica as far as I could go, beyond the farthest streetcar station in Črnomerec. On Sljeme Mountain I would carve out alternate routes from the hiking trail, pulling myself between trees and through piles of dead leaves. I did not look back once, imagining that I left manic furrows like field mice in grass.

Back in town at the end of my haphazard itineraries, people seemed distorted to me, as if I observed them through a lens. I was overly aware of people's facial structure and of their dentition. A woman would pass, and I would turn to watch her go, observing her posture, hunched from the weight of the plastic grocery bags she carried in each hand. And I would wonder how her bones might appear in the ground, and what configuration they would make.

Once, I gave my seat on a streetcar to a man with crutches and a plastered foot who had gamely hopped up the steps to board.

"Thanks." He nodded, and I looked away. *How lucky your parents, your wife, your children are*, I imagined telling him, thinking of the thin line the break would make once healed. Something to identify his remains in the event that all else failed.

I WATCHED MY OWN FACE in the mirror. I made an inventory of my body's physical attributes. Not the fullness of my breasts or the curve of my thighs, but the permanent things that are not so easily erased. I wrote them down. I broke a bone in my hand when I was fourteen, and also a toe. I was hit once with a softball in the face when I tried to catch a fly ball in the sun's glare. It had not broken the bone, however, just left a horizontal gash on my cheek. I scratched out the last item when I remembered that skin was unlikely to survive.

I stood over the bathroom's porcelain sink and opened my mouth. The teeth in my upper jaw were straight and even, subjected to years of an orthodontist's manipulations in order to close a gap I had found embarrassing as an eleven-year-old. The bottom teeth were untouched, however, and as nature had made them. I staked my hope on the front two, which crossed very slightly, a feature my lower lip usually covered.

I CONSTRUCTED A MAP of Zagreb with landmarks to be avoided at all costs. I stayed away from Gajeva Street, with its collection of funeral homes, and Mirogoj Cemetery. Since the 1995 Oluja offensive, which had retaken a third of Croatian territory, graves had been exhumed in formerly occupied territories, and reburials took place with numbing frequency.

I avoided the UN Protection Force's Zagreb base, where families of the missing and dead had built a low brick memorial wall. One woman I had met there months before explained that the red bricks had been bright crimson when the wall was built. Her twenty-year-old had been missing since 1991, from Slavonia. When she looked at the bricks, she said, she remembered him as a child falling on rocks at the sea. He had screamed, and she plucked him up. He came sailing through the air toward her. And there was his brick, she said, pointing to his name written across it in white letters.

There were black bricks in the wall as well, indicating known deaths. But five years of pollution had worn them down, so that they were all the same: soot-covered and colorless. The satin roses wedged into the wall at intervals had also faded to the same noncolor. On All Soul's Day the wall was alight with thousands of candles. *We are waiting for you*, the flames would tell the passing cars, the dark sky.

Initially the names meant nothing to me. I had even seen the photographs of these unknown people, next to a long roster of the dead. The faces were predominantly of young men, but there were some elderly and women as well.

Eventually I began seeing photographs in different settings. Sitting in refugee rooms, I would notice the smiling face atop a bureau. Women opened their wallets to show me pictures of the dead and missing: baby pictures, first Communions, weddings.

I SAW THE SAME WOMAN AGAIN a few months later, beside the open grave near Okučani. She said a few words after the memorial Mass, which was held in a town that until recently had been under occupation. But it was not her town, and her son had still not surfaced. Before she spoke, I overheard her ask a friend quite calmly, "How many more of these meetings can I be expected to survive?"

She wore a conservative suit, and her voice from the podium was alternately steady and faint. "They can beat you, they can starve you, but they cannot strip you of what you are, of what I gave you, of your history."

She was very small against the podium, and I shivered, imagining that she had been telling the ghosts these words nightly for four years. *They cannot rob you of the fact that I nursed you, read to you, held your hands in our garden, spinning you around and around so that your feet lifted off the earth and you flew.*

A few weeks after returning from Bosnia, I saw her next to the Trešnjevka market. She did not know me by name, but she would remember that I had visited her office with my friend Judita. The woman was looking in the windows of the Nama Department Store across the street, her black handbag at her side. I knew that inside the handbag was a wallet, and inside it, a picture of someone who was dead. I turned my face away from her, not thinking.

"If I had a body, at least," she had once said to me. "A body to bury. A place to light candles. That would be something."

A streetcar slid mercifully between us. I did not look to see where it was going, but clambered aboard, into a crowd of nameless people.

MY FATHER ONCE OBSERVED that I have a face stripped bare. It was not a compliment. "Some people can mask what they feel, *kćeri*. But when you go out into the world, you go naked." I am sure the diggers at the exhumations would have agreed. After returning to Zagreb I attempted to control my expressions, to cover my nakedness.

I moved into my aunts' second apartment, next door to them, and switched from working on war-related projects to translation contracts. They were few and far between, but my aunts were forgiving landlords. I spent much of my time with friends and in comfortingly meaningless pursuits.

In the bustle of my aunts' kitchen, I sat at the table and watched them while they roasted trays of coffee beans. Aunt

Katja would flick out the stunted ones with a lightning-quick hand, lifting her head a moment later to find me studying her.

"Our little girl has returned!" She almost sang the words to me in those first few weeks, leaning over to squeeze my arm, going back a moment later to her trays.

In the next room, Aunt Ljubica wept whenever she saw my face, no matter how broad my smile.

LATE IN THE SUMMER OF THAT YEAR, my family rented a house on the Adriatic. In the shade of a cypress tree I told my father about Bosnia while locusts filled the heat with their drowsy singing.

I had not been in Slavonia as he had thought, I confessed, and I described my past months in as few sentences as possible. The brighter my smile and the more I insisted that it had been fine, really, not as terrible as he might imagine, the grimmer his expression grew.

He did not speak to me for hours after that. When he finally did, he was not furious, as I had expected, but heartbroken.

"I'm *fine*," I insisted. "I got out of there okay, and I won't be doing it again. You don't have to worry."

He swung his head from side to side, looking exhausted. He placed both hands on my arms, and for a minute I thought he would shake me. But he let me go.

"Come home," he pleaded.

BUT I DID NOT GO HOME. I had lost the thread of home. How could I return to a country where people consistently asked whether Croatia and Bosnia were in Latin America?

Those savvy enough to know the region's geography would express surprise and confusion that the war had happened at all. Yugoslavia had been an idyll, hadn't it? Where the past had been forgotten and people lived as brothers? I did not relish explaining, over and over again, that the past had never been forgotten, but merely buried.

The war was over, and yet, for me, it still lived. My self-therapy was to surround myself with people whose own experiences dwarfed my own. My friend Judita was a former army nurse who had been on the front line in Slavonia and northern Bosnia. She married her husband, Milan, two months before I met her, in 1995. Initially I was a little frightened of her. She was a tall, no-nonsense redhead with a low level of tolerance.

She had put me in touch with some of the people I interviewed during my year of research in Zagreb. And it was to her that I fled when my aunts' fussing annoyed me or when I was depressed from the stories I had heard during the day. In the warmth of her kitchen she poured me tea and listened to my complaints. She patted my arm and joked with me, or told me sharply to snap out of my mood, that there was plenty to be happy about. The war was over, in theory, and I was young and healthy. She did not have sympathy for self-pity.

Sometimes she pulled out the photographs of her days on the front lines. They showed her rawboned and dressed in faded fatigues. Her bright red hair shone like a beacon, a point of light in charcoal surroundings, and I teased her. "I wouldn't have wanted to walk beside you with a sniper in the vicinity."

There were pictures of her beside the ambulance that they used to ferry the wounded, often during the shelling and shooting. There were pictures of her at work, bending down to the ground and attending men who were bandaged, dirty, and dying.

As she leafed through the photographs, her hand would hesitate over pictures of the dead. A body without a head and arms, nothing but red, ground flesh. Some were pictures of unknown men upon whom they had happened accidentally. Some were pictures of friends.

There was one lacking arms. "He was so beautiful," she told me, pointing to the photograph. "So young and beautiful and sweet."

She was lost in thought, and I shifted beside her on the couch. She closed the album abruptly and pushed it away. "I made them go back for him. I couldn't stand the thought of him lying out there, and I made them get his body and bring it back."

And I was relieved that my dead were usually faceless.

JUDITA'S HUSBAND, Milan, had been in the war four years. When Judita first met him, she told me, he shook constantly and uncontrollably. Most of their friends were people with whom they'd survived the war. In that sense, I was an anomaly in their circle, and I felt like a child beside them. *Naša mala cura*, my aunts called me. Our little girl. To Milan, I was *mala*, or little one. Not inconsequential or quiet, he seemed to be saying, but mysteriously intact.

One night a friend of his drove me home after dinner at their apartment. A man of medium height and build with a mild face, he had come late and taken the chair next to mine. He had been in the same National Guard unit as Milan at the beginning of the war. They had slept in the same barracks during rapid training, but had gone later in different directions.

"He's nice," Judita had whispered to me in the kitchen. "So quit the silent act and start being friendly."

I made a face to show what I thought of her matchmaking, but Stjepan had a shy reserve that I liked. We sat talking in his car in the dark street outside my aunts' apartment—niceties about Zagreb, my translating, books we had both read. I did not mention Bosnia. I had developed the notion that those weeks had contaminated me, and I omitted them from any description of my circumstances.

I looked at the darkened doorway of my aunts' apartment building, and at the windows. The television would be roaring, occupying their attention fully. But I imagined all the other eyes that were pressed to the glass, watching the parked car. There would be solicitous neighbors who would stop by the next day to drink coffee with my aunts, mentioning that they had seen their American niece in a parked car with a strange man while it was dark outside. I grinned in the darkness.

Stjepan saw me and, not understanding my expression, smiled as well. We were quiet and awkward, and I examined him obliquely: he had short, sandy hair and fine lines around his eyes.

"I feel old," he sighed, looking at me with resolute blue eyes. I could see their clarity and color even with little light. He blushed, focusing on his hands on the steering wheel. "Not in years. Just old. And sometimes I don't know how to communicate things, like I've been living in a zoo for so long that I've forgotten how to speak a human language."

His profile was almost stony, but his voice was raw in a way that made something in my chest expand sharply. I knew he had been a scout in the army. And he was a rarity—in four years of combat he had never been seriously wounded. But most of his friends had not been so lucky, and many were dead.

He was taking an English class at the military academy, and he tried out the words he had learned, shyly. He gave up a moment later. "I don't have the chance to speak as much as I would like," he said.

In the forest of other people's hurt, I believed that mine might be eclipsed. So I told him in English, "Practice is important."

MY AUNTS occasionally asked about my friends. "Where is that nice lady whose son died behind Zadar?" they would ask. "Did they finally find the body?" Or, more frequently, "You need a boyfriend. It's not nice to be alone."

They were enamored of a certain Mexican soap opera in which a handsome doctor was treating a critically ill child, never realizing the boy was his own son. They would turn off the television at the end of the series and, without missing a beat, say, "A medical student would be nice."

"Yes," I agreed, smothering a grin, "it would."

"You should have children," Aunt Katja would say.

And my aunt Iva would nod in agreement. "At least five!" she would add brightly, ignoring Katja's withering glare.

They cooed over babies born on their shows: babies born to poor families, to rich families. Babies born out of wedlock and under the shadow of family curses.

Initially I had been amused by the fact that they were addicted to the subtitled *sapunice*. I knew not to telephone them at certain times of day, because Aunt Katja would pick up the phone sounding far away, only vaguely aware of a voice on the other end. Conversely, I knew that news could be delivered painlessly during those holy hours. Occasionally they would relate the plotlines to the lives of people they knew. Sometimes in the shows people would disappear. A freak case of amnesia or a child kidnapped under cover of night. The shows were a fantastical land of lost people who were almost always found again.

I WAS NOT READY FOR BABIES, but I was prepared to forget. I stashed a near-empty diary I had taken to Bosnia on my bookshelf. I folded a family tree I had been mapping out, and put it between the leaves of a book. The tree was only half finished anyway, and I doubted that I would ever be able to fill it out. There were too many unknowns, too many people beside whose names I had written "presumed dead" in such and such year.

My grandmother and her sisters were the only known quantities on that piece of paper. And my father the only man in his family to approach old age.

My aunts did not like my questions anyway. "No use in digging up the past," they would tell me.

STJEPAN AND I began meeting, ostensibly to practice his English and my Croatian.

He explained the Croatian word *sa*, and the way that it can mean both "with" and "from the perspective of."

"I am 'with' you now," he told me, putting an arm around my shoulders and pulling me to the front of his jacket. "Accompanying case."

He let me go abruptly, and I felt unsteady. We were standing on the street at midday, and a woman passing by stared at us strangely. He did not notice, and I covered my laugh by coughing. He took the lessons quite seriously.

He stepped into the gloom of a building entrance. "But I am looking at you 'from the perspective of' this doorway. I am removed from the situation. Genitive case."

I nodded, but could not hide my smile any longer. He moved again into the light.

"Makes no sense," I teased. "To be 'with' and yet 'removed.' "

He shrugged. "Every language has its internal logic."

WHEN SOMEONE in his brigade committed suicide, he was summoned. When some former soldier held his wife hostage, Stjepan would stand outside the apartment with the police. This was all part of his peacetime duties. With, yet removed.

"Did you ever consider suicide yourself?" I asked bluntly.

"Never," he said with a shake of his head.

It wore on him in different ways, he admitted after some prodding, and I was naïvely relieved.

Sometimes we spoke about Herzegovina. His family came from the edge of it. I told him what I remembered of Posušje and Rakitno, which was not much. I told him stories about my parents and their childhoods, and he listened, bemused.

Once, he grabbed my hand suddenly in his. "We're a good fit," he said, grinning.

We deserve each other, I found myself thinking.

One night we drove to the top of Sljeme Mountain. We parked the car on the road beneath the radio tower and looked over the mountainside at the twinkling lights of the city. The black wind whipped my hair across his face. During the war, the Yugoslav Air Force had tried to demolish the radio tower. The bombardments had made the hill shake. The tower had been damaged but remained standing, and we stood underneath it.

HIS FAMILY had moved to Zagreb from beside Rama Lake when he was thirteen, but he remembered the still water and the profiles of boats resting onshore at dusk. He remembered the tight heat of summer and the path of falling snow, vertical and quiet, somehow different from the city snow.

He was born between Herzegovina and Bosnia, not entirely a part of either. He had told me simply that he was from "Rama," and at first I could not place it. Then I remembered an old legend, and I snapped my fingers. "Diva's tomb is there!" And he smiled with pride over that ancient martyr.

In Rama, he told me, people had their own traditions. Their temperament was somehow different from Herzegovinian razor sharpness and Bosnian humor, and he considered himself a borderlander, hailing from a versatile patch of ground between two larger fields. His accent had remained clipped, never taking on Zagreb's nasal tones.

His father was rarely home during his childhood, working as a *Gastarbeiter* in Germany. His parents' marriage was a continuous cycle of absence and presence. Sometimes, when his father was gone, he would find his mother standing stock-still as she did the dishes, a glass or plate held in one hand, her gaze fixed on some distant point.

If they discussed his father's absences at all, she would shrug as if to say, *That's the way it's always been.* But he interpreted it in still another way, *Who am I to decline the burden of history?*

He told me that there had always been an awkward period of readjustment whenever his father returned. Stjepan, as the eldest, had been expected to bow again to his authority, and the initial anticipation of his homecoming was replaced by a tense vying for position, then mutual retreat. Then his father would be gone again.

Stjepan's parents had found common ground in religion. And although he was also devout, like most Catholics from Rama, he had stopped taking Communion after the first few months of the war, though he went to confession regularly. The priests absolved him, telling him that his sins were of a relatively inoffensive nature, yet I think that he believed the stink and ooze of the war had nonetheless contaminated him. In civilian churches he watched children swinging their legs or babies lying against their mothers' shoulders, and it seemed that he did not wish to taint the air they breathed.

Sometimes he stood at the back doors during a Mass, not even sitting in a pew, and as soon as the priest said, "The Mass has ended, go now in peace," he would hurry outside. The army chaplains gave him benediction and urged him to partake of the Eucharist again, but something held him back from walking to the front of the church, opening his mouth, and allowing the host to be placed on his tongue.

One Sunday I stood across from him in Zagreb's cathedral.

"Lamb of God, you take away the sins of the world," I saw him tell his folded hands. "Have mercy on us."

HE HAD NOT ALWAYS wanted to be a soldier. He had been one of the brighter pupils in his school, an avid reader, devouring one book after another. The money his father sent from Germany was not enough to buy all the books he wanted, but he had befriended a literature teacher who lent him volumes of poetry and novels.

He had fallen in love only once, he told me, with a girl in his high school class, but she had crushed him by marrying someone else. He started to study engineering at the university but grew restless and did not finish. Instead, he joined his father in Germany, where he worked as a laborer for several months. When he spoke of that period, he described his longing for home. Home was not the house his father had spent a lifetime building on the outskirts of Zagreb. Nor was it Rama. He had left his place of birth as little more than a child and been back only infrequently. Although he did sometimes think of the fine silt that flew through the summer air around the lake, home was something altogether less defined.

"In Germany," his father had told him when he was a boy, "they have rules. Not to mention in places like America. There, no one can come and drag you away because of who you support or what you say."

Stjepan had briefly considered going to New York, where he had cousins, but he just as quickly discarded the idea. Instead, he envisioned a home whose possibilities had not yet been realized: a combination of what he knew and what could yet be.

He read Gundulić, dog-earing certain pages. He would quote the poet's verses to me: "Oh dear, sweet freedom, no one ever truly loves you nor knows your blessedness, who has not lost you."

Meeting him was like being given a key, and with it I unlocked several mysteries. It was an insight into the world from which my father had come. And Stjepan was the closest I ever got to the bodies in the ground.

"Of course I was frightened," he would answer me, hunching his shoulders somewhat defensively.

I once met a mother who proudly showed me a picture of her missing son. When people die or disappear, I had quickly realized, they fail to age. The man had been a year older than I was in 1991, the year he vanished.

"Yes," I confirmed. "He's very handsome."

"Just right for you," she said.

STJEPAN WAS eleven years older than I, but he never called me *mala.*

On the night we drove up to the radio tower, when we came back to my building, he stopped the car and took my face in his hands. I was surprised by his thirst, and by the fact that I wanted to be emptied like a glass bottle.

He had a nice taste, and it reminded me of the hill overlooking the city. I looked over my shoulder, afraid of relatives and neighbors flooding the street or watching from their windows. He misunderstood my retreat, and he sat back, blinking rapidly. He apologized. "I've forgotten how to behave like a human being."

I put a hand on his arm and undid my seat belt. I inched over until my arms encircled his middle and my chin rested on his shoulder. I remembered how he described himself as a man who had been living in a zoo. He had wandered through wild and godforsaken places, he told me. And had forgotten certain fundamental rules.

"*Što?*" he inquired softly, his voice shaking, unable to meet my eyes. "What?"

I was so certain that I could take the dark out for both of us.

IN THE DREAM, I am digging out my brother. He is perfectly preserved beneath the dirt, wholly intact. But his skin is pale and rigid, and his face has an appearance I do not recognize from the familiar pantheon of his expressions.

Sometimes it is my parents, or Judita. Increasingly it is Stjepan. Sometimes it is all of them together, and I have been left behind. There is no one left to tell.

SOMETHING HAD BEEN NAGGING at me since returning to Croatia, and in the autumn I climbed the steep hill that led to the Bosnian embassy. I explained at the desk that I wanted to speak to someone about my work in Bosnia. The man who manned the reception desk looked dumbly from my passport to my face.

A few moments later I was ushered into an office where a perspiring diplomat with a nervous smile sat behind a desk. He stood while I sat, and he offered me coffee, which I declined.

I told him about the exhumations and the site. I explained

about the workers who were present daily. This was the point I wanted to make, sitting primly across from him, my hands folded in my skirt. The words came in a flood, and I was relieved to let them out. When I finished, he was staring at me uncertainly. It occurred to me that he thought me insane.

"Do you understand?" I told him. "It isn't right."

He looked down at the pad of paper in front of him, then back at me. He nodded.

"I just thought you should know." I rose, and he stood as well.

"Thank you," he said, nodding again. "Thank you very much. I will see what I can do."

There is nothing you can do, I thought. But now you know.

Outside on the street, the sun shone. I descended into the heart of the city, past neat gardens enclosed by ornate iron gates. I descended past huge trees that had flung out their now nearly naked branches in triumph and stretched their roots until they cracked the sidewalk.

IT WAS EVENING when I heard his car. The sun had buried itself in the abandoned buildings of the Kraš chocolate factory across the street, and the lamps had just come on. I went to the balcony windows and watched him park the white Renault that had borne us up the serpentines of Sljeme. I had turned off the lights in my room, and I waited for him in the twilight, listening to reedy sounds from a radio. When he emerged from his car, he raised his face. He was smiling as he walked to my front door.

There is a selfishness to love. Something that tricks the self into believing that the slate can be wiped clean, that the dead will stand meekly by and forfeit their haunting of us. That they will be evicted like the sun dislodges shadow.

He hummed something as he approached, a few notes whose volume was amplified by a street where nothing else moved. I tried to identify the melody for a moment, before walking out from the darkness of my apartment to meet him.

MY FATHER has an attachment to wind. And the open spaces through which it runs full speed like a madwoman. And if wind were, indeed, a madwoman, I believe he would have happily invited her home to live with us.

His is a double-sided obsession: American wind, and the wind *over there*.

In his adopted country, he has turned his face into the soft wind that rolls off the Chesapeake Bay in the summer and the freezing one that blows along the winter coast of Maine. He has stood at the foot of the Black Hills, hands shoved deep in his pockets, shivering as the wind pierced his nylon jacket.

The summer I was twelve, he and my mother bought a camper and took us on a cross-country trip that lasted two months. Irritable and hot, my brother and I complained from the hills of Kentucky to the grim dustiness of Arizona's Navajo Reservation. We drove on until we saw the bright sunlight on waves off the coast of northern California. My father, contentious until then, grew suddenly at ease with the gusts that carried spray up the sheer cliffs.

You had to see this country, our father tells us whenever we joke about the trip now. *I fought hard enough to get here. You had to see it.*

We returned to Virginia with the windows rolled down, air moving freely through our station wagon and depositing gritty layers of every state onto the floor.

Then there is the wind that blows only *over there*. The *maestral*, which sighs in the evenings, lifting strands of hair and making them float as if you were underwater. A *jugo* is a warm wind that comes from the south, bringing debris to the shore. The mightiest is the *bura*, a cold wind from the north that can blow with such ferocity that bridges and roads are closed. A *bura* can lash Herzegovina's hills as well, bringing a cold that sinks its teeth into bone. It is the cleanest of winds, whisking stale sky away and replacing it with air so pure that its crystal brightness hurts the eyes. But while it blows, it attacks shutters, roofs, and windows and makes sounds like human suffering.

My father was forever opening doors and creating drafts at home. Two ceiling fans and an assortment of smaller, upright fans created wind year-round. Our mother learned to sleep with a steady draft above her head.

In Dalmatia he frequently slept outside on the terrace of whatever cottage we rented, watching the white tears of the Milky Way over his head. On some nights the wind blew hard enough to churn the sea into peaks, on other nights not at all. My brother and I invariably found him in the morning, curled up on an air mattress, snoring lightly. To this day he is uncomfortable in the prison of enclosed spaces.

Love of wind is not my father's only eccentricity.

He is ill at ease answering the questions of strangers, and he becomes unnerved when people telephone as part of surveys.

He is forever accusing my mother of saying too much to people she has just met.

"You don't know who they are!" he argues. "You always give too much information!"

He does not enter into conversations about religion with strangers, and he has sent more than a few Mormons packing. Beyond our immediate family circle he is uncomfortable forming attachments to others.

For years, almost every letter my brother and I wrote to Santa contained a common denominator: a dog. We imagined him large and brown, with floppy ears. He bore a striking resemblance to Timothy, from our favorite bedtime mystery books, *The Famous Fives*, which my mother had brought with her when she emigrated from England. But he flatly refused every request that we made. In the beginning he proffered excuses such as, "We don't live in the country. It would be cruel for the dog." Or, "Dogs are unhygienic." We considered this a great injustice and pointed out school friends with dogs that seemed both happy and hygienic. But he was adamant, and as the conniving sweetness of our faces turned into sulky whines, he would slam his fist on the table. "No dog!" he would shout. "No dog!"

But then when I was in high school, my parents bought a sturdy Dalmatian puppy. He had silky ears and a wet, warm nose. He romped with the entire family but reserved a special love for my father, who would stroke his head and feed him scraps from the kitchen.

"We should have bought one years ago," I often chided him. "Why didn't we?"

My father waved his hand at me. "You and your brother were fragile. You buy a dog, and the dog dies."

"But that's no reason not to get one," I persisted. "That doesn't even make sense."

He went on as if he had not heard me. "Dogs die, and then you and your mother . . ."

I looked at him expectantly.

"I can't stand the crying."

Our mother claimed that his reluctance had to do with past experience and the war, which also explained why he cannot bring himself to throw anything away. When I was growing up, our basement, attic, and garage became so overcrowded with the various items he hoarded that maneuvering through them was all but impossible.

"You never know when you might need something," he insisted, and we watched the piles of assorted articles most people throw into their garbage cans grow into towers and, inevitably, topple.

But the gravest crime in our household was wasting food, especially bread. Rather than throw out stale pieces, my father would run them under water and put them into the toaster oven.

He would tell us, chewing thoughtfully, "You can't even tell it's not fresh."

I would make a face.

"Don't be a princess," he would tell me. "The hungry eat anything."

There were days when we knew to stay out of his way. He would shout, banging from one end of the house to the other and upsetting furniture. Only rarely did my mother get angry in return, once coming close to throwing a cast-iron pot at his head. On only a few occasions did she weep, standing at the kitchen sink up to her elbows in soapy water as she scrubbed and rinsed the dinner dishes. Huge, silent tears rained into the dishwater, and her shoulders twitched. My father, seated at the dining-room table, from where he could see her back, would be shocked by the knowledge that she was crying, and his anger would suddenly dissipate like steam through an open window as he rose from the table to go to her.

"I'm sorry," he would tell her quietly.

"Why are you so angry?" she would demand.

The expression on his face would be one of bafflement, as if his anger were something of which he had been unaware.

"It's who I am," he would say finally. "It's where I'm from."

"That's no excuse."

"No," he would always agree.

"You made a choice when you married me, when we had children."

There would be an oddly hypnotic moment in which both stood still, and then he would break the spell by nodding. It was the strangest of dances, one that kicked dark earth from the ground and created a cloud that hovered over our house, and each time the air grew dark, the edges of the past came suddenly into view.

As I grew older, I began asking questions about that past. I wanted to know what my parents' childhoods were like, and about people in the yellow-tinted family photographs. My mother, I noted early, was an open book, and my brother and I reveled in bedtime stories from her own childhood. Like Heidi, we imagined her, running down the mountains with edelweiss in her hair, talking to goats. And she has an entirely different makeup from my father's, as if the granite of her mountains were actually softer than the limestone of Herzegovina, of which my father had once said, *It eats at the feet and doesn't stop until it devours the heart.*

We listened to stories about my mother balancing on her *Onkel's* shoulders in a swan boat he had constructed for a village feast day. When her mother remarried and our mother was forced to leave her Austrian mountains forever, we learned of the gray wetness of England's industrial north.

But my father was not as forthcoming. "Stories." He would shake his head ruefully. "You always want stories."

Now, as then, my father prefers films. De Sica's *The Bicycle Thief* and *The 400 Blows* by Truffaut. Anything by Bergman. He considers Kurosawa's films masterpieces—especially *Rashomon*, in which a man, his wife, and a thief relate three different versions of one event.

"But which was true?" I asked curiously.

"None and all," he responded, explaining the film's greatest truth.

And still I pressed him, an eleven-year-old archaeologist in search of the past.

"To be a woman over there was to suffer," he would tell me cryptically. "To suffer abuse, to be alone. To outlive the people who should have outlived you."

"Your mother?" I would ask tirelessly. "What was she like?"

And pain would burn like a low gas lamp in his eyes when he described her. He rarely talked about her lightly, and he finished each story with the soft refrain, "It was so long ago."

AT FIFTEEN, I played Rimsky-Korsakov's "Song of India" over and over on our old upright piano. Out of my entire repertoire, it was my parents' favorite, which was somewhat odd because the way I played it had nothing to do with the way it was written. I changed tempos and notes randomly. I pedaled when I should not, and played softly when I should have played loudly. My parents listened to my playing after dinner, my father sitting on the couch reading the newspaper and my mother washing the dishes with the kitchen door open.

My father dozed on the couch, awakening at intervals to listen to the notes. My mother would come up behind me in the living room and lay her hands on my shoulders. They smelled of lemon soap and rubber gloves. I could not bear to play that song for my teacher, who was a stickler for form and discipline. But it was this song, with its tender symmetry, that my mother hummed under her breath, gathering my heavy dark hair absentmindedly into a ponytail.

My parents have spent a lifetime explaining things to me. *We live precisely because we will die. We eat the fruit, skin and all. We crack the seeds open and eat out their white centers. We lick all the juice from our fingers and under our nails. There is nothing else we can do.*

DRESSED IN A WHITE SLIP, I let Stjepan through the front door after the students renting the room next to mine had gone to sleep. I placed my index finger to my lips, and he smiled, leaning forward to kiss me. He followed me down the hallway to my room, and I closed the door behind us.

"Why did your father leave?" he asked later, as we lay together on my bed beneath a picture my uncle Mile had painted of *Stari most* and a copy of the *Madonna of the Streets*.

"Political reasons," I explained to him. "Why did people usually leave?"

"Does he want to come back?"

I thought for a moment. "He wants very badly to come back. A piece of him is always here, but . . ."

Stjepan was looking at me expectantly.

"But he's so used to life in America now. It would be a difficult adjustment."

This troubled him. Stjepan had, after all, fought for the right of people like my father to come back permanently, to reclaim their lives.

But my father's life was elsewhere, I explained.

Finally he nodded and smiled. "Well, he was smart. He went to America and had a smart daughter like you . . ."

I grinned. "I am pretty smart."

"A real brain," he told me, tickling me.

"But are you saying I wouldn't have been smart if he had stayed here?" I asked him, laughing and batting at his hands.

"You wouldn't have been born if he had stayed here," he reminded me, growing suddenly serious. "You would be smart, but in a different way. In a meaner way."

Stjepan admitted that he wanted to finish a degree at the university. He had earned some of the highest grades in his high school class and had started studying engineering at the university.

"What happened?"

"Not every place is like America," was his terse reply. His eyes clouded, and he looked away from me. He shrugged his shoulders. "Later I went to Germany, and then the war came."

"You could go back now," I suggested quietly.

"Maybe"—he grinned—"but I think it's too late. Besides, I like my job, and they let me study English at the base."

"And you get to practice it with me," I teased him. "And I am a very good teacher."

"Yes." He closed his eyes and began to kiss my wrist. "And anyway, I remember all the important things."

I raised my eyebrows.

"Like poetry." His eyes opened. "I remember poetry."

"Recite some," I ordered, settling back against the pillows.

And he lowered his mouth to my ear and began to whisper. Russian poets, Croatian poets, American love songs.

STJEPAN KNEW what I had done, however briefly, in Bosnia. And I told him how upset my father had been when he learned about it. They are the only two people I've never been able to explain the details of those weeks to.

"What did he say," Stjepan asked, "when you did tell him?"

I grimaced. "That he had gone to America so we could be safe, and not so we'd turn around and do foolish things."

Stjepan laughed. "Precisely."

For my father, America represented safety as well as freedom. Of all he has achieved in his life, the birth of his children as Americans is what he is most proud of.

One childhood summer, when my brother and I had endured the gauntlet of relatives and hours of misery on car trips, we discovered a new and entertaining game for the drive from Sarajevo to the sea. We whispered in the backseat and constructed our plan. The next time a car overtook us, we unrolled the windows to shout at the passengers.

"America!" we yelled, but the car was going too fast, and the occupants had not heard us. I remember that my father swerved and looked at us sternly in the rearview mirror. We were simultaneously petulant and remorseful, each sinking down into the seat. But then a laugh escaped him, and he looked at our mother. He was soon informing us of upcoming cars about to pass.

And each time the anonymous people passed, we hung out of the car windows, one on either side, yelling, "America!" Some smiled and waved at us, and some ignored us with marked concentration. Some shook their fists. One farmer spit into the dirt as we passed.

"I hope we don't get arrested," my mother said, looking back at us, getting us to sing a song, quieter and within the confines of our car.

She was surprised that our father had not become angry. We could see it in her face. He was so careful each time we came back, so conscious of passing anonymously through the country that still kept dossiers and files on him. He avoided certain cousins who would drink too much *rakija* and become involved in animated political discussions in public places.

Driving from Zagreb, we took a wrong turn and came upon a military installation. The guard at the gate carried a submachine gun and leaned an angry face into our car, demanding identification.

My father pretended not to understand him, handing him his American passport, which nonetheless revealed his place of birth. But the fingers that gripped the steering wheel did so with such intensity that we could see the blue veins standing out on the backs of his hands. The guard finally took down our license plate number and waved us away disgustedly, knowing that the white-lipped man at the steering wheel could understand exactly what he was saying. That he had been one of the lucky ones to leave the shit-State behind.

"America! America!" we shouted, our voices growing hoarse. We were also surprised by our father's good mood, although we did not understand what caused it. He roared with laughter, and we all laughed, delighted by his high spirits. Looking at our mother, he said, "Who would've thought that one day I would be driving down these roads with my two children screaming 'America!' out the windows?" We could see his smile in the rearview mirror.

AFTER MY FLATMATES moved out and I had the apartment to myself, I would let Stjepan in through the front door, but still we did not speak. We littered the hallway with our shirts and the black elastic that held my hair in a ponytail.

In the living room, I would undo the canvas khaki belt that cinched his fatigues and drape it over an arm of the couch. In my room, he would close the door and sit on the edge of an easy chair, drawing me to him, his arms around my waist and his clean-shaven face pressed against my belly. He would hold me for a moment and breathe, and then he would get up and we would continue undressing.

Outside, the sun or the moon was always shining, and the leaves from the tree that graced the front of the building on Trpimirova Street made low, soft sounds through the open windows.

• • •

THE ARMY required Stjepan to speak to a psychologist every few months as a matter of course for all veterans still on active duty.

He had nightmares. He also tapped his foot almost uncontrollably. He seemed unaware of this tic, and once, in a café, I placed my hand on his knee under the table to still it. He was not seriously wounded in the war, he told me—as if through some mysterious oversight he had stayed whole. As if God were saving him for something and had cloaked him in invisibility so that he could walk upright without fear of bullets. But his friends had died on all sides of him like flies.

"I'm in pieces," he told me once. At first I was unsure I had heard correctly.

"Little pieces," he repeated. "But I'm here." His tone was more tired than gratified.

It might have been sheer stubbornness that saw him through, I realized, or faith. He had worn a rosary around his neck, under his fatigues. And he had fingered it by the light of days that he would forever remember as covered in dirt and blood.

I MET JOSEF FINCI'S SISTER NELA for the first time during those months, at the Lavoslav Švarc Home for the Elderly. She embraced me and urged me to sit down at a table in the room she shared with her second husband, Bencen.

"My son has brought me photographs from Sarajevo," Nela told me in excitement, winking. "You will see how beautiful I was in those days."

Her heart was like a young girl's. Her thoughts took off in three different directions at once, but there was very little that she missed. The hands were the rainbow colors of an elderly woman's hands, opals spreading under the skin. She was about the age my grandmother would be.

Nela seated me at the table, asking, "What should I call you?"

I smiled, telling her that my parents gave me two names, Courtney and Angela. The second is easier for people who speak no English, but I claim both names as my own.

Nela nodded. "Angela."

When she learned that I spoke Spanish, she switched to Ladino. But it was confusing for me, like trying to braid, holding three languages in two hands. I was groping with my Spanish vocabulary, trying to remember which words were closer to Italian. Work was not *trabajar*, but *lavorar*, and there were strange Slavicisms thrown in. Child was *ižiko*, close to the Spanish for *hijito*, little son, but with a Slavic twist. We switched to Croatian, and Nela handed me a bottle of thick, sweet brandy.

"My eyes," she said sadly, indicating that I should pour. I realized that she was almost blind.

Nela was full of questions. Did I want to stay in Zagreb? What were my long-term plans? Were my parents angry that I lived so far from them?

I laughed. "They live far from me."

"Don't you want to return to America?"

I shrugged. "I love America," I explained to Nela, "but America is dangerous." I thought of Washington, D.C., its crime, its drugs, and its homeless. I tried to explain, unsure how much an elderly European woman could grasp.

"If I were to have children," I told her honestly, "I would be scared to raise them in Washington."

Nela chuckled. "Where is it safe?" she wanted to know. "In Israel people put bombs in buses and shoot at little girls on school trips. And Sarajevo . . ." Her voice trailed off, and she shook her head.

I filled the two glasses carefully. The syrupy liquid ran from the bottle lip down the paper on the side of the bottle. I trapped it against my thumb. It stained the pad and pooled in the print. My thumb was a mystery. My brother and I both have a genetically rare print, a double sworl, and I considered it now, stained red.

I realized that Nela was saying something about my grand-mother. She was tall, very tall.

"Yes," I told her, "my father has told me that. She was even taller than I am."

"Yes, yes. Tall." She was lost in thought for a moment, and we sipped the brandy.

"Do you know how my brother died?" Nela's eyes were wet. She was grasping for words.

I nodded, forgetting that she could not see.

"He was killed with a machine gun, against the wire fence of the camp. It happened in the last days of the war."

"Yes," I told her quietly, "I have heard that." His family be-lieves that he was killed during a camp uprising.

Nela shook her head, and I became suddenly aware that her blind eyes were focused on me, as if the tears in them created prismatic lenses through which she could make out the features of my face. "I lost them all," she said. "My parents, my sister and her baby, my brother." Her voice was a loud whisper.

She brought out a photograph album. The cover was a floral print. She opened it to the first page, a portrait of her parents.

Another woman from the nursing home came in to sit beside her. "And where is Josef?" Nela asked the woman. "Where is my brother?"

"I didn't know Josef," the woman reminded her. "Is this him?" It was a picture from when he graduated from high school, shot in profile. His eyebrows were thick and arched high above a slender face.

"And me." Her finger pointed to a young face.

"Yes." She was beautiful, I agreed. "My father told me you were very pretty," I said.

Nela seemed pleased. She paused a moment, then went on. "Josef and your grandmother truly loved one another."

Our words were an exchange of gifts.

"What are your plans for the future? Do you have a boy-friend? What about your studies?" She was very interested. She closed the album and smiled. Life creaked forward.

She related a story about her teenage granddaughter, who was evacuated from Sarajevo in 1992, when the war began, and went to live in Israel. When the girl was very little, around eight, she had a crush on a boy in her class. She wore pretty dresses and shoes with shiny buckles, but to no avail. The boy would not walk home with her or even talk to her.

"I wanted to shake that little boy very hard," Nela said with a little smile, "when I saw her so small and disappointed. And now?" She had an intent expression. Balkan storytellers always have an underlying message, and she was regarding me past the filminess of her irises. "I was in Israel a few months ago to visit, and I asked my granddaughter how things were with her now that she is a grown woman. And what do you think?"

I shook my head, waiting.

"She told me, 'Love always disappoints me.' " Nela returned to me. "What is your opinion?"

I laughed. "On love?"

She looked at me expectantly.

I thought of his face. I thought of the sturdiness of his legs entwined with mine. I had tested him once, when a camp commander from Jasenovac was facing extradition to Croatia to stand trial for crimes in the Second World War.

"Poor man," I had heard some people say, "so old and frail. They should just leave him alone."

"Maybe they should just leave him alone," I parroted experimentally to Stjepan to see what he would say. "He's just an old man."

And he had been silent for a long moment before responding evenly, "He's an old man who did evil things." And my relief was so immediate that I threw my arms around his neck, and he looked at me oddly.

Now I thought of the fact that I had found him through the smell of the dead, which still followed me everywhere.

"Love is a strange country," I told Nela finally, and rose to leave. It was almost lunchtime, and she caught my hand when I bent to kiss her cheek good-bye.

"Tell me if you find it," she said. There was a twinkle in her eye, and something else. Something indefinable and infinitely sad.

"Find?"

"That land." She was regarding the photograph album. "That place where the children are safe."

I left, closing the door behind me. I could hear the clinking of the tiny brandy glasses as they were cleared from the table. A woman stopped me in the hall. There had been a steady stream of visitors, friends of Nela's and other residents curious to learn who the young visitor was.

"Are you Nela's granddaughter?" she wanted to know. "Are you a Jew?"

I smiled. "No."

When she heard that I was American, she smiled. "I was in America last year. I went to visit my son. It's very cold in America."

I said good-bye to her and retrieved my passport from the visitors' office, where I had checked in an hour before. I walked down the stairs of the residence. Spread out in front of the building was a large lawn with some trees. Spring had come, and the trees were squeezing out tiny, hard buds. They were green and sour looking as new things are. When I reached the gravel path that led to the iron gate, two cats passed, running toward the home. They paid no attention to me. They were fat and sleek, and their tails stood straight up. They had been sunning themselves in the yard, and as they passed, I caught the scent of sunlight on clean fur.

But I was remembering something, not really concentrating on the path or the trees or the cats. My family was sitting at the table. It was Christmas, and we were making ornaments for the tree, each of us with newspaper spread out beneath the clay stars and snowmen. My mother was telling us about Christmas in Austria. Her *Tante* would send her into the other room while the Christmas Angel decorated the tree. When it was finished, the doors were flung open, and the tree would be shining with candles and tinsel.

Dad smiled. Yes, it had been something like that for them,

too, in Sarajevo. And there was the little bell to tell you the angel was leaving and that you could go in. And the tree would be shining, its boughs heavy with handcrafted ornaments.

Mother looked up. She has a tenderness for sentimental objects. "What happened to all the ornaments?" she asked.

He looked down at the star that he was painting. His hand was shaking.

She asked again, tentatively.

"Like my mother and Josef," he told her quietly. "They are dust."

SOMETIMES I SHARED STORIES about my family with Stjepan. And although he told me stories about his childhood, he rarely spoke about the war. I noticed that when he did, his voice was as tightly controlled as my father's was when discussing my grandmother. For me, Stjepan's war was an imagined landscape in which he was as light as air and smoke, his body a thousand particles of dust somehow kept together in the wind. I would imagine him scouting, walking down a dark road in a dead town; then I pushed the thought from my mind.

When we made love, he hummed under his breath. It was somewhere between melody and sighing. It would give me goose bumps and send a current through my rib cage.

"Do you know you do that?" I asked him once, afterward, out of curiosity.

He was embarrassed, but I told him I liked it.

You are my reward, I thought, watching him pretend to sleep. He was observing me through eyes almost completely shut, but the ghost of a smile was playing at the corners of his mouth, and I knew that in a minute he would give up and move close to me again. The thing I have been searching for.

IN THE DREAM, my left arm is gone. I am looking through the dirt to find it, scrabbling at half capacity. I feel no pain, just pathetic emptiness and the numb weight of that phantom appendage. Other parts of me start to disappear, as if I am being slowly erased. When I am only my right hand, I waken.

"MY AUNTS have their spies everywhere," I teased Stjepan the day after my dream.

When I stumbled over to their apartment after waking, they had told me about a light-haired *vojnik* who had been seen entering my building on some evenings and leaving in the mornings.

"Have you seen the soldier?" Aunt Iva asked me as I drank tea at the kitchen table in their apartment.

I concentrated on stirring a teaspoon of sugar into the hot liquid, watching as the crystals melted in the heat. I shrugged. "What does he look like?"

"Oh, Zorica said he's light-haired and handsome." Her eyes lit up. "He is exceptionally tall and wears an officer's uniform."

I smiled into my tea. My aunts were romantics, or their neighbor was. Stjepan was my height and wore inconspicuous clothes.

"You'd tell us if you had a sweetheart, wouldn't you?" Aunt Iva burst out, and it occurred to me that the same neighbor must have craned to see which buzzer the *vojnik* had pressed.

"Of course I would."

This seemed to satisfy her.

I went into the next room to greet Aunt Ljubica. Each time I visited, her face grew thinner and whiter. Her silver hair was thick with a startling metallic sheen. The chestnut color of her dyed hair, and the transitory symbol of a previous life, had long ago grown out. I had watched it inch its way along the pillow until reaching the edges. Then one day, after Katja had cut Ljubica's hair, it was gone altogether.

But her eyes were like twin pieces of basalt, the only point of darkness in the entire bed. She watched me, bemused. A little smile played at her lips, and I wondered if she could smell him on my skin. I smiled at her, as if we shared a secret.

STJEPAN USUALLY came to the apartment after work, still dressed in his fatigues. The greens and browns were almost faded to gray, the material worn in some places so that the cloth was almost threadbare. He would hold me in the hallway of the apartment for some time, perfectly still, before I led him into my room. I would inhale the smell of him: sometimes he had showered, and I could smell the soap on his skin and in his hair; sometimes he had come directly without stopping for a shower. He would apologize for not having bathed. When I inhaled, he did not smell dirty, but tired. He liked to rest his head on my abdomen, and I would stroke his hair. Sometimes he fell asleep like that.

He checked his gun at the base each night before leaving, and I was glad that he did not bring it into the apartment. I once asked him the make, and he gave me a strange look. The name he said meant nothing to me, and I promptly forgot it.

"You carried it on the front line?"

He nodded.

"A knife too?"

He closed his eyes. "Yes."

And the rosary. I had seen it around his neck in a picture from the first year of the war. He was dressed in a uniform so new and stiff it seemed to keep him upright.

"You look so young here," I had told him.

And frightened.

MY BEDROOM WAS FILLED with ancient memorabilia. There was heavy wooden furniture that Aunt Ljubica's husband, Ante, had made years ago, before the Second World War.

In Herzegovina it was tradition for women to have a hope chest of ornately hand-carved wood, filled with the things she would take into her marriage. Sometimes, when Stjepan and I lay against the thick cotton sheets, I imagined that I smelled cedar.

The books that lined the shelves were ancient and dusty. Some had belonged to Uncle Mile, and one or two were my father's from before he had left. Some were my aunts' books. I laughed myself into hysterics one day when I found one printed in the 1930s delineating "the proper and respectable role of a young lady in the Catholic Church."

Stjepan and I spent a lot of time in bed, surveying the room and listening to the sounds from the street. In summer, children played under the balcony, and in winter, frost formed an icy lace on the windowpanes. When we made love, his hunger was so deep that it alternately elated and frightened me. "Please," he would whisper into my ear, humming under his breath.

As weeks went by, I buried Bosnia inside him.

But I artfully ignored the odd day when he would not materialize. Or the moments when he was detached from me and sad. I willed them away by teasing him, tickling him, or putting my hands on either side of his head and leaning my face until our noses were tip to tip. An Eskimo kiss, I had told him, and he chuckled at the idea.

"Where do you go?" I asked him once.

"When?"

"When you're with me but you're really somewhere else."

A smile spread slowly across his face, and he looked away. But I had seen the almost hurt look in his eyes.

With and yet removed, I thought when I realized later that he never answered me.

DURING THE WAR, he finally told me, he had continued to believe in some idea of justice. But the necessity of suffering had been buried miles and miles beneath the crusted blood, the oozing faces of his dying friends. The fear had set in slowly. And the opposite of fear, which was even worse. Lying awake in the night, emotionless. Dying tonight, tomorrow, all the same. Eyes refusing to dilate, suspended in the dull thudding glue of that strange universe. Resoluteness. Worse, resignation. A hard, amorphous skin that did not let the sunlight in.

One year out of the war, and sometimes the eyes that looked at me were flat. His disappearances grew in length and frequency. He would be gone for days at a time, then reappear unexpectedly. I would be walking on the main square and turn a second later to see him behind me, only to lose sight of him when a streetcar slid between us. Or in Maksimir Park, where I would walk off into the trees, I would hear someone following close behind me. But every time I stopped and turned, the rustling sound would stop as well. Backtracking at high speed, sometimes running, I never managed to find my shadow.

When Aunt Iva learned of my walks, she warned me, wagging a cautionary finger, "Don't go deep into the woods."

And I, a modern-day Gretel who would not listen to sense, grinned at her.

"All sorts of things can happen to a woman," she said with a furrowed brow.

When Stjepan reappeared, we never discussed the interim periods, but I had the sensation that I was being punished. All my sins were gathering, and the time for retribution had come. Among them: arrogance, narcissism, and self-pity. The belief that I could change things, and the memory of trying to see a person through a winter of war. I never told Stjepan about Antonio, or the lie of love that I had told him in my letters. I shivered often in those days, wondering what form recompense would take.

One evening when Stjepan was particularly taciturn, I gave him a playful shake. "What's wrong?" I asked him. I had not seen him in a week.

At first he insisted nothing was amiss. He rested his head on my thigh. He closed his eyes and opened them a moment later, the pupils dilating widely in the blue irises.

"What is it?" I repeated. A chill had started in my spine, but I pushed the feeling back.

"I'm so fucked up," he told me finally, groaning and turning away. "I'm so fucked up, and I ruin everything."

"No!" I almost cried the word out, and I cradled his head. "No, you're not. We're here. We're together now. Nothing else matters."

Not the war, not the dead, not the dreams, I thought foolishly. But even as I showered his face with kisses, I knew that the past had edges that could not be so easily navigated.

When I was a teenager, my father often told us that he had dreams of his intact childhood, and they were a territory strangely untouched by the war and what had come afterward. When he awoke, it would take him several minutes to remember where he was. Then, I believe, the intervening years would come at him in a flood.

I remember that when he worked the night shift at the Voice of America, he would sleep until ten, or until our children's voices roused him from those dreams, populated by the ranks of his ghosts. He would come down the stairs to find our mother sitting in the garden in a lawn chair, a book lying across her lap, watching my brother and me as we ran in circles in the grass.

Mine were still not nightmares. I continued to be an observer, for all my searching and loss of limbs. But I had daymares, strange moments when I would remember details.

A bullet embedded in a vertebra, the dull metal a shock in all that whiteness.

Or a ragged hole that pierces the aerodynamics of a scapula. Holding the thing up to the sun, watching how the light comes through the section of intact bone, warm and comforting, like a piece of amber glass. Just the hole, the shocking part. The sun glaring at me through it, washing me in the light of that hole.

THEN ONE MONTH I did not menstruate when I should have. A week went by, but I told no one. Stjepan had disappeared, and I was waiting for him to resurface. Stress could disrupt my cycle, I knew. At twenty-four, I felt too young for a baby.

When I next saw him, the way he filled the threshold of my door was a relief. But his face was ashen.

"What's wrong?" I asked him in alarm.

"Nothing," he told me dully. But he would not meet my eyes.

Whatever I carried in my belly—whether it was a thing capable of dreaming or a bunched-up ache of months—I could not let it go at that. I looked at him angrily. Like an expert interrogator, I baited him until he cracked.

Their senses have been deadened, Judita had once told me. *They are compelled to fuck the darkness back.* And the truth was that I had been warned many times. Fucking the darkness back was exactly what he had been doing, with other women. And one of them had told him she was pregnant.

I looked at him in stunned silence. "How could you?" I said in English, starting to cry. I hit him, and he flinched, but quickly withdrew into a shell, leaving the strange, lifeless eyes behind.

"The war . . ."

"The war is an excuse for everything!" I sobbed, the tears now soaking my white nightgown.

I imagined him with an unknown woman in some strange

bed. Not knowing what she looked like, I pictured them as anatomy-class skeletons, fitted together with wire. I imagined the click and clack of their bones. Oh, how merrily the living dead can fuck.

"You've polluted it," I shouted. "Can't you see that?"

I moved away when he reached for me.

"Admit it," I told him, forcing my tears back and clawing at my cheeks to dry them. "You were fucked up even before the war."

He did not know how to answer me. He had never heard me curse, and I could see my vulgarity had surprised him.

After he left, the woman who lived across the hall knocked on the door to see if I needed help. "No," I managed to say through the shut door. She went away, and I curled into a fetal position on the linoleum floor in the hall. I allowed myself the tiniest circumference and slept.

WHATEVER HAD BEEN INSIDE ME died the next morning. I looked at the petals of blood on the bathroom's white porcelain with dismay. Not you, too, I wanted to tell the thing that never really was.

I needed a project, and I started to repaint the apartment, attacking the walls in a frenzy. Standing in the kitchen, I rubbed the walls with sandpaper wrapped around a wooden block. Tiny pieces of white dust spun and pasted themselves to my skin and hair. When the doorbell rang, I was barefoot on top of the kitchen table, working on the ceiling, covered in fine flakes.

When I let him into the apartment, he looked at me in

amazement, taking one of my hands in his and turning it over. It was rubbed raw, and the fingernails were broken. I snatched it away.

He went over to the walls to inspect my work. "You're showing off," he told me mildly. "You think you can do everything on your own."

He touched the wall, which was still thick with paint. "This needs to be sanded down more. I'll show you."

I turned my back on him and washed my face and hands at the kitchen sink. I brushed past him on my way to the bathroom.

He waited outside the bathroom door as I sat on the edge of the bathtub splashing water on my arms and legs. I peeled off my clothes. My nightgown was hanging on the back of the door, and I slipped it over my head. When I emerged, he was sitting on my bed.

"Fuck you," I said in English.

He winced but was quiet.

"Fuck you," I repeated.

"Don't," he said softly.

"You think you are the only one with pain?" I spat the words at him.

He began to say something about the war, but I had stopped listening. I thought of Bosnia. Some of the bodies had been of young boys, I wanted to tell him. "Children," I interrupted him. "I held the bodies of decomposed children in my hands."

He stared at me, then rose and tried to brush my tears away with his hands. He looked stricken, and he told me again, whitely, "I've ruined everything."

I pushed him toward the door.

"Let me spend the night," he pleaded, trying to pull me toward him. "Let's just fall asleep together."

I shook his hands off.

He left me in my white nightgown and bare feet, standing at the top of the apartment building stairs. He mustered some anger. It came from that growing, dark space inside. It was beginning to match the one that had started in me.

Bitch. I could see the thought written across his face as he went. *All I wanted to do was fall asleep with you.*

FOR MANY NIGHTS it seemed that the ability to remember my dreams had left the apartment with him. I was amnesiac at daybreak, conquering the gauntlet of night like a swimmer and throwing my body on the far bank in the morning. I would lie there for some time, panting and half submerged in the shallows of sleep. A low, dense fog descended like a curtain over the water behind me, and I would find suddenly that I had misplaced the dream. I spent desperate moments attempting to regain that fading landscape, but the more I strained, the farther the dream receded. In the few feet of water visible beyond my legs, smoke twisted and rose, but there were no heads of monsters or glowing eels. There were no fins that sliced through the inky water, nor waterlogged vines curling around my ankles. No bodies, no flesh.

But when I awoke, my heart would continue like a windup toy, carving a hole with its steady percussion. And my bones ached in their elaborate casing of skin, as if a child had scraped their flared ends against a rough pavement and then replaced them one by one, in half-pulverized form.

Then one morning I woke up crying. I had dreamed of the Cezners' garden in Sarajevo, which looked remarkably like our garden at home, with the addition of the ominous unexploded shell. In the dream, people were milling about.

During the last couple of days in the Tuzla morgue, it seemed that I had laid out hundreds of articles to be photographed. There were shoes whose soles had long ago come unhinged, and underwear that had been roughly sewn from other garments. There were hand-knit socks and sweaters, whose stitching showed a woman's touch. I imagined the women who made these things, who had sat long hours in half-light to clothe their families, and I held the objects in my hands. But the smell was something that clung to the fabric and to me. I could smell it even in my sleep.

In the dream, I recognized some of these men by their homespun shirts and sweaters. They were talking and laughing with people I knew. There were plates of food and glasses of wine, and I wove through them all. My father and uncle were there as little boys. Lado and his father were bringing armloads of intact wine bottles up from the cellar, and the workers from the morgue were there, beneath a tree.

My mother sat a short distance away, under one of the fruit trees in the garden, my brother, still a toddler, on her lap. She was reading aloud to him from *Goodnight Moon*, and his eyes were growing heavy. Every few moments she would stop to check whether he had fallen asleep, and then he would squirm to indicate that she should continue.

The shell was still in the ground, dangerously close to where they sat, and I knelt beside them. "Mom, please move," I told her, a catch in my voice. "I don't think it's very safe to sit here."

The light had faded, and she could barely read, so she got up, my sleeping brother in her arms, and made her way to the house. Her departure relieved me, and I rose as well, warily circling the piece of ugly metal. Stjepan was sitting on the other side of it, and he took my hand and pulled me down beside him. We sat watching the shell, and my heart was thundering so loud that I thought the vibrations would detonate it and carry us all into the sky, scattering us in little bloody pieces.

"Let's go, Stjepan," I pleaded. But he shook his head, and in the murky twilight I could see that he was crying soundlessly.

MY AUNTS knew something was wrong. They telephoned, but I had stopped answering. After a week I crawled over to their apartment, my eyes swollen.

"Our little girl!" they cried in some alarm.

And I began to laugh in spite of myself. In their apartment, with its assortment of ceramic plates and lace tablecloths, I was more Amazon than little.

They wanted details, and for once they forfeited their soap opera.

Their faces were earnest and worried. "We knew something was wrong." They led me into the living room, and Aunt Ljubica watched me silently from her grave of a bed, crying while I cried. I told them only the outline of the story.

"You got off easy, girl," Aunt Katja told me matter-of-factly. "Be glad you weren't married to him." She thought a moment and then added, "Think only about tomorrow, and bury yesterday."

But I shook my head.

• • •

I IMAGINED that his hand shook when he dialed my number.

"Hello?"

Nothing. He was trapped inside that ocean and could not speak to me.

"Stjepan." I found that I could recognize even his silences. "Please."

Sometimes I could hear him breathing over the telephone wire. On occasion he said a few words. Once, he asked me to meet him for coffee. We met at a café across from his base and sat in silence. He drove me home and pulled up in front of the building, but I bolted from the car without saying good-bye.

He told me that he could not bear to look into my eyes, but he continued to drive past my building. I believe he hoped to find me in the arms of other men, kissing under streetlamps. He would be out of his car in a flash. He would push me to the ground and stand over me and tell me that he hated me.

I saw his shadow all over Zagreb those days, in every doorway and in each passing car. At night I imagined him reading a book I had given him. Verses of love by a dead poet. I knew that he kept it in his desk drawer.

He had warned me once, *Leave the dead where they are*.

But I had never been able to leave the dead alone. Not where they lay in Bosnia's dry fields, not the young boy who died beneath the pear tree when my train was shelled, and certainly not my grandmother and Josef Finci.

Some weeks after seeing Stjepan for the last time, I finished painting the apartment. I had started full-time work, and the painting had gone slowly. Finishing it had become a minor obsession, and I devoted all my evenings and weekends to it.

I was hoping to surprise my aunts with my work, but when they saw it, they were infuriated.

"You had no right!" they shouted at me. "Why must you meddle in our affairs!"

The venom in their words shocked me, and I lost my temper. "I did it for you!" I shouted back at them.

"You think you know everything," they cried.

"I know plenty," I retorted.

"You know nothing!" They had drawn together like a wall and stood glaring at me.

I felt suddenly uneasy. "What don't I know?"

They fell silent.

"Go on, what don't I know?"

Aunt Katja looked at me bitterly. "You don't even know about your own grandmother."

I knew my grandmother's life like a book, inside and out. "My father told me everything!" I menaced them with my words. I knew about the war; I knew about Ante; I knew about Jasenovac. I had spent a lifetime getting to know her, my grandmother who was dead when I was born.

"Do you know that she killed herself?"

It was like being stabbed. The blade went in clean, and its metal took my breath away. "That's not true," I whispered. Then, like a child, "Take it back."

My grandmother had gone to America, but she had been unhappy. She'd returned to Croatia and died there of a stroke in 1968. I spat this chronology at Aunt Katja.

"Oh no, miss," she corrected. "She hanged herself." Angry tears were filling her eyes. "But she didn't die for another five years."

I ran from their apartment. I pushed open the front door

and barreled into the hallway. I knew that my grandmother had once lived in an apartment upstairs, in this same building, but I had never wandered into the gloom of the building's upper floors. I ran down the stairs, striking the walls with my fists as I went.

I MOVED OUT and did not tell my aunts where I was going. I refused to speak to them for months.

I could not bring myself to ask my father if it was true, because I knew that it was. I told him only that we had fought and that I could not go on living next door to them another moment.

They could not have chosen a more effective way to wound me. I had been imagining my grandmother's life since childhood. Old photographs and my father's stories gave her a frame, but I had added the flesh myself. And survival was the language I attributed to her, murmuring late at night to her living and her dying children. It was what had driven her out of Herzegovina. *Survival is a talent of women in our family*, Aunt Katja had said, trying to comfort me after Stjepan and I broke up.

"For what, then, did you survive?" I asked the black marble of my grandmother's Mirogoj tomb.

My aunts told me one more thing before I fled their apartment. My father had found her. He had come home one evening and found her, half dead.

"How could you?" I asked the chiseled letters of her name.

AUNT KATJA AND I eventually made peace with each other, and over the next year my anger ebbed. I accepted that I could never really know my grandmother. I could reconstruct the facts of her life and even find some truths in them, but the dead are lost, and it is not within our means to bring them back.

When I finally broached the subject with my father at the end of that year, he was upset. It was not that I knew how she died, but that I had carried the knowledge inside me for months.

"Those things fester," he chided. "You have to let them out into the light of day."

I remembered Dr. Peerwani's words when I saw my first decomposed body. *A body left in the sun for a few days returns to good, clean earth.*

"You kept those things in," I pointed out to my father. "You didn't talk about them."

My father looked at me as if seeing my adult face for the first time. "Ask me whatever you want to know. I'll tell you now."

HE BEGAN to make tapes for me about his childhood. I wrote out pages and pages of questions, but told him to answer only what he wanted.

When I received the tapes in the mail, I listened to them over and over. Sometimes I listened to make sure that I had written down dates and names correctly. But I also listened just to hear the timbre of my father's voice. It was as if my father were peeling accumulated layers of earth away to show me what had been lying underneath. Listening to one tape, I realized he was crying. He describes looking for Ante at Žuta Tabija, so sure that if he can just find his aunt's husband, he will be able to do something. But the unit has pulled out, and my father's mission has been in vain. The tape makes a click where he turned off the recorder, and it idles for a moment until his voice begins again, steadier than before. He describes other things.

But I go back to that click, listening to the wavering silence as if it can tell me more than his words, picturing my father seated at our dining-room table in Arlington. Picturing him at twelve, as soldiers and carts thunder around him, knowing that the affliction of those days will be without end.

LJUBICA

1996–1997

If I eavesdrop on the wind
I hear your voice.
If I look at death
I hear your song.

—*Jure Kaštelan, from "Parting"*

THE SKY above Ljubica's head is white. Such an uninterrupted, smooth white that she wonders how anything so featureless can exist in nature. Some of the
time she realizes that it is the whitewashed ceiling above her
bed and that she has been lying there for two years. It is in
these rare moments of lucidity when she picks up her arms,
wasted beyond recognition. She touches her face with her yellowed nails. Her left side has not functioned properly since the
stroke, but she can trace the contours of her face with her right
hand. Each time she makes the return voyage to Earth, realizing that the white is ceiling and that she is lying in the same
old apartment, cared for by her sisters, she finds new hollows in
her face.

For six years the television in the room where she lies has
shown news of the war. In the past two years it has shown the
aftermath, and she finds that the stroke prevents her from un-

tangling the threads of this war from that war. Her sisters prop her on one side so that she can see the nightly news and the reports of the dead and the missing.

A woman on the television is crying over her sons. Her face is paper and shadow as the television announcer relays their last known location, after which every trace of them was lost.

When Milošević's face comes onto the screen, or Šljivančanin's, or Karadžić's, her sisters mutter curses. Then comes the weather forecast, then sports. The news ends, and her sisters remove the pillows that have propped her up. A beauty contest or music festival is usually next, and she sinks back into her daze amid the music.

Sometimes she meets Ante in the white fog above the bed. But she is so old. How will he recognize her? Then she realizes that in the fog she is young again. She looks down at her hands, and the skin that covers them is pale and milky. Her breasts are full and high. Those moments are the ones she likes best. She stands on the side of the road, in the fog. She can hear his motorcycle and the little sidecar in which she traveled miles and miles with him. He goes faster, and she can hear him maneuver the turns. The motorcycle comes out of the fog and stops in front of her. He cuts the engine, and as she watches him, the anger melts away. Anger at him for leaving her and for dying. Anger that she did not die as well. Better that she had died on the road with him. What is a moment of death compared to a lifetime of it?

HER SISTERS ANNOY HER. They have always annoyed her. She has been the leader among them since Anđelka died. Even in their seventies, they are like children, lost without her. In the first few months after the stroke, their anxious faces hovered over her. They kept her awake with their chatter and wailing. They piled so many blankets on her that she sweated miserably underneath them. They force-fed her, dripping food and soup all over her motionless body. Being washed was an ordeal; they scratched and bruised her. They nearly dropped her once, and she had resented them for months.

She is not happy to see their faces looking at her from the darkness. The presence of their faces precludes the possibility of Ante and his motorcycle. She hates the moments of clarity more than anything. It is then that she becomes miserably aware of the uselessness of her limbs, the smell of urine as she soils the bed, the fact that she is old, and he is dead.

Bero's daughter is there some of the time. She grasps the girl's hand. This is the only one who can be saved, Ljubica thinks to herself. The others are too old; too much time has elapsed. She holds the girl's hand against her ribs. There is something she wants to tell the girl, but the words come out garbled, and her tongue cannot separate them.

The girl waits patiently. She kisses the old woman in the bed, a kiss for each cheek, and pats her arm, nodding as if she understands. Ljubica cries with the effort of it. The girl tells her not to cry, and Ljubica waves her away angrily. The words are right there. I must tell the girl, she thinks.

The girl grows older. She is no longer so much a girl anymore as a woman. Ljubica watches when she sits on the couch across from her and talks with her sisters. Her face is thinner, but her hair is still the same dark mass that had infuriated Ljubica. With her dark skin, it makes her look like a Gypsy. Ljubica has told her this many times, telling her to pin it up so that she looks respectable. There will be a time and place for the hair to hang loose and wild, but now is not it. The girl had always laughed. She had complied for visits to her aunts, but Ljubica, watching her walk away down the street, had seen her take out the hairpins and shake her head until the darkness fell around her shoulders again.

Later there is something with the girl and a soldier, and Katja tells her that she will sew the wedding dress. "But we are not supposed to know," her sister whispers with a smile. White with lace around the collar. The girl is as light as air, and a citizen of her own invented country. Until she shows up at the apartment, face stained with tears, insisting she is well. Ljubica clasps the girl's hand to her chest. In her mind they have all been killed in the war or are wandering the roads, dazed and in bloody shoes.

Are you sure that he's dead? She wants to ask the girl. *It could be that he will return years from now.* She has, after all, been waiting for Ante through all this time. "Another woman," Katja whispers, shaking her head. Something about a baby, damn him to hell. Ljubica's eyes flicker open. Was the girl going to have a baby? She smiles before falling asleep. A baby would be nice.

SHE WAITED SO LONG for a baby with Ante. She tried so hard. She was the only one of the sisters to be educated, and she spoke a little German, a little French, and had lovely penmanship. But she turned her back on all of this. She tried every herb, salve, and remedy. Ante was not happy that there were no children, she could tell, although they never talked about it. Each month she greeted her menstruation with bitter disappointment.

Her sister Anđelka had two boys and had been pregnant a number of times, but the other babies had not survived. Ljubica saw how Ante was with the boys. When Anđelka's husband died of typhus, Ante told her that he would keep them in line as much as he could. Which, except for rare visits, was not much, because Ljubica and Ante were stuck miles away in a village in Macedonia.

Disappointment sat in Ljubica like a stone. "You are spoiling the boys," she would tell her sister. "You're making them soft, doing everything for them."

When Anđelka took her sons with her to live in Sarajevo, Ante insisted they come to him one summer to learn how to be men. Anđelka bit her tongue at this. Ante was a big, sturdy man with a bad temper. Her boys were not used to that. But Ante had insisted, reasoning that a man's hand was needed. Ljubica watched the entire exchange from a distance. Zoran came to live with them for a summer.

She could barely look at her sister because of the utter unfairness of it all. And her sister had no patience for her and for her moods. She never had, and spoke to her more sharply than she perhaps intended.

The boys were pale and scrawny. City babies, was how Ante had phrased it. She'd made them into city babies.

AND THEN THE WAR STARTED. Ante had been an officer in the Royal Army. Yugoslavia collapsed, and he was in the Domobran. They returned to Herzegovina. The previous years of exile in Macedonia following Radić's assassination in Parliament had honed Ante's anger into a sharp blade. He cut a handsome figure in his uniform, and other men listened to him, and Ljubica was proud. It was just the lack of a baby that ate at her. Ante traveled heavily, and they moved finally to Zagreb.

And Croatia had been independent for a little while. It seemed to be going so well, and then the tide was against them, and suddenly the Partisans were heading toward Zagreb as well. Four years of promise followed by fifty years of darkness when the Communists took over.

Ante left with other officers. They were going to escape westward and northward and go into exile. And from there, from some other country, they would try to put the pieces together again.

She had wanted to go with him, insisted on it, in fact. Other wives were going. Entire families were going. What would they do to so many people? To women and children? But he insisted on going alone, his face white. She had pleaded, but he raised his voice. There would be no argument. She packed his bag angrily, her hands shaking. He was going to leave her, she thought to herself. It might be years before he was able to send for her from some distant place filled with strangers.

There would be no chance for a baby now. It was already getting too late.

When he left, he kissed her. Behind the kiss was the taste of darkness. She hung on to his collar, but he pulled away from her. "I *must* go," he told her. There was a strange mosaic of color in his face, of sorrow and of anger.

She began to cry. He left her at the window, watching his

progress down the street. He left in a car with other officers. The lucky ones had cars, but thousands had to go on foot. There were the ragged faces of children at the car windows and women who beat on the glass, asking for bread. There were refugees all over Zagreb, starving and with nowhere to go. He became lost among them.

"FOUR YEARS OF PROMISE!" Anđelka had screamed the words at her after their only conversation about the war.

Josef was dead. She had waited for him for months, hoping that he was making his way slowly home to her. There had been an uprising in the camp, and some prisoners had survived. But day after day he had not appeared, and she had known.

The sisters did not speak of these matters again for as long as they both lived.

LJUBICA'S HOPES DIED with Ante. She packed away her clothes, the things that he had bought her, and she made dresses out of black. Black shoes, black hats, and matching black gloves. And then she stopped going out. She lived with Katja and Mile. They had no children either, and it was easier that way.

"*Sestro?*"

She starts suddenly. Her sister is trying to coax food into her. But she does not want any of it. And when her stomach shrivels and caves, she will shrivel and cave, and at last the ordeal will be over.

Over Katja's shoulder she catches sight of her niece, hair

around her face like a veil. Ljubica meets her eyes. Stubborn girl, she thinks at this perpetual obstinacy, but sighs a moment later. You are the brush that clings to the rocky ground.

She looks away. She watches the white sky and strains to hear the sound of a motorcycle in the distance.

Acknowledgments

I am grateful to Family Cezner, Judy Brozović and Milan Brozović. To Ledig House, where I was given the time and space to transform my ideas into these pages. To my editors, Ethan Nosowsky and Ayesha Pande, and to my agent, Sandra Dijkstra. To Catherine Kanjer Kapphahn, René Vasicek, Rose Billington, and Maria Mayo Robbins, each of whom read this book in earlier incarnations. To Ljubica Butula and Asja Armanda, who never tired of answering my endless questions. And to Nela and Bencen Pinto, who welcomed me whenever I appeared unexpectedly at their door. I owe a debt of gratitude to Flory Jagoda for her songs: together with my father's stories, they helped me see the Sarajevo of those years. To my fellow crew members in Bosnia-Herzegovina, particularly Dr. Nizam Peerwani, Juerena Hoffman, Ron Redic, Tim Curran, Clea Koff, Cyril Chan, and José Luis Baraybar. And to Ivica Lešić, who made me smile again.

To my aunts, in whose warm kitchen I will always be at home—*vaša mala vas voli*. With love for my mother, for whom one more bedtime story was never too much; and to my brother, fellow inheritor of the stories. Finally, to all the people who spoke with me about their missing and their dead.